# Using Poetry across the Curriculum

## A Whole Language Approach

D0064382

# Using Poetry across the Curriculum

## A Whole Language Approach

by Barbara Chatton

ORYX PRESS

1993

The rare Arabian Oryx is believed to have inspired the myth of the unicorn. This desert antelope became virtually extinct in the early 1960s. At that time several groups of international conservationists arranged to have 9 animals sent to the Phoenix Zoo to be the nucleus of a captive breeding herd. Today the Oryx population is nearly 800, and over 400 have been returned to reserves in the Middle East.

Copyright © 1993 by The Oryx Press
4041 North Central at Indian School Road
Phoenix, Arizona 85012-3397

Published simultaneously in Canada

Printed and Bound in the United States of America

∞ The paper used in this publication meets the minimum requirements of American National Standard for Information Science—Permanence of Paper for Printed Library Materials, ANSI Z39.48, 1984

**Library of Congress Cataloging-in-Publication Data**

Chatton, Barbara.
  Using poetry across the curriculum : a whole language approach / by Barbara Chatton
    p.     cm.
  Includes bibliographical references and index.
  ISBN 0-89774-715-1
  1. Poetry—Study and teaching (Elementary)   2. Language experience approach in education.   3. Interdisciplinary approach in education.
  I. Title.
LC1575.C53   1993
372.64—dc20                                                                93-1428
                                                                                CIP

In Memory of
Milton John Chatton
1916–1992

# Contents

# Preface

Using *Poetry across the Curriculum* offers teachers of elementary school students a formula for integrating poetry into all areas of study by exploiting their interconnections. Just as reading, writing, listening, and speaking are all parts of the experience of learning about language, each of the subjects into which this book has been divided overlaps and interconnects with the others. For example, it is difficult to teach mathematics, or any other subject, without raising the concerns of science, reading, social studies, and other disciplines. Any one of these basic subjects can be a starting point for a unit that interconnects several, or even all, of these curriculum areas.

## The Cross-Cultural Approach

The first chapter of the book, "Poetry and Thematic Units," illustrates and reinforces this cross-disciplinary approach. The chapter comprises two thematic units that can be used in classrooms to help children view material across the curriculum, and it includes a discussion of the process of finding poetry that focuses on the two themes and planning for its use in the curriculum. "Eats," the unit on food and nutrition, includes poetry about the senses of taste and smell, which might also be included in units for a science curriculum, or in units on imagery in a language arts curriculum. "Eats" also suggests poetry that could be used to augment curricula on health, nutrition, or physical education. The other unit, "Conversation," includes material on biography, dialogue, and point of view, which might also apply to social studies, literature, or language arts curricula.

## Treatment of Poetry Writing

Another example of a subject-specific chapter that crosses the disciplinary lines is the chapter on language arts (Chapter 5). Far from being designed to teach poetry writing, the focus of this chapter is on reading and using poetry to communicate and interrelate all areas of study. Although in many schools poetry writing has taken precedence over poetry reading, in whole language classrooms the opportunity to experiment with many forms and elements of poetry is not isolated from the acts of reading, listening to, and sharing poems. This integrated approach is supported in this chapter. Background material is included on teaching poetry writing, along with a list of helpful books for teachers and librarians who want to learn more about it. However, ideas for writing poems are presented in *all* chapters of this text when relevant to the subject matter. Poetry writing assignments are offered as optional activities but are never required. The remainder of the language arts chapter deals with enhancing other aspects of this particular curriculum through poetry.

## Multiculturalism

As educators become more aware of diversity and seek to honor the backgrounds and beliefs of all students, more and better multicultural literature will become available for enriching school collections. Poems authored by poets from various ethnic and cultural groups are listed in the chapter on social studies (Chapter 4). Some of these groups are poorly represented in poetry for children. Teachers and librarians may want to explore collections of poetry written for adults (but that are written on a level that can be understood and enjoyed by children) by poets from the same ethnic backgrounds as those of some of the students in their classes. They can also invite children from differing cultural traditions to share nursery rhymes, songs, and poetry from their own families. A successful approach to treating diversity in the classroom is to regard it as part of everyday life in our classrooms and not to limit it to special days of the school year. It is not uncommon, for example, for students to briefly study Native Americans during the week before Thanksgiving. All too often these studies are cursory and stereotypical.

## Chapter Organization by Subject

Although the approach of this book is to cross curricular lines, for convenience, the remainder of the book has been arranged into standard major content areas, or disciplines, as follows: science, mathematics, social studies, language arts, literature programs, art, music, physical education, and health. Within these disciplines, each chapter is broken into sections based on basic principles and concepts. For example, the chapter on mathematics (Chapter 3) is subdivided into sections on numbers, counting, patterns, and classification. Each subsection presents and discusses poems that highlight, support, or enhance the study of these concepts. At the end of each chapter, collections of poems that focus on the subject are listed, along with pertinent professional references. These bibliographical lists will assist librarians and media specialists in keeping poetry collections relating to all subject areas complete and current.

## Sources for and Citation of Poetry

The suggested poems in each chapter of this volume are discussed and then listed in a bibliographic format following the discussion. If the poem is available in the poet's own works, that edition of the work is cited. If not, one single source is cited, generally the one that is most readily available. Most of the poems, however, can be found in additional sources as well. A concerted effort has been made to cite books that are still in print and available for purchase. The chosen poems comprise only a sampling of possible choices. As teachers and librarians develop their classroom, library, and personal poetry collections, they and their students will find many other poems that are appropriate for these units of study.

# Acknowledgments

The seeds of the ideas in this book were planted in the course of graduate studies with Charlotte Huck at The Ohio State University. David Gale encouraged me to write an article on using poetry with literature, which appeared in *School Library Journal*. The editors at Oryx Press have been consistently supportive of this project.

The members of the faculty of the College of Education at the University of Wyoming granted me a sabbatical to work on this book, and the faculty of the American Studies Program provided a beautiful place to write.

A number of teachers in the Albany County School District have shared their ideas and classrooms with me. I am grateful to Julie Aegerter, Matt Davidson, Barbara Deshler, Sarah Heyen, Lynette Parkhurst, Joan Ray, Sue Sandeen, Stephanie Weigel, Stephanie Wiley, Sharon Yovich, and Shelley Yovich for their help.

Vicki Atterberry prepared and key coded the manuscript efficiently and with good humor.

The staffs of the Albany County Public Library and the Interlibrary Loan department at the University of Wyoming personify the notion of "library service." Laurn Wilhelm and his staff at the university's Learning Resource Center made this work easier by providing poetry books and cheerful help over the course of the project.

Two librarians have made working on this book a collegial pleasure. Linda Goldman and Bonnie Robertson have participated in and conducted poetry workshops, helped to search for poems, checked bibliographic references, read drafts, and offered kindly advice and unfailing support. Their work is reflected on every page of this book.

Andy Bryson has been the resident computer specialist, averting "Macrises" whenever they threatened. In the course of this writing project he has also listened carefully, responded thoughtfully, provided connections and sustenance, and made my world a better place. I believe that makes him a poet.

# Introduction

As I walked toward a kindergarten classroom one morning, I saw an aide moving a line of small children toward the entrance, encouraging them to stamp their boots against the sidewalk to knock off the snow after a surprise spring storm. The natural rhythms of stamping his feet caused one kindergartner to burst spontaneously into a chant:

> We're marching into the building,
> The building, the building
> We're marching into the building
> We're going back to school.

When I rounded the second-floor stairway of that same school several days later, I came upon a trio of third graders who were taunting their male classmates with this bit of jump rope jingle:

> California grapefruit,
> Texas cactus,
> We think the boys all
> need more practice!

Later, I sat with a group of fifth graders who were gathered in the writing center to share journal entries. They had been asked to write about what they observed as they sat under a tree. Two children read detailed chronicles and then a third child began to read. This work was a brief, dense, free verse poem with words overlapping each other and some letters used to connect several words as if they were parts of small crossword puzzles. The writer commented that so many things were happening at once around the tree—smells and sounds and things to feel—a poem just seemed a better way to put them all together.

For all of these children the world is alive with poetry. They play with the sounds, images, and rhythms of language, they like the effect it has on others, and they use it with exuberance. Poetry is a part of their lives.

## WHAT IS POETRY?

If you ask them what a poem is most children will tell you that it is something that rhymes. Others will tell you that it's not rhyme that makes a poem; it is the way the words look on the page. They will tell you that other kinds of writing go from one edge of the paper to the other but the poem sits in the middle of the page. Some children will tell you that poetry is about certain subjects. Children who tell me they don't care for poetry will say that poems are about fairies and sweet things and nature and other things they aren't interested in.

When I share Byrd Baylor's picture book, *I'm in Charge of Celebrations* (1986), with elementary school students I ask them if they think it is a poem. Few of these students are sure. Some say it is a poem because of the arrangement of the words (which look like free verse) on the page. Others say it can't be a poem because it is a whole picture book and, besides, it doesn't rhyme. Others say it's like a list and a list isn't poetry. Some say, and I agree with them, that Byrd Baylor uses words "very carefully" and that makes her book a poem.

Like these students, critics and poets have spent a great deal of time trying to define poetry in terms of its form, elements, or content. Poets try to capture what a poem is through images and comparisons, or how it makes you feel as you read or listen to it. Some poets, such as Eleanor Farjeon (1992), have suggested that we can't define poetry: "What is poetry? Who knows?" Instead, we can only give images and descriptions of what poetry does.

In this book, poetry will be defined broadly as Laurence Perrine (1977) has defined it: Poetry says more and says it more intensely "than the language we use every day." Poets work with language to carefully express thoughts and feelings in a way that the poem's readers or listeners can enter in and share them. But learning about poetry does not happen merely by learning its elements, or by writing or reading poems of various types. It comes, as Harry Behn (1968) says, from falling in love with language: We "learn to love words, to know how they look, what they mean, how they sound." Terry Eagleton (1983) has described literature as using language that "draws attention to itself." Because of its careful use of language, poetry calls attention to language more than other forms do. Schools and classrooms should be places where we are free to play with words, experiment with literary forms, read widely from all kinds and levels of literature, and use many kinds of language as we talk together. When students use the elements of poetry, for example, to create a meaningful comparison between one thing and another or when they search for a word that exactly describes something they have observed on the science table, they are paying attention to language. When they listen to or read and respond to poems, they are paying attention to language. When they share poems with others, poems they like because of their language, feelings, or rhythms, or poems they have written, they are paying attention to language. Taking joy in language is essential to poetry.

## THE YOUNG CHILD AS POET

The Russian psychologist Kornei Chukovsky (1968) calls the pre-school-age child a "linguistic genius" for his or her ability to play around with and eventually to figure out the complexities of language without being directly taught. Young children's attempts to learn language sometimes sound like poetry. They play with the poetic elements of rhythm, sound, and imagery as they learn to speak.

Like the child who invented the boot-stamping chant, young children respond to the rhythmic qualities of language. The youngest infant shakes a rattle or bangs a spoon over and over, practicing rhythm. An older child chants and sings a rhythmic accompaniment to the clicking noise of a truck moved across a wooden floor. The rhythms of "Pease porridge hot" and "Pattycake, pattycake" are understood universally, though the meanings of these words are lost in time. Some families have their own rhythmic nonsense words created by small children as they play. When I was growing up, the act of swinging your head rhythmically from side to side was accompanied by repetitions of a nonsense word, "ackenoidy." My father passed the word on to my small nephew who smilingly participated in the rhythmic activity this word evoked before he could say the word. Later, he loved the sound of the word, repeating it endlessly while swinging his head.

Like my nephew, young children respond to the sounds of words. When three-year-olds listen to the traditional Russian story *The Turnip*, a cumulative tale in which a turnip grows and grows until it is enormous and a chain of family members try to pull it out of the ground, they embrace the word "enormous" and begin to ask for this story as "The enormous story" (Milhous and Dalgliesh, 1990). "Enormous" sounds enormous. A first grader I know loved to say the word "D'Nealian" even though she hated having to create these letters in her handwriting book. "D'Nealian" represented a whole world of possibilities for her. Sound effects also seem to come naturally. Animal sounds such as "meow" and "quack" are often the earliest words children say, and onomatopoetic words such as "crash," "zoom," and "woosh" accompany many of their actions, providing language to highlight movement.

Their enjoyment of the sounds of language draws children to rhyme. Rhyme is heavily reinforced in works for young children. Most of the poetry shared with them is rhymed. Mother Goose rhymes, songs, jingles on television ads, and didactic lectures about manners and getting along are presented in rhyme. Beloved first stories such as Margaret Wise Brown's *Goodnight Moon* (1947) and Wanda Gag's *ABC Bunny* (1978) are presented in this form. Rhyme is the element of poetry most children know best when they come to school.

Young children learning to speak often use imagery and comparisons in delightful ways. A child describes an insect as a "manbug" to distinguish it from the ladybugs; another describes the wind as music for trees; another tells me she keeps an "I'm sorry" inside of her for something she once did. When a young boy asked his mother what the curved piece of plastic he had found was called, she told him it was a shoehorn, at which he grinned and said, "Honk!" These children are all creative users of language.

Certainly young children are attracted to elements of poetry. But loving the sounds and rhythms of language and finding images in the language we use, while poetic qualities, do not make children poets. They do allow children to be receptive to the more conscious, thoughtful arrangements of words and meanings that are the work of the poet. What happens to young children's interest in language when they enter school? Do they respond differently? What do elementary school age children like and dislike about poetry?

## POETRY PREFERENCES OF ELEMENTARY SCHOOL CHILDREN

Several studies have tried to find out about elementary school childrens' preferences in poetry. Ann Terry (1974) provided cassette tapes with poems of various kinds for over a thousand children in grades four, five, and six to listen to and evaluate. Carol Fisher and Margaret Natarella (1982) conducted a similar study with first, second, and third graders. The children chose their favorite and least favorite poems from among those presented. Although both studies found individual differences among children, both also found that the children as a whole had decided preferences in the form, poetic elements, content, and age of a poem. Children at all grade levels preferred the narrative form of poetry, liking poems that told some kind of story. Within this form, they liked limericks in particular. These short narratives included humor and rhyme, qualities the children enjoyed in poetry. They least liked short free verse poems, including haiku, finding these difficult to understand. Like preschool children, elementary children enjoyed rhyme, rhythm, and sound in poems. They least enjoyed imagery and figurative language, particularly when they could not understand the image or the comparison being made. They most enjoyed poems that described familiar experiences, as well as poems that were humorous or with animal characters. The younger children liked more traditional poems, perhaps because they were more familiar, while the older children liked more contemporary poems. Terry (1974) concluded that these children were less apt to like poems that contained an adult's rather than a child's point of view, were about subjects that were not familiar or relevant in their own lives, or used inappropriate or old-fashioned language. They disliked serious, sentimental poetry and poems that required thought and meditation.

Fisher and Natarella (1982) point out that these studies were somewhat contrived in that children were asked to listen to poems twice and that they never saw them. They were asked to vote on these experiences right after the listening sessions. It is not surprising that they would choose the familiar and the humorous given this set of conditions. More thoughtful poems may need to be pondered and re-read a number of times, but neither study provided this time.

In spite of these constraints, it is still revealing that the two studies were conducted eight years apart and across grade levels and yet children's preferences remained essentially the same. A later study, conducted with middle school students, has shown that they too were drawn to humorous, rhythmic, rhymed verse that did not demand much of them (Kutiper, 1985). Terry (1974) polled the teachers in the classrooms she studied and found that about half of these teachers read poetry to their students occasionally (less than once a month) and another quarter read a poem about once a month. Three-quarters of the children participating in her study might have heard fewer than nine poems during the course of the school year. Thus, their poem choices were those of inexperienced poetry listeners and readers. These children made choices about what they liked based on limited school experiences with poetry. From these results, it appears that not much is happening in elementary schools to change students' ideas about or preferences for poems.

A look at a selection of curriculum guides for language arts and literature in elementary schools around the country reveals that most elementary schools hope to provide merely some exposure to poetry. In some schools simple concepts of poetry such as rhyme and rhythm are introduced; in others an introduction to some classic poems and poets is suggested. Some schools have focused on "skills" such as defining and finding examples of elements of poetry and writing particular types of poems. In many elementary schools, poetry has simply been neglected. The studies by Terry and by Fisher and Natarella support this. Children still enjoy the aspects of poetry with which they were comfortable when they came to school but their tastes are no more sophisticated than those of preschool children.

Researchers who have looked at children's preferences for poetry in whole language classrooms and schools have found a very different kind of picture. Amy McClure (1990) and Robert Hull (1988) have given their readers a view of poetry at work in whole language classrooms. In these classrooms there is silent and oral reading of many poems by students and teachers. There are chances to try out the language and styles of poetry. There are conversations about poems, poetry, language, and poets. This kind of exposure results in a genuine liking for a greater range of poems, more sophisticated responses to poems, and more critical thought about the poems that are shared.

## A WHOLE LANGUAGE APPROACH TO POETRY

What is a whole language approach to poetry? Charlotte Huck and Janet Hickman (1983) have said that "Poetry flourishes where it is heard and read and loved and nurtured." Adults who came by their love of poetry naturally recognize these conditions. They had parents, teachers, and librarians who loved to read and recite poetry; perhaps wrote poetry themselves; encouraged them to chime in reciting verse and poetry; or quoted lines of poetry when they were happy or glum or distressed because the lines of poetry said what they felt better than they could. Robert Frost's daughter, Lesley, has published the journals she wrote as a child. It is easy to see how she came by her own love of poetry in this "whole poetry" environment, as she watched her father write and listened to him read and as he encouraged her to find her own poetic voice (Frost, 1969). As in the Frost home, poetry abides in an environment where it is fostered as a kind of continuous thread throughout the day, not as a brief interlude, or unit or skill session. Poetry is not a subject to be studied but a part of the rich language environment of classrooms and schools.

Other conditions in the Frost home fostered the spirit of the poet. Besides providing a rich language environment, Robert Frost encouraged careful observation of the natural world. Lesley said, "If we brought Papa something born of a half a look, a glance, he sent us back for a whole look" (Bober, 1991). His children read and were read to and they were encouraged to have critical opinions about their reading. Robert Frost used the farm's environs and the stars to help his children understand the larger world around them and encouraged them to play and imagine. These conditions are necessary for poets and language lovers.

In a school that fosters these conditions, you don't have to go far to find a poem to read and enjoy. Poetry is everywhere. There are hundreds of books of poetry for teachers and students to read and use. Some of these books are anthologies of poems on topics of specific interest—cats, machines, or families—and some are books of poems by well-known poets beloved for their humor, rhyme, and nonsense. Some are by poets who write in other languages, about other countries, or about their own unique backgrounds. Some of the poets are classmates, whose books have been bound and kept in the school collection for others to enjoy.

Poetry is part of the landscape of the school. Copies of favorite poems are printed on large paper and hung in classrooms, in libraries, and in hallways. Younger children practice their reading and predicting as they chant the new verses they have added to their favorite songs and rhymed picture books. Older children read and contemplate thoughtful poems and change their ideas about the meanings of the poems as they read and re-read them. Poems are printed to accompany science displays or book displays in the library, highlighting an aspect of discovery or a new thought. A poem about reading is posted in the picture book corner of the library, printed carefully by a second grader. A poem about the principal is attached to the office door. These poems are replaced as children and teachers find other poems that express their feelings about the people and places in their school.

Poetry is shared. The school library features recordings of poets reading their own poetry and talking about how and why they write. The library and the classrooms contain recordings of children reading their favorite poems for others to enjoy, as well as taped collections of poems compiled by children on topics they have studied. Teachers and librarians read poetry to children a number of times a day. Sometimes a poem is a light moment, something to make us laugh when we are tired or disgruntled. Sometimes a poem provides a thoughtful moment, a time to stop and contemplate the poet's words and feelings. Sometimes a poem piques curiosity about a subject, making us want to know more, or highlights something we've been working on by looking at it in a new way. Children share their current favorite poems during class meetings, either reading or reciting them. Dramatic presentations and choral readings bring poems alive for others to enjoy.

Poetry writing is an ongoing activity. It takes time and care to write poems that reflect what we actually think and feel. Students, teachers, and librarians keep poetry notebooks. One section contains a personal poetry collection. These are poems we love to read and re-read as we observe what the poet was trying to do. Another section is for ideas: perhaps a topic, or a single line of a poem, or even a word that appeals. Another section is for poems in progress. These may be recent drafts or poems written some time ago and now being re-worked. Sometimes we share one of these with a friend or teacher and ask them to respond to it. Sometimes a part of the notebook is private. No one is asked to deliver a poem "product," a haiku or diamonte, on demand. Students can explore them if they choose and share their drafts and polished poems when they are ready. Figure 1 shows a web of possible uses for poetry in whole language programs.

| SPEAKING POETRY | WRITING POETRY |
|---|---|
| Reading or reciting a favorite poem for classmates | Writing thoughts and ideas for poems |
| Discussing one's ideas or feelings about a favorite poem | Writing down favorite poems or lines from poems in a poetry notebook |
| Discussing the meaning of poems shared in class | Writing a response to a favorite poem |
| Dramatically presenting a favorite poem or a poem one has written | Writing a poem in response to a poem, novel, or incident |
| Presenting new verses created for poems or songs | Writing a poem using a model of a particular form |
| Sharing ideas about poems during writing conferences | Writing a poem to express a feeling or sensory experience |
| Including a poem with an oral presentation of work on a topic or theme | Writing a poem in collaboration with others |
| | Writing a poem for a class collection |

| LISTENING TO POETRY | READING POETRY |
|---|---|
| Listening to the teacher or librarian read poems aloud | Reading poetry in a variety of forms by a variety of poets |
| Listening to classmates read their favorite poems | Reading individual poems displayed in classrooms and libraries |
| Listening to classmates read drafts or finished poems they have written | Reading one's own poems in writing conferences and as finished products |
| Listening to tapes of poets reading and talking about their poetry | Reading poems written by classmates |
| Listening to tapes of classmates reading poems | Performing dramatic readings of favorite poems for others |

**Figure 1. Web: A Model for Using Poetry in Whole Language Programs**

The elements of poetry are all around us in elementary schools. Rhythm, sound, and imagery are part of playground games, conversations, and the books we read. We have not capitalized on these features in most schools; we have not called attention to the language we all use. We need to make poetry an active part of school life. It is not enough that we simply use language; we must also understand its power and be able to use it powerfully. For language to hold a powerful place in our schools, we must create an environment where poetry flourishes. We create such an environment through a use of poems and books in a variety of languages, styles, and formats; through opportunities to share our thoughts and those of others; through thinking critically about what we do and how we express ourselves; and through joyful wielding of language.

# REFERENCES

Baylor, B. (1986). *I'm in Charge of Celebrations*. New York: Charles Scribner's Sons.

Behn, H. (1968). *Chrysalis: Concerning Children and Poetry*. New York: Harcourt Brace Jovanovich, p. 19.

Bober, N.S. (1991). *A Restless Spirit: The Story of Robert Frost*. New York: Henry Holt, p. 67.

Brown, M.W. (1947). *Goodnight Moon*. New York: Harper Collins.

Chukovsky, K. (1968). *From Two to Five*. Berkeley: University of California Press, p. 7.

Eagleton, T. (1983). *Literary Theory: An Introduction*. Minneapolis: University of Minnesota, p. 2.

Edelsky, C., B. Altwerger, and B. Flores. (1991). *Whole Language: What's the Difference?* Portsmouth, NH: Heinemann.

Farjeon, E. (1992). "What is Poetry?" In *Inner Chimes: Poems on Poetry*, selected by Bobbye S. Goldstein. Honesdale, PA: Wordsong/Boyds Mills.

Fisher, C.J., and M.A. Natarella. (1982). "Young Children's Preferences in Poetry: A National Survey of First, Second, and Third Graders." *Research in the Teaching of English* 16 (December): 339-54.

Frost, L. (1969). *New Hampshire's Child: The Derry Journals of Lesley Frost*. With notes and index by Lawrence Thompson and Arnold Grade. Albany: State University of New York Press.

Gag, W. (1978). *ABC Bunny*. New York: Coward/Putnam.

Goodman, K. (1986). *What's Whole in Whole Language?* Portsmouth, NH: Heinemann.

Huck, C., and J. Hickman. (1983). "Teacher Feature: Poetry is Alive and Well in Mt. Victory." *The Web* 7 (Summer): 31.

Hull, R. (1988). *Behind the Poem: A Teacher's View of Children Writing*. London: Routledge.

Kutiper, K. S. (1985). "A Survey of the Adolescent Poetry Preferences of Seventh, Eighth, and Ninth Graders." Ed.D. diss., University of Houston. Ann Arbor: University Microfilms International. ADD86-07020.

McClure, A.A., with P. Harrison and S. Reed. (1990). *Sunrises and Songs: Reading and Writing Poetry in the Elementary Classroom*. Portsmouth, NH: Heinemann.

Milhous, K., and A. Dalgliesh. (1990). *The Turnip: An Old Russian Folktale*. New York: Putnam.

Pappas, C.C., B.Z. Kiefer, and L.S. Levstik. (1990). *An Integrated Language Perspective in the Elementary School: Theory into Action*. New York: Longman.

Perrine, L. (1977). *Sound and Sense: An Introduction to Poetry*. New York: Harcourt Brace Jovanovich, p. 3.

Rosenblatt, L. (1978). *The Reader, the Text, the Poem: The Transactional Theory of the Literary Work*. Carbondale, IL: Southern Illinois University.

Terry, A. (1964). *Children's Poetry Preferences: A National Survey of Upper Elementary Grades*. Urbana, IL: National Council of Teachers of English.

# Using Poetry across the Curriculum

## A Whole Language Approach

# Chapter 1:
# Poetry and Thematic Units

Although this book is organized around subject areas, poems do not fit neatly into a "curriculum slot." Poems lend themselves to a variety of experiences and responses. The context in which they are used and the way they are shared depend upon events in the classroom and the spontaneous ways that students and teachers use poems during the classroom day. Many whole language classrooms and library programs are not organized by discrete curriculum areas, but around themes. Poetry can be incorporated into thematic units in a variety of ways. This chapter describes two thematic units. The first of these is a unit named "Yummers" after the title of a book by James Marshall. This unit will use poems from several collections of poems about food and eating along with other literature to help students look at a commonly taught subject in the elementary curriculum. The second unit, "Conversations," was created in response to the two collections of dialogue poems by Paul Fleischman, *I Am Phoenix* and *Joyful Noise*.

## THEMATIC UNITS

Thematic units cross subject lines, sometimes incorporating several subjects and sometimes encompassing the range of topics being studied. They vary in length and may be done in small groups or by a whole class. A brief unit may arise from a response to a book or a poem. When he noticed that his third-grade students were playing with rhyme, one teacher shared one of his favorite rhymed texts, Nancy Shaw's *Sheep in a Jeep*. One group of children liked the book so much that they decided to write a rhymed picture book for younger children using Shaw's style. They called it *Pig in a Wig*. In the course of this afternoon-long unit, students worked on having their poem make sense and follow a plot, on rhyme, and on laying out their story in book form and creating a continuous flow of illustration. In the process, they learned how to cooperate to produce the book.

Units can take place over the course of a week as the sole subject of study or they may be done for a part of each day over a longer period of time. Poetry can be incorporated into standard units of study, such as units on the Civil War or on insect populations. Poetry can also be incorporated into units that use a more abstract theme and span several curriculum areas, such as a unit on "change" or "beginnings." Thematic units that focus on poetry can be created around a favorite poem, collection of poems, or a poet. Sometimes a poem can be the thought-provoking beginning to a unit. The poem may raise a question about a topic or theme; it may ask us to consider a subject in a new way or from a new point of view; or it may enrich our understanding of a subject that has become dry or help us to look at new subjects and themes.

## "YUMMERS!": A UNIT ON FOOD AND EATING

To clarify the process of planning and selecting materials for a thematic unit, I will describe the process that librarian Linda Goldman and I used to create a unit featuring poetry on the topic of food entitled "Yummers," after James Marshall's picture book. We chose the unit because, like Emily Pig in the book, we both love to eat, because several collections of "food" poems were available, and because nutrition and aspects of the growth and manufacture of food are included in the elementary curriculum. In the initial planning for the unit, we read through the poems in three collections, including *Eats* by Arnold Adoff, *Munching* by Lee Bennett Hopkins (now out of print), and *Poem Stew* by William Cole. As we read we began the webbing process by identifying the topics and forms of the poems and creating categories for them.

One poem in Adoff's collection, for example, is in the form of a recipe, thus the category "Poems as Recipes" was added to the web. One of the poems was about learning to eat with chopsticks, so the category "Utensils" was created. As we read, we saw that some poems fit into more general categories, such as "Big Eaters." This category included poems about dieting and poems about people or creatures who, like Emily Pig, get carried away in their eating. The preliminary web was an attempt to see some of the possible topics, structures, and themes in the poetry in the three collections (see Figure 2).

After this initial webbing, we began clumping items under broader topics and themes and eliminated poems from the web that did not have clear connections to other poems, topics, or activities. As we thought about the topics and themes we had discovered, we added works of fiction and nonfiction and listed some possible activities (see Figure 3). In reality, when teachers and librarians plan, these first two webs emerge simultaneously. Poems immediately suggest writing ideas, other activities, and books that make connections to them.

**POEMS AS RECIPES**
*Adoff:* "Preface Poem"
"Sunday Morning Toast"
"Grandma Ida's . . ."
"Turn the Oven On"
"Peanut Butter Batterbread"

**CHORAL READING AND CHANTS**
*Hopkins:* "Bananas and Cream"
*Cole:* "Song of the Pop Bottles
*All of Adoff*

**WRITING PARODIES**
*Cole:* "On Eating Porridge
  Made of Peas"

**COOKING**
*Adoff:* "Measuring and Mixing"
"Momma Cooks"

**INTERNATIONAL FOODS
AND COOKING**
*Adoff:* "Dinner Tonight"
"Momma Cooks"

**UTENSILS**
*Adoff:* "I Am Learning"

**MANNERS**
*Cole:* "My Wise Old
  Grandpa"
"Speak Clearly"
"Table Manners"

**TASTES**
*Adoff:* "Love Song"
*Hopkins:* "Drink a Garden"

**UNUSUAL FOODS**
*Cole:* "On Eating Porridge
  Made of Peas"
"Rhinoceros Stew"
"Skip-Scoop-Annellie"

YUMMERS!

**MAGIC FOODS**
*Cole:* "The Silver Fish"

**SPILLS**
*Cole:* "Tableau of Twilight"
"When Father Carves"
"When You Tip"

**BIG EATERS**
*Adoff:* "The Coach Said"
"The New Pants"
*Cole:* "Eat It All Elaine"
"Father Loses Weight"
"Here Lies a Greedy Girl"
*Hopkins:* "Clean Platter"

**LOVED FOODS**
*Adoff:* "The Baker" (Pizza)
"Dinner Tonight" (Spaghetti)
"Love Song" (Chocolate)
"Sunnyside Up" (Eggs)
*Cole:* "The Hot Pizza
  Serenade"
*Hopkins:* "Apple Pie"
"The Pizza"

**UNAPPETIZING FOOD**
*Cole:* "Going Too Far"
"O Sliver of Liver"
*Hopkins:* "Sunny Side Up"

**Figure 2. Web of Poems Included in Three Collections of Food Poems**

A third aspect of unit planning is to consider curriculum objectives. We scanned our local district objectives in science, social studies, and health for topics on nutrition, food manufacture and marketing, digestion, and so on. We then turned some of these objectives into questions that we might ask students or that they might ask about the topic. We also added some fanciful food questions that might generate interest in the topic (see Figure 4). These questions led to ideas for some possible activities. We selected poems that model styles of poetry or topics to write on. When children read and write poetry, they should be free to choose from among several topics, moods, or forms, although over the course of a longer unit they may eventually try many different kinds of poems. We considered poems to read aloud and poems to post in the classroom and the library. We discussed collections and

**POEMS AS RECIPES**
Use Adoff poems as
    models for writing recipe
    poems. Look at real
    recipes. Find recipes for
    favorite foods.
Create recipes for imagi-
    nary foods.
Read Seuss, *Green Eggs
    and Ham*

**CHORAL READING**
In small groups, write a
    "love song" to a favorite
    food as Adoff does and
    present it to the class.

**WRITING PARODIES**
Bring in Mother Goose
    collections and find food
    poems.
Use the first line of these
    rhymes, then alter the
    message in the rest of
    the rhyme

**COOKING**
Cook together.
Cobb, *More Science
    Experiments You Can
    Eat*
*Stone Soup* (several
    versions)

**INTERNATIONAL FOODS
AND COOKING**
Talk about students'
    favorite foods from their
    own and other cultures.
Bring a simple recipe or
    dish from home to
    share.
Invite parents to do cooking
    demonstrations.

**UTENSILS**
Use Adoff poems with
    Friedman, *How My Parents
    Learned to Eat* and
    Giblin, *Read from Hand to
    Mouth*
Practice using other types
of utensils.

**MANNERS**
Brown, *Perfect Pigs*
Joslin, *What Do You Do,
    Dear?*
Create a book of table
    manners using Joslin as
    a model.

**TASTES**
Conduct science experi-
    ments with tastes—
    sour, bitter, acid, etc.
Study the sense of taste.
Web your favorite tastes.
    Try to describe them
    carefully.
Taste unusual foods such
    as okra, kiwi fruits, rice
    candy, etc.

**UNUSUAL FOODS**
Cole: "On Eating Porridge
    Made of Peas"
"Rhinoceros Stew"
"Skip-Scoop-Annellie"

# YUMMERS!

**MAGIC FOODS**
What foods might make
    good magic foods?
What food wish would you
    wish?
Smith, *Chocolate Fever*
Catling, *The Chocolate
    Touch*

De Paola, *Strega Nona*

**SPILLS**
*Cole:* "Tableau of Twilight"
"When Father Carves"
"When You Tip"

**BIG EATERS**
Combine with picky eaters.
Big eaters in books:
Carle, *The Very Hungry
    Caterpillar*
Kent, *The Fat Cat*
Rounds, *I Know an Old
    Lady*
Marshall, *Yummers!* and
    *Yummers III!*
Picky eaters in books:
Raynor, *Mrs. Pig's Bulk
    Buy*
Hoban. *Bread and Jam for
    Frances*

**LOVED FOODS**
Read several pizza poems:
    Are they true?
Khalsa, *How Pizza Came
    to Queens*
Pillar, *Pizza Man*
Read several apple poems:
McMillan, *Apples*
Watson, *Applebet*
Survey classmates on
    favorite foods

**UNAPPETIZING FOODS**
Adoff's egg poem is
    positive, others are
    negative. Which do you
    agree with?
Hoban, *Egg Thoughts and
    Other Frances Songs*
Seuss, *Green Eggs and
    Ham*
Rockwell, *How to Eat Fried
    Worms*
Survey classmates on least
    favorite foods. Which
    foods did your parents
    dislike when they were
    your age?

**Figure 3. Web of Potential Activities and Materials**

**SURVEYS, CHARTS, GRAPHS, TABLES**

What are some of your favorite foods?

What are some of your least favorite foods?

What is your favorite meal?

What is your favorite holiday meal?

**COOKING ACTIVITIES**

What is your favorite meal?

Prepare it for parents or other students at your school.

Could you plan and cook a meal or a dish from another culture or from an earlier time?

How do recipes work?

**DISCUSSION AND WRITING ACTIVITIES: PERSONAL EXPERIENCE**

What is your favorite food? Why? Describe it in beautiful language.

What is your least favorite food? Why? Describe it in disgusting language.

What is your favorite holiday meal? Write a description of the holiday feast from preparation to clean-up.

Have you ever eaten or do you know someone who has eaten something unusual?

**WRITING ACTIVITIES: CREATIVE WRITING**

Could you design a menu for an unusual feast? A delicious feast? A holiday feast?

Could you invent an imaginary creature and describe what it likes to eat?

What kinds of poems could we write about food and eating? A recipe poem? A menu poem?

YUMMERS!

**LITERARY KNOWLEDGE**

Do you know of any interesting eaters in books?

Do you know of any good books or poems about food? Find and present a poem about your favorite food.

What foods appear in nursery rhymes? In fairy tales?

Do you know any songs about food and eating?

**RESEARCH ACTIVITIES**

What is junk food? Why isn't it good for you?

Where does our food come from? Who grows it?

What is advertising? Does it affect what we buy?

Does our diet differ from that of other times and places? Why?

How do our bodies digest food?

What do we need to eat to stay healthy?

What foods contain vitamins, minerals, and other nutritional requirements?

**INTERVIEWS**

Have you ever grown your own food or know people who have? What do they grow? Interview them about their gardens.

What's the best way to go shopping?

Have you ever visited a good factory?

Interview shoppers, a grocery store manager, or a person who helps in the manufacture of food (a baker, a butcher, a pizza maker).

**MEASUREMENT ACTIVITIES**

Does measurement make a difference in cooking?

Could we shop for nutritious foods and keep a budget?

**Figure 4. Web of Questions Arranged by Type of Experience Generated**

books to be featured in booktalks, small group discussion, and individualized reading. It is clear from the poetry, questions, and activities presented in the webs that there is material here for a lengthy unit, but the responses and questions that students generate about the subject will affect how much of this material is actually used.

This unit might be used in library sessions, for combined library and classroom work, for a short poetry unit, or for a longer integrated unit used with other materials on food and nutrition across several grade levels. In a library session, for example, the librarian might share several poems on the same topic and ask students to respond to them or read a poem and a picture book or chapter from a longer book reflecting the same topic. If the topic is covered during both library programming and classroom instruction, students gain more time to look at resources, different strategies for answering their questions, and differing perspectives on a subject. Any aspect of the web could be undertaken as a short session focusing on food in language arts, reading, social studies, or science. If children choose their own reading and writing activities and research topics, and work alone or in small groups rather than in whole class activities, many more of these ideas can be tried.

## Books in the "Yummers!" Webs

Stories and nonfiction mentioned in Figures 2 and 3 are listed here.

Brown, Marc, and Stephen Krensky. *Perfect Pigs: An Introduction to Manners*. Little, 1983.

Brown, Marcia. *Stone Soup*. Scribner/Macmillan, 1979.

Carle, Eric. *The Very Hungry Caterpillar*. Putnam, 1990.

Catling, Patrick. *The Chocolate Touch*. Illus. by Margot Apple. Morrow, 1979.

Cobb, Vicki. *More Science Experiments You Can Eat*. Illus. by Giulio Maestro. Harper, 1979.

De Paola, Tomie. *Strega Nona*. Simon, 1979.

Friedman, Ima R. *How My Parents Learned to Eat*. Illus. by Allen Say. Houghton, 1987.

Giblin, James C. *From Hand to Mouth: Or How We Invented Knives, Forks, Spoons, and Chopsticks, and the Table Manners That Go with Them*. Harper, 1987.

Hoban, Russell. *Egg Thoughts and Other Frances Songs*. Illus. by Lillian Hoban. Harper, 1972.

———. *Bread and Jam for Frances*. Illus. by Lillian Hoban. Harper, 1964.

Joslin, Seslie. *What Do You Do, Dear?* Illus. by Maurice Sendak. Harper, 1958.

Kent, Jack. *The Fat Cat*. Scholastic, 1972.

Khalsa, Dayal K. *How Pizza Came to Queens*. Crown, 1989.

Machotka, Hanna. *Pasta Factory*. Houghton, 1992.

Marshall, James. *Yummers!* Houghton, 1973.

McMillan, Bruce. *Apples: How They Grow*. Houghton, 1979.

Perl, Lila. *Slumps, Grunts, and Snickerdoodles: What Colonial America Ate and Why.* Illus. by Richard Cuffari. Houghton, 1979.

Pillar, Marjorie. *Pizza Man.* Crowell, 1990.

Raynor, Mary. *Mrs. Pig's Bulk Buy.* Macmillan, 1981.

Rockwell, Thomas. *How to Eat Fried Worms.* Illus. by Emily McCully. Watts, 1973.

Rylant, Cynthia. *This Year's Garden.* Illus. by Mary Szilagyi. Bradbury, 1984.

Seuss, Dr. *Green Eggs and Ham.* Beginner, 1960.

Smith, Robert K. *Chocolate Fever.* Illus. by Gioia Fiammenghi. Putnam, 1989.

Watson, Clyde. *Applebet: An ABC.* Illus. by Wendy Watson. Farrar, 1982.

## "Yummers!": Poetry

Units on food and nutrition are so commonly taught in the elementary school that they can become dry and boring. It is probably not surprising that when situation comedies parody what children learn in school and when pre-service teachers plan their first units, the subject is often "the four food groups." Yet it is also true that most of us like to eat and relish meals and our favorite foods. There are also foods we really don't care for. We may even like to describe how awful they are. One of the reasons that Shel Silverstein's 'Sarah Cynthia Sylvia Stout Would Not Take the Garbage Out" is so popular is that his descriptions of such unpopular foods as "withered greens" and "yellow lumps of Cream of Wheat" are so vivid. The poetry collected for this web reflects the many directions that a unit on food and eating could take aside from nutrition. Fine contemporary books and other materials on nutrition have been published and these can be incorporated into this unit. Other topics may occur to you and your students as you create your own webs for this subject.

The language of food is a varied one. Foods come to us from all cultural backgrounds, they satisfy different tastes, and they reflect our diversity. Probably more stories and poems about eating have been written for children than on any other subject. Thematic units on food may cover many of the typical subjects such as the growing and manufacture of foods, basic nutrition, the digestive system, vitamins and minerals, and so on. But in addition, both literature and poetry can expand the topic of nutrition so that these topics are "digested" along with wonderful stories and poems that explore the more playful aspects of eating and cooking.

Few topics have produced so many poetry collections as food and eating. Arnold Adoff has two collections of his own poems, *Chocolate Dreams* and *Eats*. The first poem in *Eats* discusses Adoff's love affair with food, and this poem would make a fine introduction to a unit on food. William Cole offers us *Poem Stew* and Bobbye Goldstein has collected food poems in *What's on the Menu? The Random House Book of Poetry for Children* also includes a section of poems on food and nearly every anthology available for children includes food poems.

Librarians and teachers working with young children will find many nursery rhymes that deal with food and eating, such as "Pease Porridge Hot," "Polly Put the Kettle On," "Jack Sprat," and "Little Jack Horner," and could create a small nursery rhyme unit around food. In Arnold Lobel's *Gregory Griggs and Other Nursery Rhyme People*, they will find Handy Spandy who loves sweets and Hannah Bantry who gnaws a bone in the pantry. *Arroz Con Leche: Popular Songs and Rhymes of Latin America* includes "Sawdust Song" about sugar candy and "Orange So Sweet." Contemporary nursery rhymes, such as those in *Father Fox's Pennyrhymes* by Clyde Watson and Arnold Lobel's *Whiskers and Rhymes,* are often about food as well.

## Poetry Collections on Food and Eating

Adoff, Arnold. *Chocolate Dreams.* Illus. by Turi MacCombie. Lothrop, 1989.

————.*Eats.* Illus. by Susan Russo. Lothrop, 1979.

Cole, William, sel. *Poem Stew.* Illus. by Karen Weinhaus. Lippincott/Harper, 1981.

Delacre, Lulu, sel. *Arroz Con Leche: Popular Songs and Rhymes of Latin America.* Scholastic, 1989.

Goldstein, Bobbye S. sel. *What's on the Menu?* Illus. by Chris Demarest. Viking, 1992.

Hopkins, Lee Bennett, sel. *Munching.* Illus. by Nelle Davis. Little, 1985.

Lobel, Arnold, sel. *Gregory Griggs and Other Nursery Rhyme People.* Macmillan, 1987.

————. *Whiskers and Rhymes.* Greenwillow, 1985.

Prelutsky, Jack, sel. *The Random House Book of Poetry for Children* ("I'm Hungry!" section). Illus. by Arnold Lobel. Random, 1983.

Watson, Clyde. *Father Fox's Pennyrhymes.* Illus. by Wendy Watson. Harper, 1971.

## Poems about Meals

Another small unit can be created from the topic "meals." Children may get interested in meals through units on nutrition and meal planning, through books that explore meals of different times and cultures, or through discussions of their likes and dislikes in cafeteria food. They might take surveys and graph or chart favorite meals and favorite holiday meals. Children might enjoy reading others' descriptions of and feelings about their favorite meals or creating their own descriptions of a favorite meal.

Adoff, Arnold. "Dinner Tonight," "Momma Cooks with a Wok," and "Sunday Morning Toast" in *Eats.* Illus. by Susan Russo. Lothrop, 1979.

Aldis, Dorothy. "Cookout Night" in Hopkins, Lee Bennett. *Munching.* Illus. by Nelle Davis. Little, 1985.

Bryan, Ashley. "I'm A-Going to Eat at the Welcome Table" (African-American spiritual) in *All Night, All Day.* Atheneum/Macmillan, 1991.

Hammerstein, Oscar, and Rodgers, Richard. *A Real Nice Clambake.* Illus. by Nadine Bernard Westcott. Little, 1992.

Hoban, Russell. "Homework" in Prelutsky, Jack. *The Random House Book of Poetry for Children.* Random, 1983.

Hoberman, Mary Ann. "Dinnertime" in *Fathers, Mothers, Sisters, Brothers.* Illus. by Marylin Hafner. Little, 1991.

Levy, Constance. "Menu" in *I'm Going to Pet a Worm Today.* Illus. by Ronald Himler. M.K. McElderry/Macmillan, 1991.

Merriam, Eve. "I Want My Breakfast" in *Blackberry Ink.* Illus. by Hans Wilhelm. Morrow, 1985.

————. "Toaster Time" in Prelutsky, Jack. *Read Aloud Rhymes for the Very Young.* Knopf, 1986.

Prelutsky, Jack. "Jilliky, Jolliky, Jelliky, Jee" in *Ride a Purple Pelican.* Illus. by Garth Williams. Greenwillow, 1986.

Silverstein, Shel. "Pancakes" in *Where the Sidewalk Ends.* Harper, 1974.

Turner, Ann. "Here It Is" in *Street Talk.* Houghton, 1986.

## Holiday Meals: Thanksgiving

Holiday meals make an interesting small unit of study. Holidays differ depending upon one's cultural background, but the eating of a celebratory meal is common. These occasions provide opportunities to share food customs with one another. Children who celebrate Kwanza, Christmas, Hanukkah, Tet, or the end of Ramadan might describe their favorite meals for these occasions.

Thanksgiving is considered to be the quintessentially American holiday. This feast day provides an opportunity to look at the foods American Indian cultures have contributed, not just at the first Thanksgiving but across our history. Books such as Lila Perl's *Slumps, Grunts, and Snickerdoodles: What Colonial America Ate and Why* also help us learn about foods of that time period.

Poems about Thanksgiving are often about the foods traditionally eaten on this holiday. These include silly poems such as Jack Prelutsky's poem about what happens when the turkey is stuffed with popcorn; descriptions of Thanksgiving traditions such as the poems in Wendy Watson's *Thanksgiving at Our House*; and poems that explore Thanksgiving from the turkey's point of view as both Dorothy Aldis and Shel Silverstein have done. Jane Yolen's "Old Tom" comments on the way we separate this elegant bird from the bald specimen we consume at our tables.

Aldis, Dorothy. "The Little Girl and the Turkey" in DePaola, Tomie. *Tomie De Paola's Book of Poems.* Putnam, 1988.

Child, Lydia Maria. *Over the River and through the Wood.* Illus. by Iris Van Rynback. Morrow, 1982.

———. *Over the River and through the Woods*. Illus. by Brinton Turkle. Scholastic, 1975.

Dragonwagon, Crescent. *Alligator Arrived with Apples: A Potluck Alphabet Feast*. Illus. by Jose Aruego and Ariane Dewey. Macmillan, 1987.

Farmiloe, Dorothy. "Recipe for Thanksgiving Day Soup" in Booth, David. *'Til All the Stars Have Fallen*. Viking, 1990.

Fisher, Aileen. "All in a Word" in Hopkins, Lee Bennett. *Side by Side*. Simon, 1988.

———. "When It's Thanksgiving" in *Always Wondering*. Illus. by Joan Sandin. Harper, 1991.

Hillert, Margaret. "Thanksgiving" in Hopkins, Lee Bennett. *The Sky Is Full of Song*. Harper, 1983.

Kennedy, X.J. "Setting the Thanksgiving Table" in *The Kite That Braved Old Orchard Beach*. Illus. by Marion Young. M.K. McElderry/Macmillan, 1991.

Livingston, Myra Cohn, sel. *Thanksgiving Poems*. Holiday, 1985.

Merriam, Eve. "Giving Thanks, Giving Thanks" in *Fresh Paint*. Illus. by David Frompton. Macmillan, 1986.

Prelutsky, Jack. *It's Thanksgiving*. Illus. by Marylin Hafner. Greenwillow, 1982.

———. "The Turkey Shot Out of the Oven" in *Something Big Has Been Here*. Illus. by James Stevenson. Greenwillow, 1990.

Silverstein, Shel. "Point of View" in *Where the Sidewalk Ends*. Harper, 1974.

Watson, Wendy. *Thanksgiving at Our House*. Clarion/Houghton, 1991.

Yolen, Jane. "Old Tom" in *Bird Watch*. Illus. by Ted Lewin. Philomel/Putnam, 1990.

## Favorite Foods

There are many poems about favorite foods and favorite meals. Some of these poems are silly, some are serious descriptions of the foods, and others describe why the food is so liked. When I wrote a love song to food with third graders using Arnold Adoff's "Love Song" to chocolate as a model, the children did a survey that revealed their favorite foods were ice cream, pizza, and spaghetti. Ice cream was the most popular so we all pitched in to write a group love song to ice cream. Our poem ended with lines directly modeled on Adoff's:

Ice cream, ice cream,
Your cold is heartwarming.
I'd like to keep you forever
In my built-in freezer.

Ice cream, pizza, and spaghetti are also favorite foods of the poets, along with chocolate and popcorn. Other poets express still other preferences, including a surprising one for liver by Jack Prelutsky in his "They Tell Me I'm Peculiar." Prelutsky's poem could be paired with Myra Cohn Livingston's "O Sliver of Liver" to show two sides to the "taste" question. Gary Soto has written odes to some of the foods from his California Mexican-American background and Grace Nichols has several poems about foods of the

Caribbean. Students might want to find or write poems in honor of their particular family favorites.

## Chocolate

Adoff, Arnold. *Chocolate Dreams*. Illus. by Turi MacCombie. Lothrop, 1989.

———. "Love Song" in *Eats*. Illus. by Susan Russo. Lothrop, 1979.

Giovanni, Nikki. "The Reason I Like Chocolate" in *Vacation Time*. Illus. by Marisabina Russo. Morrow, 1981.

Kennedy, X.J. "Chocolate Rabbit" in *The Kite That Braved Old Orchard Beach*. Illus. by Marion Young. M.K. McElderry/Macmillan, 1991.

Prelutsky, Jack. "Chocolate Milk" and "Fudge" in *Rainy Rainy Saturday*. Illus. by Marylin Hafner. Greenwillow, 1980.

"Rima de Chocolate" in Griego, Margot. *Tortillitas Para Mama*. Illus. by Barbara Cooney. Holt, 1981.

## Ice Cream

Ciardi, John. "Doing a Good Deed" in *Doodle Soup*. Illus. by Merle Nacht. Houghton, 1985.

Kuskin, Karla. "Chocolate, Vanilla, Coffee, and Peach" in *Soap Soup and Other Verses*. Harper, 1992.

———. "I Like Growing" in *Dogs and Dragons, Trees and Dreams*. Harper, 1980.

Lee, Dennis. "The Ice Cream Store" in *The Ice Cream Store*. Illus. by David McPhail. Scholastic, 1992.

Merriam, Eve. "The Ice Cream Fountain Mountain" in *A Poem for a Pickle*. Illus. by Sheila Hamanaka. Morrow, 1989.

Nash, Ogden. "Tableau at Twilight" in Cole, William. *Poem Stew*. Illus. by Karen Weinhaus. Harper, 1981.

Prelutsky, Jack. "Bleezer's Ice Cream" in *The New Kid on the Block*. Illus. by James Stevenson. Greenwillow, 1984.

Silverstein, Shel. "Eighteen Flavors" in *Where the Sidewalk Ends*. Harper, 1974.

Worth, Valerie. "Ice Cream" in Moore, Lilian. *Sunflakes*. Clarion/Houghton, 1992.

## Pizza

Adoff, Arnold. "The Baker" in *Eats*. Illus. by Susan Russo. Lothrop, 1979.

Jacobs, Frank. "The Hot Pizza Serenade" in Cole, William. *Poem Stew*. Lippincott/Harper, 1981.

Merriam, Eve. "How Do You Make a Pizza Grow?" in *Blackberry Ink*. Illus. by Hans Wilhelm. Morrow, 1985.

———. "A Matter of Taste" in *Jamboree*. Illus. by Walter Gaffney-Kessell. Dell, 1989.

Nash, Ogden. "The Pizza" in Hopkins, Lee Bennett. *Munching*. Little, 1985.

## Popcorn

Adoff, Arnold. "There Is a Place" in *Eats*. Illus. by Susan Russo. Lothrop, 1979.

Ciardi, John. "Betty Bopper" in *Mummy Took Cooking Lessons*. Illus. by Merle Nacht. Houghton, 1990.

Kennedy, X.J. "Popping Popcorn" in *The Kite That Braved Old Orchard Beach.* Illus. by Marion Young. M.K. McElderry/Macmillan, 1991.

Lee, Dennis. "Popping Popcorn" in *The Ice Cream Store.* Illus. by David McPhail. Scholastic, 1992.

Prelutsky, Jack. "The Turkey Shot Out of the Oven" in *Something Big Has Been Here.* Illus. by James Stevenson. Greenwillow, 1990.

Turner, Nancy Byrd. "A Popcorn Song" in Ferris, Helen. *Favorite Poems Old and New.* Doubleday, 1957.

———. From "A Popcorn Song" in De Regniers, Beatrice Schenk. *Sing a Song of Popcorn.* Scholastic, 1988.

## Spaghetti

Lee, Dennis. "Betty, Betty" in *The Ice Cream Store.* Illus. by David McPhail. Scholastic, 1992.

Merriam, Eve. "A Round" in *A Sky Full of Poems.* Illus. by Walter Gaffney-Kessell. Dell, 1986.

Prelutsky, Jack. "Spaghetti, Spaghetti" in *Rainy Rainy Saturday.* Illus. by Marylin Hafner. Greenwillow, 1980.

———. "The Spaghetti Nut" in De Regniers, Beatrice Schenk. *Sing a Song of Popcorn.* Scholastic, 1988.

Silverstein, Shel. "Spaghetti" in *Where the Sidewalk Ends.* Harper, 1974.

West, Colin. "When Betty Eats Spaghetti" in Foster, John. *A Very First Poetry Book.* Oxford, 1987.

## Particular Food Favorites

Adoff, Arnold. "A Green Monster Face" (lentil soup) and "Greens to the Left of Me" (greens and beans) in *Greens.* Illus. by Betsy Lewin. Lothrop, 1988.

Carlstrom, Nancy White. "Sprouts" in *It's about Time, Jesse Bear and Other Rhymes.* Illus. by Bruce Degen. Macmillan, 1986.

Kitching, John. "I Like Soft-Boiled Eggs" in Foster, John. *A Very First Poetry Book.* Oxford, 1987.

Merriam, Eve. "Peculiar" and "A Vote for Vanilla" in *Jamboree.* Illus. by Walter Gaffney-Kessell. Dell, 1984.

———. "A Vote for Vanilla" also in *The Singing Green.* Illus. by Kathleen Collins Howell. Morrow, 1992.

Nichols, Grace. "Drinking Water-Coconut" and "Mango" in *Come on into My Tropical Garden.* Illus. by Caroline Binch. Harper, 1990.

Prelutsky, Jack. "They Tell Me I'm Peculiar" in *Something Big Has Been Here.* Illus. by James Stevenson. Greenwillow, 1990.

Soto, Gary. "Ode to Los Chicharrones," "Ode to Los Raspados," "Ode to Pomegranates," and "Ode to La Tortilla" in *Neighborhood Odes.* Illus. by David Diaz. Harcourt, 1992.

## Least Favorite Foods

Blount, Roy, Jr. "Song against Broccoli" in Janeczko, Paul. *Pocket Poems.* Bradbury/Macmillan, 1985.

Ciardi, John. "Mummy Slept Late and Daddy Fixed Breakfast" in *You Read to Me, I'll Read to You*. Illus. by Edward Gorey. Lippincott/Harper, 1962.

Cole, William. "Two Sad" in Prelutsky, Jack. *Read Aloud Rhymes for the Very Young*. Knopf, 1986.

Heide, Florence Perry. "Spinach" in *Grim and Ghastly Goings On*. Illus. by Victoria Chess. Lothrop, 1992.

Hoban, Russell. "Egg Thoughts" in *Egg Thoughts and Other Frances Songs*. Illus. by Lillian Hoban. Harper, 1972.

Hoberman, Mary Ann. "Eat It, It's Good For You" in *Fathers, Mothers, Sisters, Brothers*. Illus. by Marylin Hafner. Little, 1991.

Hoffman, Heinrich. "The Story of Augustus Who Would Not Have Any Soup" in Prelutsky, Jack. *Random House Book of Poetry for Children*. Random, 1983.

Lee, Dennis. "Gumbo Stew" in *The Ice Cream Store*. Illus. by David McPhail. Scholastic, 1992.

Prelutsky, Jack. "Eggs," "Gussie's Greasy Spoon," and "I'd Never Eat a Beet" in *The New Kid on the Block*. Illus. by James Stevenson. Greenwillow, 1984.

Kuskin, Karla. "To Eat an Egg" in *Soap Soup and Other Verses*. Harper, 1992.

Little, Jean. "Parsnips" in *Hey World, Here I Am!* Illus. by Sue Truesdell. Harper, 1989.

Livingston, Myra Cohn. "O Sliver of Liver" in Cole, William. *Poem Stew*. Harper, 1981.

Phillips, Louis. "On Eating Porridge Made of Peas" in Cole, William. *Poem Stew*. Harper, 1981.

Silverstein, Shel. "Sky Seasoning" in *Where the Sidewalk Ends*. Harper, 1974.

## Playing with Food: Unusual Foods and Unusual Meals

Another possible topic is "playing with food." Some of this is actual play such as making mud pies. Art activities involving "food play" include creating plaster of Paris food items and other artistic facsimiles of food through photography, painting and drawing, or using fruits and vegetables to create art such as potato prints and apple dolls. Poems about this kind of food play can be found or written. We might create a whole meal of play foods, one full of nonsense or unpalatable items. As they try out menu planning using nutritionally sound foods, students might also create their own menus of strange foods, nonsense foods, or gross foods.

Carlstrom, Nancy White. "Nitty Gritty Sand Song" and "Yum Yum" in *It's About Time, Jesse Bear and Other Rhymes*. Illus. by Bruce Degen. Macmillan, 1990.

Ciardi, John. "Some Cook" in Prelutsky, Jack. *For Laughing Out Loud*. Knopf, 1981.

Heide, Florence Parry. "What You Don"t Know About Food" in *Grim and Ghastly Goings-On*. Illus. by Victoria Chess. Lothrop, 1992.

Kennedy, X.J. "Snowflake Souffle" in Prelutsky, Jack. *For Laughing Out Loud*. Knopf, 1991.

Kuskin, Karla. "Catherine" and "The Meal" in *Dogs and Dragons, Trees and Dreams*. Harper, 1980.

————. "I Am Making Stew for You" and "I Am Making Soup of Soap" in *Soap Soup and Other Verses*. Harper, 1992.

Luton, Mildred. "Rhinoceros Stew" in Prelutsky, Jack. *For Laughing Out Loud*. Knopf, 1991.

Nash, Ogden. "Rattlesnake Meat" in Prelutsky, Jack. *For Laughing Out Loud*. Knopf, 1991.

Prelutsky, Jack. "Jellyfish Stew" in *The New Kid on the Block*. Illus. by James Stevenson. Greenwillow, 1984.

Silverstein, Shel. "Recipe for a Hippopotamus Sandwich" in *Where the Sidewalk Ends*. Harper, 1974.

Yolen, Jane. "Witch Pizza" in *Best Witches*. Illus. by Elise Primavera. Putnam, 1989.

## Playing with Food: Language Play

Still another type of food play involves playing with the language of food. One simple game to expand our understanding of the names of foods is to try to come up with names of foods for each letter of the alphabet. Could students, for example, come up with a fruit, vegetable, starch, dairy product, and protein source that start with the letter "c" (cantaloupe, cabbage, canola, cottage cheese, and corned beef)? Students might create a chart and see how many of the letters they could fill in for each of these categories.

Several poets have played with the names of foods. Eve Merriam creates food rhymes in her "I"m Sweet Says the Beet" and David McCord creates, "A rhyme for ham? Jam." in "Jamboree." Sometimes food play results in parodies of traditional rhymes. Two versions of "Mary Had a Little Lamb" both insinuate that she ate the lamb, along with a few other things, rather than taking it to school, and in a retelling of Humpty Dumpty, *he* gets eaten for breakfast. Students may want to create their own parodies of nursery rhymes about foods.

Bodecker, N.M. "Nut" and "Radish" in *Snowman Sniffles*. M.K. McElderry/Macmillan, 1983.

"Humpty Dumpty" in Prelutsky, Jack. *For Laughing Out Loud*. Knopf, 1991.

Lee, Dennis. "There Was an Old Lady" in Cole, William. *Poem Stew*. Lippincott/ Harper, 1981.

McCord, David. "Jamboree" and "Pease Porridge Poems" in *One at a Time*. Little, 1986.

"Mary Had a Little Lamb" in Prelutsky, Jack. *For Laughing Out Loud*. Knopf, 1991.

"Mary Had a Little Lamb" in Prelutsky, Jack. *Poems of A. Nonny Mouse*. Knopf, 1989.

Merriam, Eve. "I'm Sweet Says the Beet" in *Blackberry Ink*. Illus. by Hans Wilhelm. Morrow, 1985.

Phillips, Louis. "On Eating Porridge Made of Peas" in Cole, William. *Poem Stew*. Lippincott/Harper, 1981.

Prelutsky, Jack. "Potato, Potato" in *Ride a Purple Pelican*. Illus. by Garth Williams. Greenwillow, 1986.

"There Was an Old Woman of Ryde" in Prelutsky, Jack. *Poems of A. Nonny Mouse.* Knopf, 1989.

## Other Aspects of a "Yummers" Unit

Other aspects of the "Yummers" unit are the topics of cooking, big eaters, and table manners. Because of the wealth of poems about food and eating, this unit is limited only by the time and imagination of teachers, librarians, and students. I have included examples of books, poems, themes, and questions, but other topics and arrangements could be added to the unit.

### Cooking: Recipes and Directions

Cooking is an aspect of a "Yummers" unit that crosses the curriculum from science to health to language arts. Some poems in Arnold Adoff's *Eats*, among others, give directions for cooking and are written as recipes. Some show the pleasures of cooking; others show what can go wrong.

Adoff, Arnold. *Eats*. Illus. by Susan Russo. Lothrop, 1979.
Ciardi, John. "Lemonade for Sale" in *Mummy Took Cooking Lessons*. Illus. by Merle Nacht. Houghton, 1990.
———. "Mummy Slept Late and Daddy Cooked Breakfast" in *You Read to Me, I'll Read to You*. Illus. by Edward Gorey. Lippincott/Harper, 1962.
———. "Some Cook!" in Larrick, Nancy. *Piping Down the Valleys Wild*. Delacorte, 1985.
Duggan, John Paul. "Licorice" in Booth, David. *'Til All the Stars Have Fallen*. Viking, 1990.
Irwin, Wallace. "Aunt Nerissa's Muffin" in Cole, William. *Poem Stew*. Lippincott/ Harper, 1981.
Katz, Bobbi. "Recipe" in Cole, William. *Poem Stew*. Lippincott/Harper, 1981.
Merriam, Eve. "Five Little Monsters" in *Blackberry Ink*. Illus. by Hans Wilhelm. Morrow, 1985.
Prelutsky, Jack. "My Mother Made a Meatloaf" in *Something Big Has Been Here*. Illus. by James Stevenson. Greenwillow, 1990.
Worth, Valerie. "Pie" in *All the Small Poems*. Illus. by Natalie Babbitt. Farrar, 1987.

### Big Eaters

Another topic is "Big Eaters," some of whom eat for a purpose, such as Eric Carle's fantasy caterpillar in his picture book *The Very Hungry Caterpillar*. Some of them are the big eaters of traditional stories such as *The Fat Cat* and *I Know an Old Lady Who Swallowed a Fly*. Some are overeaters, like Emily Pig in James Marshall's *Yummers,* and some are eating on a dare, like Billy in *How to Eat Fried Worms*. A selection of poems about big eaters includes examples of all of these types. Students may want to look for other poems and stories about big eaters.

Belloc, Hillaire. "The Vulture" in Elledge, Scott. *Wider Than the Sky*. Harper, 1990.

Ciardi, John. "The Shark" in *Fast and Slow*. Illus. by Becky Gaver. Houghton, 1978.

Cole, William. "Piggy" in *Poem Stew*. Lippincott/Harper, 1981.

Heide, Florence Parry. "Hungry Jake" in *Grim and Ghastly Goings-On*. Illus. by Victoria Chess. Lothrop, 1992.

"Here Lies a Greedy Girl" in Cole, William. *Poem Stew*. Lippincott/Harper, 1981.

Kenward, Jean. "Betsy Pud" in Foster, John. *A Very First Poetry Book*. Oxford, 1980.

Kuskin, Karla. "Come Picture This Lovely and Frightening Scene" in *Any Me I Want to Be*. Harper, 1972.

Merriam, Eve. "I Want My Breakfast" in *Blackberry Ink*. Illus. by Hans Wilhelm. Morrow, 1985.

Prelutsky, Jack. "Herbert Glerbert" in Cole, William. *Poem Stew*. Lippincott/Harper, 1981.

———. "Twickham Tweer in" *The Random House Book of Poetry for Children*. Random, 1983.

———. "Mabel, Remarkable Mabel" in *The New Kid on the Block*. Illus. by James Stevenson. Greenwillow, 1984.

———. "My Younger Brother's Appetite" in *Something Big Has Been Here*. Illus. by James Stevenson. Greenwillow, 1990.

Starbird, Kaye. "Eat-It-All-Elaine" in Prelutsky, Jack. *The Random House Book of Poetry for Children*. Random, 1983.

West, Colin. "Tiny Tony and His Pony" in Prelutsky, Jack. *For Laughing Out Loud*. Knopf, 1991.

## Table Manners

One of the traditional uses of rhymed verse for children was to teach them manners, expecially table manners. Students might enjoy looking at books of manners for children of the eighteenth and nineteenth centuries and comparing these with books such as *The Goops* by Gelett Burgess and other classic rhymed books of instruction. They can then appreciate the parodies of this didactic instruction that poets such as Shel Silverstein and John Ciardi have created and may want to write their own books of table manners.

Baruch, Dorothy. "To Sup Like a Pup" in Moore, Lilian. *Sunflakes*. Clarion/Houghton, 1992.

Bold, Alan. "The Hiccup" in Foster, John. *A Very First Poetry Book*. Oxford, 1980.

Burgess, Gelett. "Table Manners" in Prelutsky, Jack. *Read Aloud Rhymes for the Very Young*. Knopf, 1986.

Cole, William. "Sneaky Bill" in *Poem Stew*. Lippincott/Harper, 1981.

Gardner, Martin. "Speak Clearly" in Cole, William. *Poem Stew*. Lippincott/Harper, 1981.

"I Eat My Peas with Honey" in Prelutsky, Jack. *The Random House Book of Poetry for Children*. Random, 1983.

Lewis, J. Patrick. "The Culture of the Vulture" in *A Hippopotamustn't*. Illus. by Victoria Chess. Dial, 1990.

McCord, David. "Food and Drink" in *One at a Time*. Little, 1986.

Merriam, Eve. "Company Manners" in *The Singing Green*. Illus. by Kathleen Collins Howell. Morrow, 1992.

Prelutsky, Jack. "My Mother Says I'm Sickening" in *For Laughing Out Loud*. Knopf, 1991.

———. "You're Eating Like a Pig Again" in *Something Big Has Been Here*. Illus. by James Stevenson. Greenwillow, 1990.

Schmeltz, Susan Alton. "Never Take a Pig to Lunch" in Prelutsky, Jack. *For Laughing Out Loud*. Knopf, 1991.

Shaw, Nancy. *Sheep Out to Eat*. Illus. by Margot Apple. Houghton, 1992.

Silverstein, Shel. "Ridiculous Rose" in *Where the Sidewalk Ends*. Harper, 1974.

Viorst, Judith. "Learning" in *If I Were in Charge of the World and Other Worries*. Atheneum/Macmillan, 1984.

Wright, Kit. "Dave Dirt Came to Dinner" in Prelutsky, Jack. *For Laughing Out Loud*. Knopf, 1991.

## CONVERSATIONS UNIT

Thematic units can be created from a topic in the curriculum and expanded across a number of curriculum areas as is the case with the unit "Eats," which encompasses language arts, reading, health, nutrition, and science skills and strategies. Other units might start with a particular aspect of literature study, such as studying an author, poet, or illustrator; studying a stylistic device such as imagery or dialogue; or studying an aspect of a literary genre such as alphabet books, animal fantasy, or narrative poetry. This unit, "Conversations," was created to highlight the use of dialogue and point of view in novels and poetry. The "Conversations" web is shown in Figure 5

The unit was created in response to Paul Fleischman's *Joyful Noise*. In this collection and in his earlier *I Am Phoenix*, Fleischman writes poems intended to be read by two voices, sometimes alternating lines, sometimes saying lines together. In many of the poems this dialogue makes listeners aware of sounds, rhythms, numbers, and life spans of the insects and birds he portrays.

*Joyful Noise* includes several poems that clearly express two differing points of view in conversation. In the poem "Book Lice," for example, two book lice describe how they found happiness together even though their "tastes" in reading are very different. In the poem "Honeybees," a queen bee and a drone describe their day. While the Queen bee says "Being a bee is a joy," the worker bee says "Being a bee is a pain" and the differences between their lives unfold. This "conversation" between two characters with differing points of view is found throughout literature, not only in the many poems that include dialogue but also in picture books and novels with several points of view. A recent collection of poems, *Taking Turns*, places two poems with differing perspectives on the same topic on facing pages so that readers can

**CONVERSATION BETWEEN TWO CHARACTERS WITH DIFFERENT POINTS OF VIEW**

Fleischman, "Book Lice" and "Honeybees" in *Joyful Noise*

Lobel, *Frog and Toad* books

Marshall, *George and Martha* books

Rylant, *Henry and Mudge* books

McNulty, *Mouse and Tim*

Viorst, *Rosie and Michael* "The Southpaw"

**POETRY: NONSENSE CONVERSATIONS**

Bodecker, "Ruth Luce and Bruce Booth"

Smith, "Said Dorothy Hughes to Helen Hocking"

**INVITATIONS**

Silverstein, "Invitation"

Frost, "You Come, Too"

**GOSSIP AND SECRETS**

Hutchins, *The Surprise Party*

Aardma, *Why Mosquitoes Buzz in People's Ears*

Prelutsky, "I Had a Little Secret"

## CONVERSATIONS

**BOOKS THAT HOLD CONVERSATIONS**

Benchley, *George the Drummer Boy* and *Sam the Minuteman*

Lowry, *Anastasia Krupnik* and *All About Sam*

Voigt, *Dicey's Song* and *A Solitary Blue*

**WORDS AND PICTURES HOLD A CONVERSATION**

Burningham, *Come Away from the Water, Shirley* and *Time to Get Out of the Bath, Shirley*

Noble, *The Day Jimmy's Boa Constrictor Ate the Wash*

**POETRY: CLASSIC CONVERSATIONS**

Nursery Rhymes

Carroll, *The Walrus and the Carpenter*

Field, *The Duel*

Lean, *The Owl and the Pussycat*

**POETRY: QUESTIONS AND ANSWERS**

Carlson, *Goodbye Geese*

Kuskin, "Where Have You Been, Dear?"

Sandburg, "Why Did the Children Put Beans in Their Ears?"

**OTHER CONVERSATIONS**

Wordless? Wordless picture books, body language, and pantomime

Conversations using signs—sign language, street signs, and pantomime

Bilingual conversations—several languages or animals and humans

Arguments

**CHORAL READING CONVERSATIONS**

Fleischman, *I am Phoenix* and *Joyful Noise*

Hopkins, *Side by Side: Poems to Read Together*

Wolman, *Taking Turns*

**Figure 5. Conversations Web**

read aloud poems that hold a "conversation" about a subject. Students may want to make their own or a class anthology of poems that feature several points of view on a topic.

The concept of "conversation" in literature is familiar to children. Some picture books show, through conversation and actions, that two very different characters are friends. In the *George and Martha* stories by James Marshall and the *Frog and Toad* stories by Arnold Lobel, the differences between the personalities of the characters are quickly apparent to children. In other books the narrative alternates between two points of view. In Cynthia Rylant's *Henry and Mudge,* a chapter narrated from the boy Henry's point of view alternates with one narrated from the point of view (through sensory experiences rather than thoughts and feelings) of Henry's big dog, Mudge. In Judith Viorst's *Rosie and Michael* two children alternate telling why they are best friends.

Sometimes the conversation is actually an argument. Judy Blume's *Pain and the Great One* shows family life from the point of view of a big sister and a little brother, each of whom thinks the other is better off. Judith Viorst's short story, "The Southpaw," told in the form of handwritten notes, is an argument between a boy and a girl who insists she is good enough to play on his baseball team.

Students might also read pairs of books that hold a conversation. Nathaniel Benchley's *George the Drummer Boy* and *Sam the Minute Man* are easy readers designed to help children see the Revolutionary War from the perspective of a child from each 'side." Middle grade students who love Lois Lowry's *Anastasia Krupnik* books will enjoy reading *All About Sam,* which retells many of their favorite incidents from the Anastasia books from her younger brother's point of view.

Benchley, Nathaniel. *George the Drummer Boy.* Illus. by Don Bolognese. Harper, 1977.
———. *Sam the Minute Man.* Illus. by Arnold Lobel. Harper, 1977.
Blume, Judy. *The Pain and the Great One.* Illus. by Irene Trivas. Bradbury/Macmillan, 1984.
Burningham, John. *Come Away from the Water, Shirley.* Harper, 1977.
———. *Time to Get Out of the Bath, Shirley.* Harper, 1978.
Lowry, Lois. *Anastasia Krupnik.* Houghton, 1977.
———. *All about Sam.* Houghton, 1988.
Noble, Trinca Hakes. *The Day Jimmy's Boa Constrictor Ate the Wash.* Dial, 1980.
Rylant, Cynthia. *Henry and Mudge: The First Book.* Illus. by Sucie Stevenson. Bradbury, 1988.
Viorst, Judith. *Rosie and Michael.* Illus. by Lorna Tomei. Atheneum/Macmillan, 1974.
———. The "Southpaw" in Thomas, Marlo. *Free to Be You and Me.* McGraw, 1987.
Voigt, Cynthia. *Dicey's Song.* Atheneum, 1983.
———. *A Solitary Blue.* Atheneum, 1984.

## Conversational Poetry

Just as there are several types of conversations in books, there are different kinds of conversations in poems. There are poems about gossip and secrets and poems about conversations between children and animals, children and parents, and children and teachers. There are poems about conversations without words, about arguments, and nonsense conversations. Lists of selected poems on some of these topics are included here. Teachers, librarians, and students may want to browse collections of poems for other examples.

### *Classic Conversation Poems*

Classic poems are often conversations. Nursery rhymes such as "Baa Baa Black Sheep," "Mary, Mary, Quite Contrary," "Pussycat, Pussycat, Where Have You Been?" and "Who Made the Pie?" are conversations. "The Death and Burial of Cock Robin" is an extended question-and-answer conversation. Other nursery rhymes, such as "Three Little Kittens," contain dialogue between characters. Lewis Carroll's "Walrus and the Carpenter" is a conversation, as is Edward Lear's "Owl and the Pussycat." In "The Duel" by Eugene Field, the argument between the gingham dog and the calico cat is another, less friendly conversation. All of these classic poems are available in many collections.

Carroll, Lewis. "The Walrus and the Carpenter" in Elledge, Scott. *Wider Than the Sky*. Harper, 1990.

Field, Eugene. "The Duel" in Ferris, Helen. *Favorite Poems Old and New*. Doubleday, 1957.

Howitt, Mary. "The Spider and the Fly" in Elledge, Scott. *Wider Than the Sky*. Harper, 1990.

Lear, Edward. "The Owl and the Pussycat" and "The Table and the Chair" in *Of Pelicans and Pussycats*. Illus. by Jill Newton. Dial, 1990.

Milne, A.A. "Puppy and I" in *When We Were Very Young*. Illus. by Ernest H. Shepard. Dutton, 1988.

Paxton, Tom. "Town Mouse and Country Mouse" in *Belling the Cat*. Illus. by Robert Rayevsky. Morrow, 1990.

Sharpe, Richard Schrafton. "The Country Mouse and the City Mouse" in Elledge, Scott. *Wider Than the Sky* Harper, 1990.

## Questions and Answers

Many conversations in poetry consist of questions and answers. Some poems ask questions and then provide their own answers, such as William Blake's "Little Lamb Who Made Thee?" Others, like "The Tyger" by Blake, ask a rhetorical question and provide no answer. A classic nonsense question, "Why did the children put beans in their ears?" was asked in a poem by Carl Sandburg. Some questions provide answers without the questions, such as Beatrice Schenk de Regniers' poem "An Important Conversation," in which the reader sees a child's answers to a series of unheard questions by a neighbor. In some conversations an adult asks the questions and a child tries to answer them. Sometimes the child asks questions and the adult tries to answer them as in Nancy White Carlstrom's *Goodbye Geese* and in Wendy Cheyette Lewison's *Going to Sleep on the Farm*. The poems listed here use questions and answers as part of a conversation between two people. For a discussion of poems arranged in the form of a question, see the section "Questions" in Chapter 5.

Alexander, Martha. *Where Does the Sky End, Grandpa?* Harcourt, 1992.

Blake, William. "The Lamb" in Booth, David. *Voices on the Wind.* Morrow, 1990.

———. "The Tyger" in Blishen, Edward. *The Oxford Book of Poetry for Children.* Oxford, 1987.

Calhoun, Mary. *While I Sleep.* Illus. by Ed Young. Morrow, 1992.

Carlstrom, Nancy White. *Goodbye Geese.* Illustrated by Ed Young. Philomel/Putnam, 1991.

———. *Jesse Bear, What Will You Wear?* Illus. by Bruce Degen. Macmillan, 1986.

Cattermull, Jane. "Who?" in Foster, John. *A First Poetry Book.* Oxford, 1980.

Ciardi, John. "The Army Horse and the Army Jeep" in Larrick, Nancy. *Bring Me All of Your Dreams.* M. Evans, 1980.

De Regniers, Beatrice Schenk. "An Important Conversation" in *The Way I Feel...Sometimes.* Houghton, 1988.

Fyleman, Rose. "Conversation" in Booth, David. *Voices on the Wind.* Illus. by Michele Lemieux. Morrow, 1990.

Guy, Ginger Foglesong. *Black Crow, Black Crow.* Illus. by Nancy Winslow Parker. Greenwillow, 1991.

Hopkins, Lee Bennett, sel. *Questions.* Illus. by Carolyn Crull. Harper, 1992.

Jones, Brian. "Banana Talk" in Foster, John. *A Very First Poetry Book.* Oxford, 1987.

Kraus, Robert. *Whose Mouse Are You?* Collier, 1970.

Kuskin, Karla. "The Question" and "Where Have You Been Dear?" in *Dogs and Dragons, Trees and Dreams.* Harper, 1980.

Lewison, Wendy Cheyette. *Going to Sleep on the Farm.* Illus. by Juan Wijngaard. Dial, 1992.

Merriam, Eve. "Interview" in *A Sky Full of Poems.* Illus. by Walter Gaffney-Kessell. Dell, 1986.

———. Nightlight, Nightlight, What Do You See?" in *Blackberry Ink.* Illus. by Hans Wilhelm. Morrow, 1985.

Milne, A.A. "Puppy and I" in *When We Were Very Young.* Illus. by Ernest H. Shepard. Dutton, 1924.

Sandburg, Carl. "The Little Girl Saw Her First Troop Parade" and "Why Did the Children Put Beans in Their Ears?" in Hopkins, Lee Bennett. *Rainbows Are Made.* Harcourt, 1982.

———. "What's the Matter Up There?" in Hopkins, Lee Bennett. *Morning, Noon, and Nighttime, Too.* Harper, 1980.

Serfozo, Mary. *Who Said Red?* Illus. by Keiko Narahashi. Macmillan, 1988.

Serraillier, Ian. "The Tickle Rhyme" in Prelutsky, Jack. *The Random House Book of Poetry for Children*. Random, 1983.

Weil, Zaro. "Questions and Answers" in *Mud, Moon, and Me*. Illus. by Jo Burroughs. Houghton, 1992.

"What's in There?" in Mitchell, Adrian. *Strawberry Drums*. Illus. by Frances Lloyd. Delacorte, 1991.

## Conversations between Adults and Children

Some conversations between adults and children take the form of question-and-answer sessions; many of them do not. In some poems, a question is included but the focus of the conversation is on something larger than the question asked. Some of these conversations show how adults don't always listen to children. In Kalli Dakos' "There's a Cobra in the Bathroom" and in Judith Nicholls' "Storytime," teachers clearly have their minds on something else when they should be paying better attention to the child who is talking to them.

Carlstrom, Nancy White. *Better Not Get Wet, Jesse Bear*. Illus. by Bruce Degen. Macmillan, 1988.

Ciardi, John. "At the Beach" in Prelutsky, Jack. *For Laughing Out Loud*. Knopf, 1991.

Dakos, Kalli. "There's a Cobra in the Bathroom" and "Were You Ever Fat Like Me?" in *If You're Not Here, Please Raise Your Hand*. Illus. by G. Brian Karas. Four Winds Press/Macmillan, 1990.

Joseph, Lynn. "Miss Teacher" in *Coconut Kind of Day*. Illus. by Sandra Speidel. Lothrop, 1990.

Martin, Bill, Jr., and John Archambault. *Knots on a Counting Rope*. Illus. by Ted Rand. Holt, 1987.

———. *White Dynamite and Curly Kidd*. Illus. by Ted Rand. Holt, 1986.

McCord, David. "Conversation" and "Father and I in the Woods" in *One at a Time*. Little, 1977.

Nicholls, Judith. "Storytime" in Harrison, Michael. *The Oxford Book of Story Poems*. Oxford University Press, 1990.

## Nonsense and Wordplay in Conversations

Some conversations are just nonsense. William Jay Smith's rhymed name poem, "Said Dorothy Hughes to Helen Hocking," rhymes the last name "Hughes" with "shoes" and the last name "Hocking" with "stocking." Pairs of students can create rhymes for their own first or last names using this form and create a short conversation in the process. N.M. Bodecker's "Ruth Luce and Bruce Booth" is a conversation based on two tongue twister names. Students might want to think of other pairings of names that would make good tongue twisters. The nonsense wordplay Shel Silverstein uses in "What Did?" is similar to lots of riddles children tell and many more lines could be added to it.

Bodecker, N.M. "Ruth Luce and Bruce Booth" and "Harry Perry Boysenberry" in *Snowman Sniffles*. Atheneum, 1983.

Ciardi, John. "This Man Talked about You" in *I Met a Man*. Illus. by Robert Osborn. Houghton, 1973.

Merriam, Eve. "Flummery" in *A Sky Full of Poems*. Illus. by Walter Gaffney-Kessell. Dell, 1986.

Silverstein, Shel. "What Did?" in *A Light in the Attic*. Harper, 1981.

Smith, William Jay. "Said Dorothy Hughes to Helen Hocking" in Kennedy, X.J. *Knock at a Star*. Little, 1982.

## Gossip and Secrets

Conversations involving gossip and secrets imply that someone is being left out. Children enjoy playing the "gossip" game in which some word or name is whispered from one person to another as they sit in a circle. The laughter about how garbled the message can get is often followed by discussions about how hurtful the same kind of misinformation can be when passed as gossip or secrets. Poets, too, comment on the repercussions of gossip and the difficulties of keeping secrets.

Ciardi, John. "This Man Talked about You" in *I Met a Man*. Illus. by Robert Osborn. Houghton, 1973.

Kennedy, X.J. "Telephone Talk" in *The Kite That Braved Old Orchard Beach*. Illus. by Marion Young. M.K. McElderry/Macmillan, 1991.

Lee, Dennis. "The Secret Place" and "Secrets" in *The Ice Cream Store*. Illus. by David McPhail. Scholastic, 1991.

Livingston, Myra Cohn. "I Never Told" in *I Never Told and Other Poems*. M.K. McElderry/Macmillan, 1992.

———. "Secret Passageway" in *Worlds I Know and Other Poems*. Illus. by Tim Arnold. M.K. McElderry/Macmillan, 1985.

McCord, David. "Secret" in *All Small*. Illus. by Madelaine Gill Linden. Little, 1986.

Prelutsky, Jack. "I Had a Little Secret" in *Beneath a Blue Umbrella*. Illus. by Garth Williams. Greenwillow, 1990.

Seabrooke, Brenda. "Clues" and "Secrets" in *Judy Scuppernong*. Illus. by Ted Lewin. Cobblehill/Dutton, 1990.

Viorst, Judith. "Secrets" in *If I Were in Charge of the World and Other Worries*. Illus. by Lynn Cherry. Atheneum/Macmillan, 1981.

## Invitations

Some poems are written as an invitation from the writer to a reader. This invitation implies that a conversation will take place sometime in the future. Probably the best-known classic poem that invites the reader to participate is "The Pasture" by Robert Frost in which he explains that he is going out to do some chores and invites the reader: "You come too." Shel Silverstein's poem "Invitation" invites "dreamers" and others to enjoy his poetry. Children might want to consider why he includes "liars" in the list of those invited.

Chandra, Deborah. "Shell" in *Balloons*. Illus. by Leslie Bowman. Farrar, 1990.

Frost, Robert. "The Pasture" in *You Come Too*. Illus. by Thomas W. Nason. Holt, 1959.

Howitt, Mary. "The Spider and the Fly" in Elledge, Scott. *Wider Than the Sky*. Harper, 1990.

Kennedy, X.J. "Earth's Birthday" in *The Kite That Braved Old Orchard Beach*. Illus. by Marion Young. M.K. McElderry/Macmillan, 1991.

Lewis, J. Patrick. "Dolphin" in *Two-Legged, Four-Legged, No-Legged Rhymes*. Illus. by Pamela Paparone. Knopf, 1991.

Livingston, Myra Cohn. "Invitation" in *Birthday Poems*. Illus. by Margot Tomes. Holiday, 1989.

———. "Invitation" in *There Was a Place and Other Poems*. M.K. McElderry/Macmillan, 1988.

———. "We Could Be Friends" in Janeczko, Paul. *The Place My Words Are Looking For*. Bradbury/Macmillan, 1990.

Mack, Marguerite. "If You Don't Come" in Booth, David. *"Til All the Stars Have Fallen*. Viking, 1990.

Moore, Lilian. "Letter to a Friend" in *Something New Begins*. Illus. by Mary J. Dunton. Atheneum, 1982.

Rieu, E.V. "The Flattered Flying Fish" in Prelutsky, Jack. *The Random House Book of Poetry for Children*. Random, 1983.

Seabrooke, Brenda. "Judy's Birthday" in *Judy Scuppernong*. Illus. by Ted Lewin. Cobblehill/Dutton, 1990.

Silverstein, Shel. "Invitation" in *Where the Sidewalk Ends*. Harper, 1974.

## Other Conversations

Sometimes conversations are arguments; sometimes they are dialogues involving two people, objects, or animals. Some poems provide a unique example of a conversation; it might be one without words or a monologue such as Eve Merriam's "Conversation with Myself." Examples of these are included here. Conversations in several languages are listed in the section "Dialect and Multilingual Poems" in Chapter 5.

### *Arguments*

Hopkins, Lee Bennett. "Girls Can Too!" in *Morning, Noon, and Nighttime, Too*. Illus. by Nancy Hannans. Harper, 1980.

Merriam, Eve. "Argument" in *A Sky Full of Poems*. Illus. by Walter Gaffney-Kessell. Dell, 1986.

Paxton, Tom. "Who's Helping Whom?" in *Belling the Cat*. Illus. by Robert Rayevsky. Morrow, 1990.

Prelutsky, Jack. "The Disputatious Deeble" and "Four Vain and Ancient Tortoises" in *Something Big Has Been Here*. Illus. by James Stevenson. Greenwillow, 1990.

## Animal and Object Conversations

Bodecker, N.M. "Daddy Longlegs" and "The Glowworm and the Firefly" in *Water Pennies*. Illus. by Erik Blegvad. Macmillan, 1991.

Ciardi, John. "The Light-House Keeper's White Mouse" in *You Read to Me, I'll Read to You*. Illus. by Edward Gorey. Lippincott/Harper, 1962.

Fisher, Aileen. "Bird Talk" in *Always Wondering*. Illus. by Joan Sandin. Harper, 1991.

Fyleman, Rose. "Conversation" in Booth, David. *Voices on the Wind*. Morrow, 1990.

Heard, Georgia. "Fishes: Poem for Two Voices" and "Frog Serenade" in *Creatures of Earth, Sea and Sky*. Illus. by Jennifer Owings Dewey. Wordsong/Boyds Mills, 1992.

Merriam, Eve. "Night-light, Night-light, What Do You See? in" *Blackberry Ink*. Illus. by Hans Wilhelm. Morrow, 1985.

## Unique Conversations

Ciardi, John. "Sometimes I Feel This Way" in *You Read to Me, I'll Read to You*. Illus. by Edward Gorey. Lippincott/Harper, 1961. (interior monologue)

Esbensen, Barbara Juster. "Snow Print Two: Hieroglyphics" in *Cold Stars and Fireflies*. Illus. by Susan Bonners. Harper, 1984. (messages left by birds)

Field, Rachel. "My Inside Self" in Bober, Natalie S. *Let's Pretend*. Illus. by Bill Bell. Viking, 1986. (interior monologue)

Martin, Bill, Jr., and John Archambault. *The Ghost-Eye Tree*. Illus. by Ted Rand. Holt, 1985. (ghostly conversation)

McCord, David. "Innuendo" in *All Small*. Illus. by Madelaine Gill Linden. Little, 1986. (bilingual conversation)

Merriam, Eve. "Conversation with Myself" in *A Sky Full of Poems*. Illus. by Walter Gaffney-Kessell. Dell, 1986. (monologue)

——. "Teevee" in *Jamboree*. Illus. by Walter Gaffney-Kessell. Dell, 1984. (lack of conversation due to television)

Seabrooke, Brenda. "From the Grape Arbor" in *Judy Scuppernong*. Illus. by Ted Lewin. Dutton, 1990. (conversations among friends)

Yolen, Jane. "Knick, Knock" in *Best Witches*. Illus. by Elise Primavera. Putnam, 1989. (person and ghost)

## Conversational Poems for Choral Reading

Conversation poems are perfectly suited to choral reading presentations because two people or two groups of people can provide voices for the two points of view. Any of the poems listed in this section can be used for dialogues and dramatic presentations. I have included some good collections and some of my favorite poems for shared readings here.

Ciardi, John. *You Read to Me, I'll Read to You*. Illus. by Edward Gorey. Lippincott/ Harper, 1961.

Fleischman, Paul. *I Am Phoenix*. Illus. by Ken Nutt. Harper, 1985.

——. *Joyful Noise*. Illus. by Eric Beddows. Harper, 1988.

Hoberman, Mary Ann. "An Only Child" in *Fathers, Mothers, Sisters, Brothers*. Illus. by Marylin Hafner. Little, 1991.

Hopkins, Lee Bennett. *Side by Side: Poems to Read Together*. Illus. by Hilary Knight. Simon, 1988.

Joseph, Lynn. "Pulling Seine" in *Coconut Kind of Day*. Illus. by Sandra Speidel. Lothrop, 1990.

Merriam, Eve. *You Be Good and I'll Be Night*. Illus. by Karen L. Schmidt. Morrow, 1988.

————."Windshield Wiper" in Kennedy, X.J. *Knock at a Star*. Little, 1982.

"O Won't You Sit Down," African-American spiritual, in Bryan, Ashley. *All Night, All Day*. Atheneum, 1991.

*There's a Hole in the Bucket*. Illus. by Nadine Bernard Westcott. Harper, 1990.

Weil, Zaro. *Mud, Moon, and Me*. Illus. by Jo Burroughs. Houghton, 1992.

Wolman, Bernice, sel. *Taking Turns: Poetry to Share*. Illus. by Catherine Stock. Atheneum, 1992.

# REFERENCES

Cordeiro, P. (1990). "Problem-based thematic instruction." *Language Arts* 67 : 26–34.

Cullinan, B.E. (1987). *Children's Literature in the Reading Program*. Newark, DE: International Reading Association.

Gamberg, R., et al. (1988). *Learning and Loving It: Theme Studies in the Classroom*. Portsmouth, NH: Heinemann.

Hickman, J., and B. Cullinan. (1989). *Children's Literature in the Classroom: Weaving Charlotte's Web*. Needham Heights, MA: Christopher-Gordon Publishers.

Huck, C.S., S. Hepler, and J. Hickman. (1993). *Children's Literature in the Elementary School*. 5th ed. New York: Holt, Rinehart and Winston.

Moss, J. F. (1984.). *Focus Units in Literature: A Handbook for Elementary School Teachers*. Urbana, IL: National Council of Teachers of English.

Pappas, C.C., B.Z. Kiefer, and L.S. Levstik. (1990). *An Integrated Language Perspective in the Elementary School: Theory into Action*. New York: Longman.

Parsons, L. (1992). *Poetry Themes and Activities: Exploring the Fun and Fantasy of Language*. Portsmouth, NH: Heinemann.

*The Web* (Four times per year). Columbus, OH: The Center for Language and Reading, College of Education, Ohio State University.

# Chapter 2:
# Poetry and Science

Science and poetry are closely allied. Both the scientist and the poet are close observers and chroniclers of the world around them. Scientists investigate and interpret events in the natural and physical environment. Poets investigate and interpret these same events with a slightly different eye. Poetry about nature, the physical world, animals, humans, and the workings of the world enhance the study of science.

The science teacher creates a classroom environment in which the excitement of exploring the workings of the world leads to a sense of wonder about it. Children are free to closely observe the natural world, to ask questions about what they see, and are given time to try to answer these questions. Poems about the concrete subjects of science, animals, plants, or physical objects encourage children to closely observe the world around them. The following units demonstrate close observation of several aspects of nature and science.

## CRICKETS

A student brings a cricket into the classroom to share. The teacher might read Rebecca Caudill's gentle story, *A Pocketful of Cricket*, which describes a young boy's interest in this small insect and the important place it earns in his classroom. Children may then want to look at the ways poets have observed crickets as they observe their class cricket. X.J. Kennedy's "Cricket" suggests that a cricket's point of view of the world is different than ours because of its different anatomy. In *Joyful Noise*, Paul Fleischman includes two poems that give insight into cricket behavior. "House Crickets" uses the word "cricket" as an onomatopoetic device to help the listener "hear" these insects who live year-round near the warmth of a pilot light, while "Requiem" is an elegy for all the crickets who lose their lives in the fall. J. Patrick Lewis' "Grasshopper" talks about crickets who seem to

respectfully stop their noisy displays when the grasshopper plays its "solo."
In William Stafford's *Animal That Drank Up Sound*, the tiny cricket has the
courage to make the first music that starts sound in the world again. Eric
Carle focuses on the sound of the cricket in his picture book, *The Very Quiet
Cricket*, which includes a small device that repeats the cricket's call at the
end of the book.

Aldis, Dorothy. "Singing" in De Paola, Tomie. *Tomie De Paola's Book of Poems*.
Putnam, 1988.

Andrade, Jorge Carrera. "Life of the Cricket" in Nye, Naomi Shihab. *This Same Sky*.
Four Winds/Macmillan, 1992.

Behn, Harry. "Crickets" in Hopkins, Lee Bennett. *Flit, Flutter, Fly*. Doubleday, 1992.

Carle, Eric. *The Very Quiet Cricket*. Putnam, 1990. (fiction)

Caudill, Rebecca. *A Pocketful of Cricket*. Illus. by Evaline Ness. Holt, 1964. (fiction)

De Gasztold, Carmen Bernos. "The Prayer of the Cricket" in *Prayers from the Ark*.
French and European, n.d.

Fisher, Aileen. "Halloween Concert" in *Always Wondering*. Illus. by Joan Sandin.
Harper, 1991.

Fleischman, Paul. "House Crickets" and "Requiem" in *Joyful Noise*. Illus. by Eric
Beddows. Harper, 1988.

Kennedy, X.J. "Cricket" in *The Kite That Braved Old Orchard Beach*. Illus. by Marion
Young. M. K. McElderry/Macmillan, 1991.

Lewis, J. Patrick. "Grasshopper" in *Earth Verses and Water Rhymes*. Illus. by Robert
Sabuda. Macmillan, 1991.

Moore, Lilian. "Fiddler" in *Adam Mouse's Book of Poems*. Illus. by Kathleen Garry
McCord. Atheneum/Macmillan, 1992.

Rodman, Francis. "Spring Cricket" in Ferris, Helen. *Favorite Poems Old and New*.
Doubleday, 1957.

Sandburg, Carl. "Splinter" in Hopkins, Lee Bennett. *Rainbows Are Made*. Harcourt,
1982.

Stafford, William. *The Animal That Drank Up Sound*. Illus. by Debra Frasier.
Harcourt, 1992.

Worth, Valerie. "Crickets" in *All the Small Poems*. Illus. by Natalie Babbitt. Farrar,
1987.

## SPIDERS

This small creature is popular in poetry but the search for poems
reflecting scientific observation of spiders is more difficult. Shirley Climo's
collection of stories and facts, *Someone Saw a Spider,* invites children to
explore the ways authors and storytellers from several cultures have thought
about spiders as well as the "truth" about spiders. It is particularly useful to
do this kind of careful observation of creatures with a less-than-attractive
reputation. Spiders are scary to many, as are bats and snakes. A careful
scientific study of these creatures, coupled with poems that present a variety
of images, can give children a new understanding of them and an apprecia-
tion for their important place in the natural world. Mary Ann Hoberman

focuses on the spider's natural qualities in a poem called "Spiders," which gives a list of their characteristics showing that these creatures are not insects. In "The Web," Brenda Seabrooke reveals our contradictory feelings about spiders when she describes the web as a "snowflake of spider spit."

Spider poems are frequently paired with readings from E. B. White's *Charlotte's Web*, but not all poems about spiders capture the conflict Wilbur feels about his friend who is both a loving friend and grisly eater. E. B. White has used some natural descriptions of Charlotte and her behavior, but has also given her human qualities. Students might want to make a collection of spider poems and then try to arrange the poems into categories. Which are accurate scientific looks at the spider? Which dwell on our fears? Which, if any, capture a sense of Charlotte?

Adoff, Arnold. "Volunteers II" in *In for Winter, Out for Spring*. Illus. by Jerry Pinkney. Harcourt, 1991.

Bodecker, N. M. "Drifting Summer" in *Water Pennies*. Illus. by Eric Blegvad. M. K. McElderry/Macmillan, 1991.

Climo, Shirley. *Someone Saw a Spider*. Illus. by Dirk Zimmer. Crowell, 1985. (Nonfiction)

De Gasztold, Carmen Bernos. "The Spider" in *The Creatures' Choir*. French and European, n.d.

Esbensen, Barbara Juster. "Her silken name woven..." in *Words with Wrinkled Knees*. Illus. by John Stadler. Crowell/Harper, 1987.

Fisher, Aileen. "Spiders" in *Always Wondering*. Illus. by Joan Sandin. Harper, 1991.

Fisher, Lillian M. "Lady Spider" in Hopkins, Lee Bennett. *Flit, Flutter, Fly*. Doubleday, 1992.

Hoberman, Mary Ann. "Spiders" in Booth, David. *Voices on the Wind*. Morrow, 1990.
———. "The Spider's Web" in *A Fine Fat Pig*. Illus. by Malcah Zaldis. Harper, 1991.

Johnston, Tony. "Which Shoes to Choose" in *I'm Gonna Tell Mama I Want an Iguana*. Illus. by Lillian Hoban. Putnam, 1990.

Levy, Constance. "Connection" in *I'm Going to Pet a Worm Today*. Illus. by Ronald Himler. M. K. McElderry/Macmillan, 1991.

Lewis, J. Patrick. "Spider" in *Two-Legged, Four-Legged, No-Legged Rhymes*. Illus. by Pamela Paparone. Knopf, 1991.

Moore, Lilian. "Spider" in *Something New Begins*. Illus. by Mary Jane Dunton. Atheneum/Macmillan, 1982.

Prelutsky, Jack. "The Spider" in *Something Big Has Been Here*. Illus. by James Stevenson. Greenwillow, 1990.

Seabrooke, Brenda. "The Web" in *Judy Scuppernong*. Illus. by Ted Lewin. Cobblehill/Dutton, 1990.

## FROGS AND TOADS

Frogs and toads are often given homes in primary classrooms, making them naturals for close observation through science and poetry. For younger children, reading the *Frog and Toad* stories by Arnold Lobel may lead to a conversation about the differences between these two characters' personalities. Is Frog, cheerful and outgoing, typical of real frogs? Is Toad, grumpy and methodical, typical of toads? Why has Arnold Lobel given them these characteristics? What are these animals truly like? Why would we have these two images of these creatures? What can we observe about them? Treatments of frogs and toads in folklore and literature might be combined with nature study. Why do we use idioms such as "having a frog in your throat," "playing leapfrog," or "croaking voice"? Do toads give people warts? If you cut off a frog's leg does it grow another? Are there really frogs and toads that can lie dormant in the dirt and then come alive when it rains? We can share Aesop's fables of "The Frogs Who Wanted a King" and "The Frog and the Ox," and Arnold Lobel's fictional fable, "Frogs at the Rainbow's End." The story of the Frog Prince can be read in conjunction with two parodies, Fred Gwynne's *Pondlarker* and *The Frog Prince...Continued* by Jon Scieska. Why does the story of the frog prince continue to be so popular? Why does the image of kissing the frog seem so unappealing? Younger children can find picture books with frog characters such as the magical flying frogs in William Steig's *Gorky Rises* and in David Wiesner's *Tuesday*. Older readers might read the adventures of Toad in *The Wind in the Willows* and enjoy the toad in *Abel's Island* as well as the "celebrated frog" in "The Celebrated Jumping Frog of Calaveras County" by Mark Twain. A toad plays a small but significant role in Natalie Babbitt's *Tuck Everlasting*. Lilian Moore's poem "Odd" describes a "piece of the road" hopping away and could be used with discussions of the image of the toad in this novel. What does the toad symbolize?

Works of nonfiction about frogs and toads can be consulted to answer these questions. Books such as Ginny Johnston's *Slippery Babies* and *A Frog's Body* by Joanna Cole, among others, use color photographs and interesting text to invite us to share the world of these creatures.

Poems can round out the study of frogs and toads by providing multiple images of these creatures. In "The Frog" by Hilaire Belloc, the frog is sensitive to name-calling. In her frog poem, Barbara Juster Esbensen suggests that the frog's name sounds "wet and squat." In other poems, such as the frog haiku in *Red Dragonfly on My Shoulder* and Valerie Worth's "Frog" in *Small Poems*, the beauty and mystery of these small reptiles are revealed.

Adoff, Arnold. "For Kermit" and "One Night" in *Greens*. Illus. by Betsy Lewin. Lothrop, 1988.

Aesop. "The Frog and the Ox" and "The Frogs Who Wanted a King" in many Aesop's fables collections. (traditional)

Babbitt, Natalie. *Tuck Everlasting*. Farrar, 1975. (fiction)

Belloc, Hilaire. "The Frog" in Clark, Emma. *I Never Saw a Purple Cow*. Little, 1991.

Bodecker, N.M. "The Toad" in *Water Pennies*. Illus. by Eric Blegvad. M.K. McElderry/ Macmillan, 1991.

Bruchac, Joseph and Jonathan London. "Frog Moon" in *Thirteen Moons on a Turtle's Back*. Illus. by Thomas Locker. Philomel/Putnam, 1992.

Clarke, Barry. *Amazing Frogs and Toads*. Illus. by Jerry Young. Knopf, 1990. (nonfiction)

Coldrey, Jennifer. *The Frog in the Pond*. Illus. by Oxford Scientific Films. Gareth Stevens, 1986. (nonfiction)

Cole, Joanna. *A Frog's Body*. Illus. by Jerome Wexler. Morrow, 1980. (nonfiction)

Esbensen, Barbara Juster. "Touch It with Your Pen" in *Words with Wrinkled Knees*. Illus. by John Stadler. Crowell/Harper, 1987.

Finlay, Ian Hamilton. "Great Frog Race" in Kennedy, X. J. *Knock at a Star*. Little, 1985.

Grahame, Kenneth. *The Wind in the Willows*. Macmillan, 1983. (fiction)

Gwynne, Fred. *Pondlarker*. Simon, 1990. (fiction)

Jennings, Elizabeth. "The Frogs' History" in Harvey, Anne. *Shades of Green*. Greenwillow, 1992.

Johnston, Ginny. *Slippery Babies: Young Frogs, Toads, and Salamanders*. Morrow, 1991. (nonfiction)

Johnston, Tony. "Among the Water Lilies" and "Frog Eggs" in *I'm Gonna Tell Mama I Want an Iguana*. Illus. by Lillian Hoban. Putnam, 1990.

Kuskin, Karla. "Over a Stone" in *Any Me I Want to Be*. Harper, 1972.

Lobel, Arnold. *Frog and Toad Are Friends*. Harper, 1970. (fiction)

———. "The Frogs at the Rainbow's End" in *Fables*. Harper, 1980. (fiction)

MacCaig, Norman. "Toad" in Mitchell, Adrian. *Strawberry Drums*. Delacorte, 1991.

Moore, Lilian. "Song of the Tree Frogs" and "Odd" in *Something New Begins*. Illus. by Mary Jane Dunton. Atheneum/Macmillan, 1982.

———. "How Frog Feels about It" in *Adam Mouse's Book of Poems*. Illus. by Kathleen Garry McCord. Atheneum/Macmillan, 1992.

Parker, Nancy Winslow, and Joan Richards Wright. *Frogs, Toads, Lizards and Salamanders*. Greenwillow, 1990. (nonfiction)

"Raising Frogs for Profit" in Prelutsky, Jack. *For Laughing Out Loud*. Knopf, 1991.

Scieska, John. *The Frog Prince...Continued*. Illus. by Steve Johnson. Viking, 1991. (fiction)

Shannon, Monica. "The Tree Toad" in Ferris, Helen. *Favorite Poems Old and New*. Doubleday, 1957.

Steig, William. *Abel's Island*. Farrar, 1985. (fiction)

———. *Gorky Rises*. Farrar, 1980. (fiction)

Twain, Mark. "The Celebrated Jumping Frog of Calaveras Country" in many collections of Mark Twain's works. (fiction)

Wiesner, David. *Tuesday*. Houghton, 1991. (fiction)

Worth, Valerie. "Frogs" and "Toad" in *All the Small Poems*. Illus. by Natalie Babbitt. Farrar, 1987.

Yayu. "Haiku" in De Paola, Tomie. *Tomie De Paola's Book of Poems*. Putnam, 1988.

# CAMELS

We have a hard time taking camels seriously because of their unusual looks. Mark Twain said of the camel: "When he is down on all his knees, flat on his breast to receive his load, he looks something like a goose swimming; and when he is upright he looks like an ostrich with an extra set of legs" (Geismar, 1976). An anonymous quotation says, "A camel is a horse designed by a committee" *(Oxford Dictionary of Modern Quotations, 1991).* Students who have loved Mithoo in Suzanne Fisher Staples' *Shabanu* will see another side to the camel and understand the importance of this aloof creature in desert climates. But most authors and poets are hard on the camel. Some comment on its strange physical appearance. Rudyard Kipling's story "How the Camel Got His Hump" describes both the camel's appearance and its personality as does the traditional tale "How the Camel Got Its Proud Look." Ogden Nash and J. Patrick Lewis have written poems on the humps of the camel and Shel Silverstein's sassy poem, "They've Put a Brassiere on the Camel," looks at the humps in a different way. Others, such as N. M. Bodecker in "Camel," have written about the camel's unpleasant personality.

A few writers and poets have praised the camel in their writing. In Arnold Lobel's short fable "The Camel Dances," the camel is not resigned to its bulky, impossible appearance but instead enjoys itself. Carmen Bernos de Gasztold, in a poem in the form of a prayer from a camel, shows both the camel's role in the Christmas story and its singular adaptation to its desert home. X.J. Kennedy's "Camel" also focuses on the camel's role at the manger. Students might want to study more about the camel, closely observe one if a zoo is nearby, and write a poem in praise of the camel.

Bodecker, N. M. "Camel" in *Snowman Sniffles*. M. K. McElderry/Macmillan, 1983.

Carryl, Charles E. "The Camel's Complaint" in Hall, Donald. *The Oxford Book of Children's Verse in America*. Oxford, 1985.

De Gasztold, Carmen Bernos. "The Camel" in *The Creatures' Choir*. French and European, n.d.

Esbensen, Barbara Juster. "Tonk, Tonk! Do You Hear Bells?" in *Words with Wrinkled Knees*. Illus. by John Stadler. Crowell/Harper, 1987.

Kennedy, X. J. "Camel" in *The Beasts of Bethlehem*. Illus. by Michael McCurdy. M. K. McElderry/Macmillan, 1992.

Kipling, Rudyard. "Commissariat Camels" in Whipple, Laura. *Animals, Animals*. Philomel/Putnam, 1989.

———. "How the Camel Got His Hump" in *Just So Stories*. Illus. by Etienne Delessert. Doubleday, 1972. (fiction)

Kumin, Maxine. "Camel" in Hopkins, Lee Bennett. *To the Zoo*. Little, 1992.

Lewis, J. Patrick. "How to Tell a Camel" in *A Hippopotamustn't*. Illus. by Victoria Chess. Dial, 1990.

Lobel, Arnold. "The Camel Dances" in *Fables*. Harper, 1980. (fiction)

Nash, Ogden. "The Camel" in De Regniers, Beatrice Schenk. *Sing a Song of Popcorn*. Scholastic, 1988.

Norris, Leslie. "Camels of the Kings" in Carter, Ann. *Birds, Beasts and Fishes*. Macmillan, 1991.

Prelutsky, Jack. "A Dromedary Standing Still" in *Zoo Doings*. Greenwillow, 1983.

Ross, Eulalie Steinmetz. "How the Camel Got His Proud Look" in *The Buried Treasure and Other Picture Tales*. Illus. by Josef Cellini. Lippincott, 1958. (traditional)

Shakespeare, William. "Song of the Camels" in Ferris, Helen. *Favorite Poems Old and New*. Doubleday, 1957.

Silverstein, Shel. "They've Put a Brassiere on the Camel" in *A Light in the Attic*. Harper, 1981.

Staples, Suzanne Fisher. *Shabanu*. Knopf, 1989. (fiction)

Steig, Jeanne. "The Camel" in *Consider the Lemming*. Illus. by William Steig. Farrar, 1988.

## TREES

Students may be familiar with Joyce Kilmer's much-used poem "Trees." Kilmer's description, "A poem as lovely as a tree," invites discussions of this comparison. How is a poem like a tree? A tree like a poem? Collecting poems about trees reveals some of the aspects of trees that appeal to poets: their sturdiness, longevity, and changing nature over the seasons. In "Everything Changes" poet Cicely Herbert talks about how trees represent the future to many of us: "we plant trees for those born later." This poem can be used with Tony Johnston's picture book, *Yonder*, in which the family plants a tree for each special occasion and by the end of the book, a lovely stand of trees surrounds the old farmhouse and the new generations. It might also be used with Chris Van Allsburg's *Just a Dream*, which uses tree planting as a symbol for willingness to clean up the environment and look to a better future. Janice May Udry's free verse picture book, *A Tree Is Nice*, provides a format for thinking about the qualities of trees. The book uses the title line, "A tree is nice," several times and then describes the reasons why this is so. Myra Cohn Livingston's *Monkey Puzzle and Other Poems* is a collection of her poems about trees and Anne Harvey's collection, *Shades of Green*, contains many others. After students have looked at many aspects of trees, they may enjoy Ogden Nash's parody of Kilmer's poem, "Song of the Open Road," in which Nash complains about billboards blocking his view of those poem-like trees.

Behn, Harry. "Trees" in Booth, David. *Voices on the Wind*. Morrow, 1990.

Fisher, Aileen. "The Seed" and "Windy Tree" in *Always Wondering*. Illus. by Joan Sandin. Harper, 1991.

Frost, Robert. *Birches*. Illus. by Ed Young. Holt, 1988.

———. *Christmas Trees*. Illus. by Ted Rand. Holt, 1990.

Greenfield, Eloise. "The Tree" and "Under the Sunday Tree" in *Under the Sunday Tree*. Illus. by Amos Ferguson. Harper, 1988.

Herbert, Cicely. "Everything Changes" in Harvey, Anne. *Shades of Green*. Greenwillow, 1992.

Johnston, Tony. *Yonder*. Illus. by Lloyd Bloom. Dial, 1988. (fiction)

Levy, Constance. "Tree Coming Up" in *I'm Going to Pet a Worm Today*. Illus. by Ronald Himler. M. K. McElderry/Macmillan, 1991.

Lewis, J. Patrick. "A Charm to Trees" in *Earth Verses and Water Rhymes*. Illus. by Robert Sabuda. Macmillan, 1991.

Livingston, Myra Cohn. *Monkey Puzzle and Other Poems*. Illus. by Antonio Frasconi. M. K. McElderry/Atheneum, 1984.

Millay, Edna St. Vincent. "City Trees" in *Edna St. Vincent Millay's Poems Selected for Young People*. Illus. by Ronald Keller. Harper, 1979.

Moore, Lilian. "The Tree on the Corner" and "Tree Shadows" in *Something New Begins*. Illus. by Mary Jane Dunton. Atheneum/Macmillan, 1982.

Nash, Ogden. "Song of the Open Road" in Janeczko, Paul. *Pocket Poems*. Bradbury/Macmillan, 1985.

Norman, Charles. "The Hornbeam Tree at Merrillton" in *The Hornbeam Tree*. Illus. by Ted Rand. Holt, 1988.

Steele, Mary Q. *Anna's Summer Songs*. Illus. by Lena Anderson. Greenwillow, 1988.

Udry, Janice May. *A Tree Is Nice*. Illus. by Marc Simont. Harper, 1956.

Van Allsburg, Chris. *Just a Dream*. Houghton, 1990. (fiction)

## ROCKS AND STONES

"Rocks" is a rich topic for exploration of the physical world. A simple free verse book, Byrd Baylor's *Everybody Needs a Rock*, asks listeners to look for the perfect rock using all their senses: the rock must feel exactly right, smell right, and be looked "right in the eye" to be perfect. Other poets see the mysteries in rocks—the fossils embedded in them, the geodes hidden inside, or their magnetic qualities. A thematic unit can be developed around rocks in fact and fiction because of the rich literature about the power hidden in stone. Traditional stories about rocks and stones that act as magical talismans are echoed in William Steig's *Sylvester and the Magic Pebble* and Leo Lionni's *Alexander and the Wind-Up Mouse*. Lucille Clifton traces the "lucky stone" cherished by three generations of an African-American family in her short novel, *The Lucky Stone*. Some traditional stories and fantasy novels focus on standing stones and, in the case of Patricia Wrightson's Australian novel, *The Nargun and the Stars*, on the Nargun, a rock-like creature that has taken aeons to move through the countryside. Some poets are fascinated with the age of rocks, which, as Zaro Weil says in "When I Was the Wind," have "a lot of time inside." Examples of other poems about things that have survived for long ages are included in "Time" in Chapter 3.

Baylor, Byrd. *Everybody Needs a Rock*. Illus. by Peter Parnell. Scribner/Macmillan, 1974.

Clifton, Lucille. *The Lucky Stone*. Illus. by Dale Payson. Delacorte, 1979. (fiction)

Cooper, Susan. *Over Sea, Under Stone*. Harcourt, 1965. (fiction)

Esbensen, Barbara Juster. "Geode" in *Who Shrank My Grandmother's House?* Illus. by Eric Beddows. Harper, 1992.

Hoban, Russell. "Stupid Old Myself" in Prelutsky, Jack. *The Random House Book of Poetry for Children*. Random, 1983.

Hunter, Molly. *The Walking Stones.* Harper, 1970. (fiction)

Kennedy, X. J. "Valuables" in *The Kite That Braved Old Orchard Beach.* Illus. by Marion Young. M. K. McElderry/Macmillan, 1991.

Lionni, Leo. *Alexander and the Wind-Up Mouse.* Random, 1969. (fiction)

McCord, David. "This Is My Rock" in Hopkins, Lee Bennett *Morning, Noon and Nighttime Too.* Harper, 1980.

Millay, Edna St. Vincent. "Second Fig" in *Edna St. Vincent Millay's Poems Selected for Young People.* Illus. by Ronald Keller. Harper, 1979.

Moore, Lilian. "Fossils" in *Something New Begins.* Illus. by Mary Jane Dunton. Atheneum/Macmillan, 1982.

Newton, Pam. *The Stonecutter.* Putnam, 1990. (traditional)

Prelutsky, Jack. "Grubby Grebbles Eat Rocks" in *The Baby Uggs Are Hatching.* Illus. by James Stevenson. Greenwillow, 1982.

Raine, Kathleen. "From 'Rock' in Plotz, Helen. *Imagination's Other Place.* Crowell/Harper, 1987.

Rossetti, Christina. "Flint" in Elledge, Scott. *Wider Than the Sky.* Harper, 1990.

Singer, Isaac Bashevis. *The Golem.* Illus. by Uri Shulevitz. Farrar, 1982. (traditional)

Steig, William. *Sylvester and the Magic Pebble.* Simon, 1988. (fiction)

Stewig, John Warren. *Stone Soup.* Illus. by Margot Tomes. Holiday, 1991. (traditional)

Van Allsburg, Chris. *The Wretched Stone.* Houghton, 1991. (fiction)

Weil, Zaro. "When I Was the Wind" in *Mud, Moon, and Me.* Illus. by Jo Burroughs. Houghton, 1992.

Worth, Valerie. "Pebbles" and "Rocks" in *All the Small Poems.* Illus. by Natalie Babbitt. Farrar, 1987.

Wrightson, Patricia. *The Nargun and the Stars.* Atheneum, 1979.

Yacowitz, Caryn. *The Jade Stone: A Chinese Folktale.* Illus. by Ju-Hong Chen. Holiday, 1992. (traditional)

## FLIGHT

Some thematic units allow students to explore both the physical and the natural sciences. The theme of "flight" for example, includes material from mythology, folklore, literature, the history of aviation, and biographies of pioneers in flight. It includes the physics of flight and airplanes, the natural flight of birds, the wind and air currents, kites, and balloons. Many poets are fascinated by flight. Poets have watched birds fly and marveled. In "Eagle Flight," Alonzo Lopez feels he is flying with the eagle as he watches. Byrd Baylor's *Hawk, I'm Your Brother* and Herman Melville's lines from *Moby Dick* captured in his picture book, *Catskill Eagle,* echo Lopez's feelings. Carl Sandburg wonders in "Wingtip" if humans will really ever understand the world as birds do.

Some poems discuss mythical flight, as Alden Nowlan's "I, Icarus." Others imagine flying. Others try to capture the feeling of flying in an airplane. Myra Cohn Livingston, in "First Flight" and "Flying West," describes her changing perspective on the landscape below as she flies, while

Eve Merriam suggests, in "Flying for the First Time," that flying in an airplane is like swimming in the ocean. Still other poets have looked at the flight of kites, balloons, and insects.

Poems about different forms of flight are so numerous that even the youngest students will be able to collect many for a "flight" unit. I have included only a representative sample of the possibilities for this topic.

Adoff, Arnold. "Green Kite" in *Greens*. Illus. by Betsy Lewin. Lothrop, 1988.

Baylor, Byrd. *Hawk, I'm Your Brother*. Illus. by Peter Parnell. Scribner/Macmillan, 1976.

Bronte, Emily. "Ladybird! Ladybird!" in Booth, David. *Voices on the Wind*. Morrow, 1990.

Chandra, Deborah. "Balloons" and "Look!" in *Balloons*. Illus. by Leslie Bowman. Farrar, 1990.

Ciardi, John. "Wouldn't You?" in *You Read to Me, I'll Read to You*. Illus. by Edward Gorey. Lippincott/Harper, 1961.

Esbensen, Barbara Juster. "Glimpse This Word" in *Words with Wrinkled Knees*. Illus. by John Stadler. Crowell/Harper, 1987.

———. "Two Ways to Look at Kites" in *Cold Stars and Fireflies*. Illus. by Susan Bonners. Harper, 1991.

Fleischman, Paul. "Dawn" and "The Watchers" in *I Am Phoenix*. Illus. by Ken Nutt. Harper, 1985.

Green, Mary McB. "Taking Off" in Booth, David. *Voices on the Wind*. Morrow, 1990.

Kennedy, X.J. "The Kite That Braved Old Orchard Beach" and "Meteor Shower" in *The Kite That Braved Old Orchard Beach*. Illus. by Marion Young. M.K.McElderry/Macmillan, 1991.

Kuskin, Karla. "I'm Up Here" in *Any Me I Want to Be*. Harper, 1972.

Lewis, J. Patrick. "Dragonflier" in *A Hippopotamustn't*. Illus. by Victoria Chess. Dial, 1990.

Lindbergh, Reeve. *View from the Air: Charles Lindbergh's Earth and Sky*. Illus. by Richard Brown. Viking, 1992.

Livingston, Myra Cohn. "First Flight" and "Flying West" in *I Never Told*. M.K. McElderry/Macmillan, 1992.

Livingston, Myra Cohn, sel. "II: Owls in Flight" in *If the Owl Calls Again*. Illus. by Antonio Frasconi. M. K. McElderry/Macmillan, 1990.

———. *Up in the Air*. Illus. by Leonard Everett Fisher. Holiday, 1989.

Lopez, Alonzo. "Eagle Flight" in De Paola, Tomie. *Tomie De Paola's Book of Poems*. Putnam, 1988.

McCord, David. "Melvin, Martin Riley Smith" and "August 28" in *All Small*. Illus. by Madelaine Gill Linden. Little, 1986.

Melville, Herman. *Catskill Eagle*. Illus. by Thomas Locker. Putnam, 1991.

Merriam, Eve. "Flying for the First Time" in *Fresh Paint*. Illus. by David Frampton. Macmillan, 1986.

———. "Wind Takes the World" in *You Be Good and I'll Be Night*. Illus. by Karen Lee Schmidt. Morrow, 1988.

Moore, Lilian. "Flight," "Pigeons," and "To a Red Kite" in *Something New Begins*. Illus. by Mary Jane Dunton. Atheneum/Macmillan, 1982.

Norman, Charles. "Chickadees" in *The Hornbeam Tree*. Illus. by Ted Rand. Holt, 1988.

"Now Let Me Fly" in Bryan, Ashley. *All Night All Day*. Atheneum/Macmillan, 1991.

Nowlan, Alden. "I, Icarus" in Larrick, Nancy. *Bring Me All of Your Dreams*. M. Evans, 1988.

Sandburg, Carl. "Wingtip" in Hopkins, Lee Bennett. *Rainbows Are Made*. Harcourt, 1982.

Schmeltz, Susan Alton. "Paper Dragons" in Bauer, Carolyn. *Windy Day*. Harper, 1988.

Sneve, Virginia Driving Hawk. "I Watched an Eagle Soar" in *Dancing Teepees*. Illus. by Steven Gammell. Holiday, 1989.

Stevenson, Robert Louis. "Nest Eggs" in *A Child's Garden of Verses*. Illus. by Michael Foreman. Delacorte, 1985.

Troupe, Quincy. "Flying Kites (for Nathan Dixon)" in Slier, Deborah. *Make a Joyful Sound*. Checkerboard, 1991.

Worth, Valerie. "Kite" and "Crows" in *All the Small Poems*. Illus. by Natalie Babbitt. Farrar, 1987.

# CHANGES IN NATURE

Some units use an abstract concept as an organizing principle and make links across the curriculum. A unit on change, for example, links the sciences with social studies, poetry, folklore, and literature. Poets have addressed change in a number of ways. Joan Blos' picture book poem, *A Seed, a Flower, a Minute, an Hour,* provides an introduction to this unit, showing in simple rhyme how all natural things change over time. Students might then web some of the changes they observe around them and look for poems and books about these changes. Individual poems address a number of specific kinds of change.

The process of metamorphosis from caterpillar into butterfly or moth, for example, has fascinated poets. Paul Fleischman looks at this process in his poem "Chrysalis Dairy," in which an insect records its reactions to its metamorphosis. David McCord's "Cocoon" is a more lighthearted observation of the several changes an insect undergoes. In Lilian Moore's "Message from a Caterpillar," the caterpillar cannot be disturbed in its cocoon because it is growing wings. Christina Rossetti's classic poem "The Caterpillar" describes the caterpillar walking to its chosen spot to "spin and die" and then to be reborn.

Hatching is another process of change. Jack Prelutsky suggests the commonalities of this process in "The Egg," in which we are prepared to find a chick hatching from an egg only to discover that it is a goose. Karla Kuskin's "My Home Is a White Dome/Under Me" in *Any Me I Want to Be* asks young readers to imagine themselves inside that egg and then waking as the shell cracks. A concrete poem in the shape of an egg, written by Stephen Cavanaugh, a fourth grader, titled "I Am an Egg," also takes the bird's point of view. Valerie Worth's poem "Egg" compares the "quirk and freak and whim" of the hen with the solid calm of the egg, which will hatch to produce another hen.

Even water changes. Carl Sandburg wonders if water remembers being ice and ice, water, in "Metamorphosis." Barbara Juster Esbensen remembers the sensation of movement of summer water on a lake while skating on the icy surface above in "The Lake." Jack Prelutsky takes a lighter note in "The Snowman's Lament." The snowman starts out boldly in large type explaining how in December he was handsome, round, and tall, and as the seasons begin to change and he begins to melt, the type in the poem becomes smaller and smaller.

Two of the most common subjects of poems about change are the changing weather and changing seasons. Two picture books use a similar refrain to suggest the excitement when there is a change in the air. Charlotte Zolotow's *Something Is Going to Happen* describes the morning activities of a family waking up to their first snow of the season. Edith Thatcher Hurd and Clement Hurd also use the phrase "something is going to happen" in *The Day the Sun Danced*, a picture book about the coming of spring.

*The Fledgling* by Jane Langton and E.B. White's *Trumpet of the Swan* address the theme of change through the change from autumn to winter and the migration of birds. Many free verse poems and picture books also use migrating birds as symbols for change. Nancy White Carlstrom's *Goodbye Geese* is a series of poetic questions and answers about the season when the geese leave for the south. The image is also found in Jane Yolen's "Autumn Song of the Goose" and "Bird Watcher." Rachel Field's classic poem "Something Told the Wild Geese" also uses this imagery. Barbara Juster Esbensen's "Flyway: For Robert" uses the image of the feather of a flying goose to help us feel the changing temperatures. Jon Stallworth's "Winter Was a White Page" shows the inevitable changing of the seasons. This concrete poem echoes the shape of the geese as they fly north in formation across the winter sky, a foreshadowing of spring.

Some changes come from the impact of humans. Carl Sandburg's "Buffalo Dusk" describes the impact that the hunting and settlement of thousands of people had on the buffalo population. Vachel Lindsay's "Flower-fed Buffaloes" suggests that not only are the buffaloes gone, but the Blackfeet and Pawnee who made their living from these immense creatures have been changed irreparably as well. Paul Fleischman's "The Passenger Pigeon" tells the tragic story of the death of this species. Muriel Spark's contemplative poem, "The Fall," describes extinction as the story of innocents who "failed the finals in history." This poem, when used with Ann Jonas' *Aardvarks Disembark*, a picture book litany of extinct and endangered species, will give children a chance to explore the changes around them as more species are lost.

Eve Merriam's "Landscape" describes the junkyard we may find at the edge of the world if we don't take better care of our planet. X.J. Kennedy's seemingly light poem "Dodos" is actually a stern warning that humans may well end up as dead as the dodo if they do not stop polluting the environment. In "Autumn with a Daughter Who's Just Catching On" Gary Soto takes his daughter to feed the birds, hoping that they are unaware that humans are the ones who are ruining their world. James Marsh writes in "Future Ark" that we should try to imagine a world where humans work for the good of the planet instead of hoping that computers will save us. John Ciardi tells a grim fairy tale, "And They Lived Happily Ever After for Awhile," in which the loving couple hold hands watching television in a world full of pollution.

Nicki Weiss's simple poem picture book, *An Egg Is an Egg,* in which her refrain is "Everything can change," is a fitting conclusion to this unit because it implies that some things are constants. Lucille Clifton also sees change optimistically in "December," a poem that suggests that "the end of a thing is never the end."

Blos, Joan. *A Seed, a Flower, a Minute, an Hour.* Illus. by Hans Poppel. Simon, 1992.

Carlstrom, Nancy White. *Goodbye Geese.* Illus. by Ed Young. Philomel/Putnam, 1991.

Cavanaugh, Stephen. "I Am an Egg" in Gensler, Kinereth. *The Poetry Connection.* Teachers and Writers, 1978.

Ciardi, John. "And They Lived Happily Ever After for Awhile" in *Fast and Slow.* Illus. by Becky Gaver. Houghton, 1978.

Clifton, Lucille. "December" in *Everett Anderson's Year.* Illus. by Ann Grifalconi. Holt, 1974.

Esbensen, Barbara Juster. "Flyway: For Robert" and "The Lake" in *Cold Stars and Fireflies.* Illus. by Susan Bonners. Harper, 1991.

Field, Rachel. "Something Told the Wild Geese" in Frank, Josette. *Snow Towards Evening.* Dial, 1990.

Fisher, Aileen. "Caterpillar" in Hopkins, Lee Bennett. *Surprises.* Harper, 1984.

Fisher, Lillian M. "A Magic House" in Hopkins, Lee Bennett. *Flit, Flutter, Fly.* Doubleday, 1992.

Fleischman, Paul. "Chrysalis Dairy" in *Joyful Noise.* Illus. by Eric Beddows. Harper, 1988.

———. "The Passenger Pigeon" in *I Am Phoenix.* Illus. by Ken Nutt. Harper, 1985.

Hurd, Edith Thatcher. *The Day the Sun Danced.* Illus. by Clement Hurd. Harper, 1965.

Jonas, Ann. *Aardvarks Disembark.* Greenwillow, 1990.

Kennedy, X.J. "Dodos" in *The Kite That Braved Old Orchard Beach.* Illus. by Marion Young. M.K. McElderry/Macmillan, 1991.

Kuskin, Karla. "My Home Is a White Dome/Under Me" in *Any Me I Want to Be*. Harper, 1972.

Langton, Jane. *The Fledgling*. Harper, 1980. (fiction)

Lindsay, Vachel. "The Flower-fed Buffaloes" in Mitchell, Adrian. *Strawberry Drums*. Delacorte, 1991.

Marsh, James. "Future Ark" in *Bizarre Birds and Beasts*. Dial, 1991.

McCord, David. "Cocoon" in *All Small*. Illus. by Madelaine Gill Linden. Little, 1986.

———. "The Importance of Eggs" in *One at a Time*. Little, 1986.

Merriam, Eve. "Landscape" in *A Sky Full of Poems*. Illus. by Walter Gaffney-Kessell. Dell, 1976.

Moore, Lilian. "Message from a Caterpillar" in *Something New Begins*. Illus. by Mary Jane Dunton. Atheneum/Macmillan, 1982.

Prelutsky, Jack. "The Egg" in *Zoo Doings*. Illus. by Paul Zelinsky. Greenwillow, 1983.

———. "The Snowman's Lament" in *It's Snowing, It's Snowing*. Illus. by Jeanne Tith. Greenwillow, 1984.

Rossetti, Christina. "Caterpillar" in Hopkins, Lee Bennett. *Flit, Flutter, Fly*. Doubleday, 1992.

Sandburg, Carl. "Buffalo Dusk" and "Metamorphosis" in Hopkins, Lee Bennett. *Rainbows Are Made*. Harcourt, 1982.

Soto, Gary. "Autumn with a Daughter Who's Just Catching On" in *A Fire in My Hands*. Illus. by James M. Cardillo. Scholastic, 1991.

Stallworth, Jon. "Winter Was a White Page" in Elledge, Scott. *Wider Than the Sky*. Harper, 1990.

Steig, Jeanne. "The Enigmatic Egg" in *Alpha Beta Chowder*. Illus. by William Steig. Harper, 1992.

Weiss, Nikki. *An Egg Is an Egg*. Putnam, 1990.

White, E.B. *The Trumpet of the Swan*. Harper, 1970. (fiction)

Worth, Valerie. "Egg" in *All the Small Poems*. Illus. by Natalie Babbitt. Farrar, 1978.

Yolen, Jane. "Autumn Song of the Goose" in *Ring of Earth*. Illus. by John Wallner. Harcourt, 1986.

———. "Birdwatcher" in *Bird Watch*. Illus. by Ted Lewin. Philomel/Putnam, 1990.

Zolotow, Charlotte. *Something Is Going to Happen*. Illus. by Catherine Stock. Harper, 1988.

## THE SENSES

Scientists must closely observe the world using their senses. Sensory exploration of the world, or imagery, is also a major tool of the poet who seeks to help the reader see, hear, taste, feel, or smell the world in a new way. Classrooms and libraries should hold rich troves of natural treasures. Small animals, fish, insects, birds, growing and preserved plants and flowers, rocks and shells, vegetables and fruits, wool, cotton, silk and other natural materials, feathers, and abandoned nests all encourage sensory observations by the young scientist and poet. Opportunities for children to record observations about these treasures should be provided. In *Wild Mouse*, Irene Brady recorded her observations of a mouse in pictures and text. Books like this can help children learn to keep daily records of their observations about changes in the natural world. Observation guides such as those provided by Ellen Doris in *Doing What Scientists Do: Children Learn to Investigate Their World* can help children study inanimate objects more closely. Guides to sensory observation that ask children to look carefully, smell, listen to, touch, and, when appropriate, taste the object can encourage them in their observations.

Nature walks, field trips, and science camps all allow children to explore the natural and physical world, examining, wondering, asking questions, and recording observations that may later lead to poems. Poetry that encourages close observation may be used before, during, or after these experiences. Charlotte Zolotow's poetic prose in *Say It!* and Jane Yolen's free verse text in *Owl Moon* describe an autumn and a winter walk and can be shared before or after walks.

Many poets use several senses to create images to help readers learn what they have observed about an object, creature, feeling, or person. Byrd Baylor's *Everybody Needs a Rock* and *Guess Who My Favorite Person Is* ask students to consider things with all of their senses. Mary Ann Hoberman's *Cozy Book*, an extended rumination on coziness, includes things that feel, sound, smell, taste, and look cozy. Rose Rauter's "Peach" uses two senses, touch and taste, first describing the soft "velvet" of the peach's skin and then the "runny honey" taste. Food poems, which often appeal to our senses of taste and smell, are listed in the "Eats" unit in Chapter 1.

Some poems focus on a single sense. John Moffitt's "To Look at Anything" is the classic poem on "seeing," asking us to enter into the things we see to know them. Ashley Wolff's picture book, *Only the Cat Saw*, uses pictures that show the activities of a family and how much of the natural world around them they miss as the cat carefully observes butterflies, sunsets, and other natural events. Margaret Wise Brown's "Secret Song" gives a similar message: animals observe the dropping of petals, the weather, and the rising and setting of the sun in ways that humans do not. Valerie Worth's "Magnifying Glass" invites close visual exploration of the world as she uses the glass to explore a stone, a moth's wing, and her thumb. Many poems not only give ideas on how to look at things but also use strong visual images so that the reader or listener can "see" too. All of the poems in Myra Cohn Livingston's *Light and Shadow* use visual images, treating light as if it were a living, moving thing. Paul Fleischman's "Fireflies" describes these tiny night creatures using words such as "flickering," "flitting," and "flashing" throughout the poem to help us see fireflies in summer flight.

Some poems focus on the careful listening that the scientist and poet must do. Byrd Baylor suggests in *The Other Way to Listen* that if we learn to listen very carefully we can even hear the delicate singing of plants and stones. William Stafford's prose work, *The Animal That Drank Up Sound,* provides an introduction to the sounds of nature as he focuses on the silent world of a winter without sound and the tiny, rescuing tune of a cricket. Some poems ask readers to listen in the darkness. Felice Holman's "Night Sounds" and Myra Cohn Livingston's "In Quiet Night" describe night sounds, as does Cynthia Rylant's picture book, *Night in the Country.*

Some poems focus on the sense of touch. Joanne Ryder's free verse picture book, *Under Your Feet,* asks us to explore what happens underground by repeating a question appealing to the sense of touch. "Can you feel..?" she asks, the actions of small creatures who live in the ground beneath you as you walk. The feeling of this extended poem is echoed in Rhoda W. Bacmeister's "Under the Ground," in which she wonders if the "little pink worms" can feel us moving about above them.

Poems about animals often use the sense of touch, asking the reader to imagine the feel of an animal. Cats seem to be favorite "touchable" animals. Beatrice Schenk de Regniers suggests that looks are deceiving in her poem about the difference between the soft look of the cat's tongue and its rough texture. In "Cat's Whiskers" she writes about feeling whiskers in your ear as a cat rubs against you, "whispering." Denise Levertov in "To the Snake" describes the pleasure of feeling the dry weight of a snake as she holds it hissing around her neck. Monica Shannon in "Only My Opinion" wonders if the caterpillar itself feels texture; is it ticklish?

Some poems invite us to imagine the smell of things. Some poems expand our ideas about smells by offering interesting odors. Eve Merriam says in her poem "Mushroom" that a mushroom "smells more like the earth than the earth itself." In Marci Ridlon's poem, "That Was Summer," she describes the smells that help us remember this season. This poem might encourage students to consider the smells that they associate with each season of the year, both the natural smells of growth and decay, as well as smells such as cooking odors, woodsmoke, and such favorite things as crayons, paste, and clay.

Bacmeister, Rhonda W. "Under the Ground" in Booth, David. *Voices on the Wind.* Morrow, 1990.

Baylor, Byrd. *Everybody Needs a Rock.* Illus. by Peter Parnell. Macmillan, 1974.

———. *Guess Who My Favorite Person Is.* Illus. by Robert Andrew Parker. Macmillan, 1977.

———. *The Other Way to Listen.* Illus. by Peter Parnell. Macmillan, 1978.

Brady, Irene. *Wild Mouse.* Scribner, 1976. (nonfiction)

Brown, Margaret Wise. "The Secret Song" in Larrick, Nancy. *Piping Down the Valleys Wild.* Delacorte, 1985.

De Regniers, Beatrice Schenk. "Cat's Whiskers" and "Looks Are Deceiving" in *This Big Cat.* Crown, 1985.

Fleischman, Paul. "Fireflies" in *Joyful Noise.* Illus. by Eric Beddows. Harper, 1988.

Hoberman, Mary Ann. *The Cozy Book.* Illus. by Tony Chen. Viking, 1982.

Holman, Felice. "Night Sounds" in Larrick, Nancy. *When the Dark Comes Dancing*. Philomel/Putnam, 1983.

Levertov, Denise. "To a Snake" in Elledge, Scott. *Wider Than the Sky*. Harper, 1990.

Livingston, Myra Cohn. "In Quiet Night" in Larrick, Nancy. *When the Dark Comes Dancing*. Philomel/Putnam, 1983.

———. *Light and Shadow*. Illus. by Barbara Rogasky. Holiday, 1992.

Merriam, Eve. "Mushroom" in *Fresh Paint*. Illus. by David Frampton. Macmillan, 1986.

Moffitt, John. "To Look at Anything" in Dunning, Steven. *Reflections on a Gift of Watermelon Pickle*. Lothrop, 1966.

Rauter, Rose. "Peach" in Kennedy, X.J. *Knock at a Star*. Little, 1982.

Ridlon, Marci. "That Was Summer" in Booth, David. *Voices on the Wind*. Morrow, 1990.

Ryder, Joanne. *Under Your Feet*. Illus. by Dennis Nolan. Four Winds/Macmillan, 1990.

Rylant, Cynthia. *Night in the Country*. Illus. by Mary Szilagyi. Bradbury/Macmillan, 1986.

Shannon, Monica. "Only My Opinion" in Prelutsky, Jack. *Read-Aloud Rhymes for the Very Young*. Knopf, 1986.

Stafford, William. *The Animal That Drank Up Sound*. Illus. by Debra Frasier. Harcourt, 1992. (fiction)

Wolff, Ashley. *Only the Cat Saw*. Putnam, 1985. (fiction)

Worth, Valerie. "Magnifying Glass" in *All the Small Poems*. Illus. by Natalie Babbitt. Farrar, 1987.

Yolen, Jane. *Owl Moon*. Illus. by John Schoenherr. Philomel/Putnam, 1987.

Zolotow, Charlotte. *Say It!* Illus. by James Stevenson. Greenwillow, 1980.

## CRITICAL THINKING

Curiosity is the greatest tool of the scientist and the poet. Barbara Juster Esbensen's collection of poems, *Who Shrank My Grandmother's House? and Other Poems of Discovery,* explores aspects of an object, creature, or concept, and then attempts to discover an explanation for what has been explored. Aileen Fisher's *Always Wondering* reveals by its title that the poet is filled with curiosity about the world around her. Natalie S. Bober includes a selection of poems titled "Wondering: 'Who Knows If the Moon's a Balloon'" in her collection, *Let's Pretend*. Dr. Seuss has written an extended poem about curiosity in *Oh, the Thinks You Can Think*.

Scientists also think critically about the world by trying to see the connections among things. Scientists organize what they observe into catalogues or taxonomies. Poets also make catalogues as they observe the world around them. One of the classic catalogs is Christopher Smart's "For I Will Consider My Cat, Geoffrey." In this poem, Smart describes his cat in a series of observations beginning with "For he is." The cat provides other possibilities for cataloging. Rosalie Moore's "Catalog" is a description of both good and bad qualities of cats. Beatrice Schenk de Regniers has written several of these catalogs including "Some Things I Know about Cats" and "A Special Dictionary to Help You Understand Cats." Other poems that give a catalog of features of a person, animal, or object are included in the section on list poems in Chapter 5.

Sometimes storytellers' and poets' explanations are very different from those of the scientist. The *pourquoi* stories from traditional literature, for example, provide logical but unlikely explanations of natural phenomena. Why do cats purr? Storyteller Ashley Bryan suggests in *The Cat's Purr* that it goes back to when a cat and rat were friends and a tiny drum almost came between them. Phyllis McGinley has written a poem, "Legend of the Cat," suggesting that the purr is but the dim, tamed reminder of the wild cat of the past. Arthur Guiterman in "What the Gray Cat Sings" suggests the purr is the thrum of a weaver's song, left after a witch turned the weaver into a cat. After listening to these poetic explanations we might pursue a more scientific one or write our own poetic one.

Students might look and listen for the verses nonscientists use to explain or categorize things in the natural world. One of the best known of these is the traditional nursery rhyme, "Red sky at night, sailor's (or farmer's) delight, red sky at morning, sailor (or farmer) take warning." Mother Goose and nursery rhyme collections include others. Alice and Martin Provensen's *Mother Goose Book* includes, for example, rhymes on which direction the wind should be blowing to catch fish, in what months it's good to have a swarm of bees, and the value of March winds and April showers. Alvin Schwartz' *And the Green Grass Grew All Around: Folk Poetry for Everyone* also includes a section of traditional weather rhymes. Students could make a collection of these rhymes, both from written sources and from asking adults if they know some. They could explore the truth of the rhymes.

Scientists also use poetic devices to help explain what they see and feel. One way of telling the difference between several types of evergreens, for example, is to slide one's hand along a handful of needles and to remember that "spruce is sticky" and "fir is friendly." Or one can look closely at a tiny leaf and remember that "spruce is sided" and "fir is flat." Scouts who head out into the woods will be told about the poisonous plants with this little rhyme: "Leaves of three, let it be; berries white, a poisonous sight."

Bober, Natalie S. "Wondering: 'Who Knows If the Moon's a Balloon'?" in *Let's Pretend: Poems of Flight and Fancy*. Illus. by Bill Bell. Viking, 1986.

Bryan, Ashley. *The Cat's Purr*. Atheneum/Macmillan, 1985. (traditional)

De Regniers, Beatrice Schenk. "Some Things I Know about Cats" and "A Special Dictionary to Help You Understand Cats" in *This Big Cat and Other Cats I've Known*. Illus. by Alan Daniel. Crown, 1985.

Esbensen, Barbara Juster. *Who Shrank My Grandmother's House?* Illus. by Eric Beddows. Harper, 1992.

Fisher, Aileen. *Always Wondering*. Illus. by Joan Sandin. Harper, 1991.

Guiterman, Arthur. "What the Gray Cat Sings" in Larrick, Nancy. *Cats Are Cats*. Philomel/Putnam, 1988.

Johnson, Georgia Douglas. "Your World" in Slier, Deborah. *Make a Joyful Sound*. Checkerboard, 1991.

McGinley, Phyllis. "The Legend of the Cat" in *A Wreath of Christmas Legends*. Illus. by Leonard Weisgard. Macmillan, 1967.

Moore, Rosalie. "Catalog" in Livingston, Myra Cohn. *Cat Poems*. Holiday, 1987.

*The Mother Goose Book*. Illus. by Alice and Martin Provensen. Random, 1976.

Schwartz, Alvin, sel. *And the Green Grass Grew All Around*. Illus. by Sue Truesdell. Harper, 1992.

Seuss, Dr. *Oh, the Thinks You Can Think*. Random, 1975.

Silverstein, Shel. "Listen to the Musn'ts" in *Where the Sidewalk Ends*. Harper, 1974.

Smart, Christopher. "For I Will Consider My Cat, Geoffrey" in Blishen, Edward. *The Oxford Book of Poetry for Children*. Oxford, 1984.

Worth, Valerie. "Dinosaur" in *All the Small Poems*. Illus. by Natalie Babbitt. Farrar, 1987.

## FRAME OF REFERENCE

Scientists talk about viewing things from different frames of reference and poets talk about taking a point of view. Both ask us to imagine the world from a different perspective. How would it feel? How would we act? Mary Ann Hoberman says in "Changing" that she wants to know how it feels to be someone or something else. Tony Johnston suggests in "Upside-Downer" that she might get at a spider's feelings if she could hang from a thread and do what a spider does. In "Reflection," Shel Silverstein suggests that his reflection in the water, the "upside-down man," may have a different perspective on the world.

Joanne Ryder's free verse picture books in the "Just for a Day" series invite us to wake and spend a day as a creature: to feel with the lizard the cool leaf beneath our stomach, to imagine the ocean all around us as we swim. Byrd Baylor's *Desert Voices* is a collection of first-person poems from the point of view of the creatures and people who inhabit the deserts of the southwest. In Karla Kuskin's *Any Me I Want to Be* she tries on the point of view of animals, plants, and objects. Carmen Bernos de Gasztold's *Prayers from the Ark* and *The Creatures' Choir* allow us to see the world from the point of view of various animals as we listen to their prayers: the tortoise prays slowly while the butterfly keeps losing its place as it prays. Similarly, X.J. Kennedy's collection of animal poems, *The Beasts of Bethlehem*, focuses on the thoughts of various animals who visit the manger at Christmas. Even the smallest beings have a point of view for poets. Lillian Morrison's "Oh, To Be an Earthworm" invites us to be a creature that lives its life "savoring it/inch by inch."

Our frame of reference also depends upon where we are in the world. Ellen Kandoian's book, *Under the Sun*, asks the reader in simple prose to follow the path of the sun around the earth in the course of a day and to see that some children are sleeping, while others are up and at school or at play. "The Sun's Travels" by Robert Louis Stevenson captures the same image. In "Until We Built a Cabin," Aileen Fisher talks about her broadening frame of reference; she never knew there were so many stars until she moved to the country.

Baylor, Byrd. *Desert Voices*. Illus. by Peter Parnell. Macmillan, 1981.

De Gasztold, Carmen Bernos. *Prayers from the Ark*. French and European, n.d.

———. *Prayers from the Ark: Selected Poems*. Illus. by Barry Moser. Viking, 1992.

Fisher, Aileen. "Until We Built a Cabin" in *Always Wondering*. Illus. by Joan Sandin. Harper, 1991.

Hoberman, Mary Ann. "Changing" in Bober, Natalie. *Let's Pretend*. Viking, 1986.

Johnston, Tony. "Upside-Downer" in *I'm Gonna Tell Mama I Want an Iguana*. Illus. by Lillian Hoban. Putnam, 1990.

Kandoian, Ellen. *Under the Sun*. Putnam, 1987. (nonfiction)

Kennedy, X.J. *The Beasts of Bethlehem*. Illus. by Michael McCurdy. M.K. McElderry/ Macmillan, 1992.

Kuskin, Karla. *Any Me I Want to Be*. Harper, 1972.

Morrison, Lillian. "Oh, To Be an Earthworm" in *Whistling the Morning In*. Illus. by Joel Cook. Wordsong/Boyds Mills, 1992.

Ryder, Joanne. *Catching the Wind*. Illus. by Michael Rothman. Morrow. 1989.

———. *Lizard in the Sun*. Illus. by Michael Rothman. Morrow. 1990.

———. *White Bear, Ice Bear*. Illus. by Michael Rothman. Morrow, 1989.

———. *Winter Whale*. Illus. by Michael Rothman. Morrow, 1991.

Silverstein, Shel. "Reflection" in *A Light in the Attic*. Harper, 1981.

Stevenson, Robert Louis. "The Sun's Travels" in *A Child's Garden of Verses*. Illus. by Michael Foreman. Delacorte, 1985.

As poets and scientists learn more about the world around them, as they closely observe, see connections, and think critically about it, they may be moved to honor our relationship with the natural world. Richard Lewis' free verse poem, *In the Night Still Dark*, is taken from the traditional Hawaiian creation chant, the Kumulipo, which was recited at the birth of a child to bond it to all other living things. Debra Frasier creates a similar feeling with her free verse picture book, *On the Day You Were Born*. In *The Way to Start a Day*, by Byrd Baylor parents hold their newborn child to the morning sun for a blessing "when all the power of life is in the sky." The poetic language of Chief Seattle's message in *Brother Eagle, Sister Sky* speaks of these connections. Nancy Luenn's metaphorical picture book *Mother Earth* describes the earth as our mother with mountains for bones, "listening stones" for ears, and insects for thoughts who gives us many things. Luenn then suggests some things we can give back to our mother. Norman Jordan in "August 8" suggests that all things, times, and relationships are part of each other and that the poet expresses this by writing poems that connect with the reader.

Baylor, Byrd. *The Way to Start a Day*. Illus. by Peter Parnell. Macmillan, 1978.

Frasier, Debra. *On the Day You Were Born*. Harcourt, 1991.

Jordan, Norman. "August 8" in Slier, Deborah. *Make a Joyful Sound*. Checkerboard, 1991.

Lewis, Richard. *In the Night Still Dark*. Illus. by Ed Young. Atheneum/Macmillan, 1988.

Luenn, Nancy. *Mother Earth*. Illus. by Neil Waldman. Atheneum/Macmillan, 1992.

Seattle, Chief. *Brother Eagle, Sister Sky: A Message from Chief Seattle*. Illus. by Susan Jeffers. Dial, 1991.

## COLLECTIONS OF SCIENCE POEMS

Nature, seasons, animals, and plants are frequently the subjects of poetry. The collections listed here include poems on these and other topics of science.

### General Collections

De Regniers, Beatrice Schenk, et al. sels. *Sing a Song of Popcorn*. Illus. by Caldecott Artists. Scholastic, 1988.

Ferris, Helen, sel. *Favorite Poems Old and New*. Doubleday, 1957.

Kennedy, X.J. sel. *Talking Like the Rain*. Illus. by Jane Dyer. Little, 1992.

Plotz, Helen, sel. *Imagination's Other Place: Poems of Science and Mathematics*. Crowell/Harper, 1987.

Prelutsky, Jack, sel. *The Random House Book of Poetry for Children*. Illus. by Arnold Lobel. Random, 1983.

———. *Read-Aloud Rhymes for the Very Young*. Illus. by Marc Brown. Knopf, 1986.

### Nature

Bodecker, N.M. *Water Pennies and Other Poems*. Illus. by Eric Blegvad. M.K. McElderry/Macmillan, 1991.

Brown, Margaret Wise. *Nibble, Nibble*. Illus. by Leonard Weisgard. Harper, 1959, 1985.

Esbensen, Barbara Juster. *Cold Stars and Fireflies*. Illus. by Susan Bonners. Harper, 1991.

Fisher, Aileen. *Always Wondering*. Illus. by Joan Sandin. Harper, 1991.

Harvey, Anne, sel. *Shades of Green*. Illus. by John Lawrence. Greenwillow, 1992.

Lewis, J. Patrick. *Earth Verses and Water Rhymes*. Illus. by Robert Sabuda. Macmillan, 1991.

Morrison, Lillian. *Whistling the Morning In*. Illus. by Joel Cook. Wordsong/Boyds Mills, 1992.

Norman, Charles. *The Hornbeam Tree*. Illus. by Ted Rand. Holt, 1988.

## Seasons

Adoff, Arnold. *In for Winter, Out for Spring*. Illus. by Jerry Pinkney. Harcourt, 1991.

Booth, David, sel. *Voices on the Wind: Poems for all Seasons*. Illus. by Michelle LeMieux. Morrow, 1990.

Bruchac, Joseph and Jonathan London. *Thirteen Moons on Turtle's Back: A Native American Year of Moons*. Illus. by Thomas Locker. Philomel/Putnam, 1992.

Dickinson, Emily. *A Brighter Garden*. Illus. by Tasha Tudor. Philomel/Putnam, 1990.

Esbensen, Barbara Juster. *Cold Stars and Fireflies: Poems of the Four Seasons*. Illus. by Susan Bonner. Harper, 1991.

Frank, Josette, sel. *Snow toward Evening: A Year in a River Valley*. Illus. by Thomas Locker. Dial, 1990.

Higginson, William J., sel. *Wind in the Long Grass: A Collection of Haiku*. Illus. by Sandra Speidel. Simon, 1991.

Hopkins, Lee Bennett, sel. *The Sky Is Full of Song*. Illus. by Dick Zimmer. Harper, 1983.

Hughes, Shirley. *Out and About*. Lothrop, 1988.

Katz, Bobbi. *Puddle Wonderful: Poems to Welcome Spring*. Illus. by Mary Morgan. Random, 1992.

Livingston, Myra Cohn. *A Circle of Seasons*. Illus. by Leonard Everett Fisher. Holiday, 1982.

Steele, Mary Q. *Anna's Summer Songs*. Illus. by Lena Anderson. Greenwillow, 1988.

Yolen, Jane. *Ring of Earth: A Child's Book of Seasons*. Illus. by John Wallner. Harcourt, 1986.

## Animals

Carter, Anne, sel. *Birds, Beasts, and Fishes: A Selection of Animal Poems*. Illus. by Reg Cartwright. Macmillan, 1991.

De Gasztold, Carmen Bernos. *The Creatures' Choir*. French and European, n.d.

————. *Prayers from the Ark*. French and European, n.d.

————. *Prayers from the Ark: Selected Poems*. Illus. by Barry Moser. Viking, 1992.

De Regniers, Beatrice Schenk. *It Does Not Say Meow, and Other Animal Rhymes*. Illus. by Paul Galdone. Clarion/Houghton, 1979.

————. *This Big Cat and Other Cats I've Known*. Illus. by Alan Daniel. Crown, 1985.

Esbensen, Barbara Juster. *Words with Wrinkled Knees*. Illus. by John Stadler. Crowell/Harper, 1987.

Farber, Norma. *As I Was Crossing Boston Common*. Illus. by Arnold Lobel. Dutton, 1975, 1992.

Fisher, Aileen. *The House of a Mouse*. Illus. by Joan Sandin. Harper, 1988.

————. *Listen Rabbit*. Illus. by Symeon Shimin. Crowell/Harper, 1964.

————. *Rabbits, Rabbits*. Illus. by Gail Niemann. Harper, 1983.

Goldstein, Bobbye S., sel. *Bear in Mind: A Book of Bear Poems*. Illus. by William Pene Du Bois. Viking, 1989.

Heard, Georgia. *Creatures of Earth, Sea, and Sky*. Illus. by Jennifer Owings Dewey. Wordsong/Boyds Mills, 1992.

Hoberman, Mary Ann. *A Fine Fat Pig and Other Animal Poems*. Illus. by Malcah Zeldis. Harper, 1991.

Hooper, Patricia. *A Bundle of Beasts*. Illus. by Mark Steele. Houghton, 1987.

Hopkins, Lee Bennett, sel. *On the Farm*. Illus. by Laurel Molk. Little, 1991.

———. *To the Zoo: Animal Poems*. Illus. by John Wallner. Little, 1992.

Hubbell, Patricia. *A Green Grass Gallop*. Illus. by Ronald Himler. Atheneum/Macmillan, 1990.

King-Smith, Dick. *Alphabeasts*. Illus. by Quentin Blake. Macmillan, 1992.

Larrick, Nancy, sel. *Cats Are Cats*. Illus. by Ed Young. Philomel/Putnam, 1988.

———. *Mice Are Nice*. Illus. by Ed Young. Philomel/Putnam, 1990.

Lewis, J. Patrick. *A Hippopotamustn't and Other Animal Verse*. Illus. by Victoria Chess. Dial, 1990.

———. *Two-Legged, Four-Legged, No-Legged Rhymes*. Illus. by Pamela Papparone. Knopf, 1991.

Livingston, Myra Cohn, sel. *Cat Poems*. Illus. by Trina Schart Hyman. Holiday, 1987.

———. *Dog Poems*. Illus. by Leslie Morrill. Holiday, 1990.

———. *If You Ever Meet a Whale*. Illus. by Leonard Everett Fisher. Holiday, 1992.

Mado, Michio. *The Animals: Selected Poems*. Illus. by Mitsumasa Anno. M.K. McElderry/Macmillan, 1992.

Marsh, James. *Bizarre Birds and Beasts*. Dial, 1991.

Prelutsky, Jack. *Zoo Doings: Animal Poems*. Illus. by Paul O. Zelinsky. Greenwillow, 1983.

Steig, Jeanne. *Consider the Lemming*. Illus. by William Steig. Farrar, 1988.

Whipple, Laura, sel. *Animals, Animals*. Illus. by Eric Carle. Philomel/Putnam, 1989.

# Birds

Adoff, Arnold. *Birds: Poems*. Illus. by Troy Howell. Harper, 1982.

Fleischman, Paul. *I Am Phoenix*. Illus. by Ken Nutt. Harper, 1985.

Livingston, Myra Cohn. *If the Owl Calls Again: A Collection of Owl Poems*. Illus. by Antonio Frasconi. M.K. McElderry/Macmillan, 1990.

Norman, Charles. *The Hornbeam Tree and Other Poems*. Illus. by Ted Rand. Holt, 1988.

Yolen, Jane. *Bird Watch*. Illus. by Ted Lewin. Philomel/Putnam, 1990.

# Insects

Bodecker, N.M. *Water Pennies and Other Poems*. Illus. by Eric Blegvad. M.K. McElderry/Macmillan, 1990.

Fisher, Aileen. *When It Comes to Bugs*. Illus. by Chris and Bruce Degen. Harper, 1986.

Fleischman, Paul. *Joyful Noise*. Illus. by Eric Beddows. Harper, 1988.

Hopkins, Lee Bennett, sel. *Flit, Flutter, Fly!* Illus. by Peter Palagonia. Doubleday, 1992.

Parker, Nancy Winslow, and Joan Richards Wright. *Bugs*. Greenwillow, 1987.

## Weather

Bauer, Caroline Feller, sel. *Rainy Day: Stories and Poems*. Illus. by Michele Chessare. Harper, 1986.

———. *Snowy Day: Stories and Poems*. Illus. by Margot Tomes. Harper, 1986.

———. *Windy Day: Stories and Poems*. Illus. by Dick Zimmer. Harper, 1988.

Prelutsky, Jack. *It's Snowing, It's Snowing*. Illus. by Jeanne Titherington. Greenwillow, 1984.

———. *Rainy, Rainy Saturday*. Illus. by Marylin Hafner. Greenwillow, 1980.

Radley, Gail. *Rainy Day Rhymes*. Illus. by Ellen Kandoian. Houghton, 1992.

## Physical World

Livingston, Myra Cohn. *Earth Songs*. Illus. by Leonard Everett Fisher. Holiday, 1986.

———. *Sea Songs*. Illus. by Leonard Everett Fisher. Holiday, 1986.

———. *Sky Songs*. Illus. by Leonard Everett Fisher. Holiday, 1984.

———. *Space Songs*. Illus. by Leonard Everett Fisher. Holiday, 1988.

## REFERENCES

Barnes, D. (1976). "Ways of Thinking about Classroom Learning" *From Communication to Curriculum*. New York: Penguin.

Carey, M. (1989). "Catalog Poem" in *Poetry: Starting from Scratch*. Lincoln, NE: Foundation Books.

Doris, E. (1991). *Doing What Scientists Do: Children Learn to Investigate Their World*. Portsmouth, NH: Heinemann.

Esbensen, B.J. (1975). *A Celebration of Bees: Helping Children to Write Poetry*. Minneapolis: Winston Press.

Geismar, M. (1976). *The Higher Animals: A Mark Twain Bestiary*. Illus. by Jean-Claude Suares. New York: Crowell.

Kennedy, X.J., and D. Kennedy. (1982). "What Do Poems Do?: Start You Wondering" in *Knock at a Star: A Child's Introduction to Poetry*. Boston: Little.

*Oxford Dictionary of Modern Quotations*. (1991). Oxford: Oxford University Press, p. 5.

# Chapter 3:
# Poetry and Mathematics

Modern methods of mathematics instruction stress the use of mathematical concepts and logic in authentic situations just as whole language has encouraged authentic experiences with reading and writing. Learning by doing leads to a richer, longer-lasting understanding of both mathematics and language concepts and skills. Poetry is one of the ways we can link the language of letters and words with the language of numbers.

> I count the beats in every line.
> I count them and I list them:
> Iambic pentameter, and rhyme.
> Is this the metric system? (Chatton, 1992)

As this poet has noticed, mathematics and poetry have a piece of shared language. The word "meter" simply means measurement, and measurement is critical in both fields. The mathematical meter is a unit of length and the poetic meter is a unit of rhythm. Children can develop a different understanding of the vocabulary of mathematics through poems that explore numbers, counting, and mathematical processes. Some poems introduce children to the concepts underlying these terms, as the poet tries to put mathematics into "writing." Poems can introduce children to problem solving, classification, patterns, and even logic. The nursery rhyme "As I was going to St. Ives," for example, presents a classic logic problem that delights children who enjoy riddles. A selection of other riddle poems involving logic is included in Chapter 5.

## COUNTING

The simple rhymed texts in concept counting books and counting out rhymes for young children provide an obvious link between poetry and mathematics. Typically, in these rhymes a number sequence is used as a framework for a simple story and the mnemonic device of rhyme helps children to remember the counting scheme. The Mother Goose counting rhyme "One, two, buckle my shoe" performs this function. A two-year-old will joyously repeat the rhymed line "Buckle my shoe" after "One, two" is given. Children who enjoyed this rhyme when they were younger laugh at Shel Silverstein's parody of it, "One Two," in which someone yells back, "'Buckle your own shoe!'" Counting is implicit in "This Little Pig Went to Market," as the parent or child traditionally counts toes as the rhyme is being recited. Although we generally think of Mother Goose rhymes for very young children, they are so much a part of our culture that five- and six-year-olds still enjoy them. Michael Jay Katz has collected counting rhymes in *Ten Potatoes in a Pot and Other Counting Rhymes*. Others can be located in comprehensive collections of Mother Goose rhymes. Counting-out rhymes appear in all languages and cultures. Jane Yolen's *Street Rhymes around the World* contains several international examples as does *Miss Mary Mack and Other Children's Street Rhymes* by Joanna Cole and Stephanie Calmenson.

Most counting books are organized around a common subject or theme. Olive Wadsworth's classic *Over in the Meadow* counts animals while S.T. Garnes' *One White Sail* counts things found in the Caribbean. Some counting books are designed to teach numbers and counting; others use numbers merely as a frame for a creative story or art work. These "artistic" counting books can be used with older students. Students studying Australia, for example, might like Rod Trinca's *One Woolly Wombat,* which includes different animals and plants of that continent. Fulvio Testa's *If You Take a Pencil* is a counting book that includes an art lesson. Some poems for older students also use the conventions of counting and numbers as a pattern.

Children may discover that there are differences among counting books when they have a chance to look through several of them at one time. Some books include the numbers 1 to 10; others use 1 to 12. Still others use 1 to 10 then skip to higher numbers. Molly Bang's *Ten, Nine, Eight* counts backwards. Students might want to try to sort and categorize counting books as they notice these differences.

## Counting Books

Alda, Arlene. *Sheep, Sheep, Sheep: Help Me Fall Asleep.* Doubleday, 1992.
Aylesworth, Jim. *One Crow: A Counting Rhyme.* Illus. by Ruth Young. Harper, 1988.
Bang, Molly. *Ten, Nine, Eight.* Greenwillow, 1983.
Becker, John. *Seven Little Rabbits.* Illus. by Barbara Cooney. Scholastic, 1973.
Calmenson, Stephanie. *Dinner at the Panda Palace.* Illus. by Nadine Bernard Westcott. Harper, 1992.
Christelow, Eileen. *Five Little Monkeys Sitting in a Tree.* Clarion/Houghton, 1991.
Crews, Donald. *Ten Black Dots.* Greenwillow, 1986.

De Regniers, Beatrice Schenk. *So Many Cats!* Illus. by Ellen Weiss. Clarion/Ticknor and Fields, 1988.

Eichenberg, Fritz. *Dancing in the Moon: A Counting Book.* Harcourt, 1975.

Enderle, Judith Ross, and Stephanie Gordon Tessler. *Six Creepy Sheep.* Illus. by John O'Brien. Caroline/Boyds Mills, 1992.

Garne, S. T. *One White Sail: A Caribbean Counting Book.* Illus. by Lisa Etre. Green Tiger, 1992.

Leedy, Loreen. *A Number of Dragons.* Holiday, 1985.

LeSieg, Theo. *Ten Apples Up on Top!* Illus. by Ray McKie. Random, 1961.

Lewin, Betsy. *Cat Count.* Putnam, 1981.

Lindbergh, Reeve. *The Midnight Farm.* Illus. by Susan Jeffers. Dial, 1987.

Linden, Anne Marie. *One Smiling Grandma: A Caribbean Counting Book.* Illus. by Lynne Russell. Dial, 1992.

Samton, Sheila White. *The World from My Window.* Boyds Mills, 1991.

Sendak, Maurice. *One Was Johnny: A Counting Book.* Harper, 1962.

Testa, Fulvio. *If You Take a Pencil.* Dial, 1982.

Thornhill, Jan. *The Wildlife 1-2-3: A Nature Counting Book.* Simon, 1989.

Trinca, Rod. *One Woolly Wombat.* Illus. by Kerry Argent. Kane/Miller, 1985.

Tudor, Tasha. *1 Is One.* Macmillan, 1988.

Wadsworth, Olive A. *Over in the Meadow.* Illus. by Ezra Jack Keats. Scholastic, 1985.

————. *Over in the Meadow: An Old Counting Rhyme.* Illus. by David A. Carter. Scholastic, 1992.

Yolen, Jane. *An Invitation to the Butterfly Ball: A Counting Rhyme.* Illus. by Jane Breskin Zalben. Caroline/Boyds Mills, 1992.

## Counting Poems for Older Readers

Poets sometimes use the counting out scheme as a method of organizing a poem for older readers. A few counting poems that would be enjoyed by upper elementary childdren are included here.

Fleischman, Paul. "Morning" in *I Am Phoenix.* Illus. by Ken Nutt. Harper, 1985.

Johnston, Tony. *Whale Song.* Illus. by Ed Young. Putnam, 1987.

Lewis, J. Patrick. "Blue Herons" in *Earth Verses and Water Rhymes.* Illus. by Robert Sabuda. Atheneum/Macmillan, 1991.

Millay, Edna St. Vincent. "Counting-Out Rhyme" in Dunning, Stephen. *Reflections on a Gift of Watermelon Pickle.* Lothrop, 1966.

Silverstein, Shel. "One, Two" in *A Light in the Attic.* Harper, 1981.

Soto, Gary. "Teaching Numbers" in *A Fire in My Hands.* Illus. by James M. Cardillo. Scholastic, 1991.

## Fingerplays and Action Rhymes

Many fingerplays involve counting from 1 to 10 using fingers or toes. Joanna Cole and Stephanie Calmenson include several of these in *The Eentsy Weentsy Spider: Fingerplays and Action Rhymes.* Individual fingerplays and counting rhymes also appear in many other collections.

Ciardi, John. "Guess" in *I Met a Man.* Illus. by Robert Osborn. Houghton, 1973.

Cole, Joanna, and Stephanie Calmenson, sels. *The Eentsy, Weentsy Spider: Fingerplays and Action Rhymes.* Illus. by Alan Tiegreen. Morrow, 1991.

———. *Miss Mary Mack and Other Children's Street Rhymes.* Illus. by Alan Tiegreen. Morrow, 1990.

Eastwick, Ivy O. "Ten to One" in Prelutsky, Jack. *Read-Aloud Rhymes for the Very Young.* Random, 1983.

"Five Little Chickens" in Prelutsky, Jack. *Read-Aloud Rhymes for the Very Young.* Random, 1983.

"Five Little Monkeys" in Bennett, Jill. *Tiny Tim.* Delacorte, 1982.

"Five Little Squirrels" in De Regniers, Beatrice Schenk. *Sing a Song of Popcorn.* Scholastic, 1988.

"Jack Jingle" in Opie, Peter and Iona. *Tail Feathers from Mother Goose.* Little, 1988.

Katz, Michael Jay, sel. *Ten Potatoes in a Pot and Other Counting Rhymes.* Illus. by June Otani. Harper, 1990.

Kuskin, Karla. "One Jay, Two Jay" in *Something Sleeping in the Hall.* Harper, 1985.

McCord, David. "Alphabet (Eta Z)" and "Five Little Bats" in *One at a Time.* Little, 1986.

Merriam, Eve. "Ten Little Apples" in *You Be Good and I'll Be Night.* Illus. by Karen Lee Schmidt. Morrow, 1988.

" One, Two, Three, Four, Five" in Briggs, Raymond. *The Mother Goose Treasury.* Coward/Putnam, 1966.

Reeves, James. "Poor Jane Higgins" in Bennett, Jill. *Tiny Tim.* Delacorte, 1982.

Roberts, Elizabeth Madox. "The Dark" in Larrick, Nancy. *When the Dark Comes Dancing.* Philomel/Putnam, 1983.

Withers, Carl, sel. "Counting Out Rhymes" in *A Rocket in My Pocket.* Holt, 1988.

Yolen, Jane. *Street Rhymes around the World.* Illus. by Jeanette Winter and 17 international artists. Wordsong/Boyds Mills, 1992.

## Counting Song Books

Some counting books are also song books. Counting songs use rhythm and rhyme to help establish number names and series. The nursery song best known as "Knick Knack Paddywack," which uses a counting theme, is available in three picture book versions. A traditional version titled "Jack Jingle" appears in *Tail Feathers from Mother Goose.* Marissa Moss's *Knick Knack Paddywack* starts with the traditional song, adds verses, and has the character blast off to become the man in the moon after a lovely 10-to-1 countdown. There are two picture book versions of *Roll Over* or *Ten in the Bed* and several versions of *The Twelve Days of Christmas.* Students may want to compare retellings and styles of art among these books or they may want to create their own illustrations for a favorite counting song or poem.

Cole, Joanna, and Stephanie Calmenson, sels. *The Eentsy, Weentsy Spider: Fingerplays and Actions Rhymes.* Illus. by Alan Tiegreen. Morrow, 1991.

Moss, Marissa. *Knick Knack Paddywack.* Houghton, 1992.

*Roll Over!: A Counting Song.* Illus. by Merle Peek. Clarion/Houghton, 1981.
*Ten in a Bed.* Illus. by Mary Rees. Joy Street/Little, 1988.
*This Old Man.* Illus. by Carol Jones. Houghton, 1990.
*This Old Man: The Counting Song.* Illus. by Robin M. Koontz. Putnam, 1988.
*The Twelve Days of Christmas.* Illus. by Joanna Isles. Hyperion, 1992.
*The Twelve Days of Christmas.* Illus. by Jan Brett. Putnam, 1990.

## NUMBERS

Some poems discuss a single number in a poetic way. Carl Sandburg, Aliki Barnstone, and Eve Merriam have all written poems about the number zero. Some books and poems are about large numbers. Poems such as Karla Kuskin's "Counting," in which she discusses the difficulty of counting stars, and Beatrice Schenk de Regniers' "I Want To," in which she talks about counting sheep beyond a million, can be used with David M. Schwartz's nonfiction book *How Much Is a Million?* which describes large numbers using a litany of "if" statements.

Barnstone, Aliki. "Zero Makes Me Hungry" in Lueders, Edward. *Zero Makes Me Hungry.* Scott, 1976.

De Regniers, Beatrice Schenk. "I Want To" in Larrick, Nancy. *When the Dark Comes Dancing.* Philomel/Putnam, 1983.

Kuskin, Karla. "Counting" in *Dogs and Dragons, Trees and Dreams.* Harper, 1980.

Merriam, Eve. "Arithmetrix" in *The Singing Green.* Illus. by Kathleen Collins Howell. Morrow, 1992.

———. "A Number of Numbers" in *Jamboree.* Illus. by Walter G. Kessell. Dell, 1984.

———. "A Number of Words" in *Chortles: New and Selected Word Play Poems.* Illus. by Sheila Hamanaka. Morrow, 1989.

———. "A Short Note" in *A Sky Full of Poems.* Illus. by Walter G. Kessell. Dell, 1986.

———. "Zero" in *Halloween ABC.* Illus. by Lane Smith. Macmillan, 1987.

" My Hat It Has Three Corners" in Cole, Joanna. *Eentsy Weentsy Spider.* Morrow, 1991.

Prelutsky, Jack. "Eight Big Black Bears" in Goldstein, Bobbye. *Bear in Mind.* Viking, 1989.

Sandburg, Carl. "I Am Zero, Naught, One Cipher" in *The People, Yes.* Harcourt, 1990.

Schwartz, David M. *How Much Is a Million?* Illus. by Steven Kellogg. Lothrop, 1985. (nonfiction)

Soto, Gary. "Teaching the Numbers" in *A Fire in My Hands.* Illus. by James M. Cardillo. Scholastic, 1991.

"Three Young Rats with Black Felt Hats" in Sutherland, Zena. *The Orchard Book of Nursery Rhymes.* Orchard, 1990.

## MATHEMATICAL OPERATIONS

Sometimes poems allude to or discuss a mathematical operation. Sometimes a mathematical process is a pattern within a poem. Children may realize that the little one in the counting-out rhyme *Roll Over!* is subtracting one each time it yells out, "Roll over!" even as they enjoy the use of simple numbers to tell this story. Other poems in the counting section can be used with lessons on addition and subtraction as well. Sometimes poets make fun of numbers and the processes of using them. John Ciardi, for example, has written a number of poems showing how even simple math can be confusing. Students enjoy the mock turtle's description of the four processes of mathematics in Lewis Carroll's *Alice's Adventures in Wonderland:* "Ambition, distraction, uglification, and derision." They also enjoy Carroll's pun on school lessons, a comment on subtraction:

"And how many hours did you do lessons?" said Alice, in a hurry to change the subject.
"Ten hours the first day," said the Mock Turtle: "nine the next, and so on."
" What a curious plan!" exclaimed Alice.
" That's the reason they're called lessons," the Gryphon remarked: "because they lessen from day to day." (Carroll, 1960)

Some poets use a mathematical operation as a pattern to tell a story. Beatrice Schenk de Regniers in *So Many Cats* and Betsy Lewin in *Cat Count* comment on people's tendency to "collect" cats by using addition. These poem picture books can be used with Wanda Gag's *Millions of Cats* for a short unit on "cat collecting."

Adoff, Arnold. "The Old Math: Two" in *Chocolate Dreams.* Illus. by Turie MacCombie. Lothrop, 1989. (subtraction)

Carroll, Lewis. "A Sum" in Harrison, Michael. *Splinters.* Oxford, 1988. (fractions)

"The Cats of Kilkenny" in Elledge, Scott. *Wider Than the Sky.* Harper, 1990. (subtraction)

"Chook, Chook" in Prelutsky, Jack. *Read Aloud Rhymes for the Very Young.* Knopf, 1986. (addition)

Ciardi, John. "About Being Very Good and Far Better Than Most But Still Not Quite Good Enough to Take on the Atlantic Ocean" (subtraction), and "There's Nothing to It" (fractions) in *Doodle Soup.* Illus. by Merle Nacht. Houghton, 1985.

———. "Chang McTang McQuarter Cat" (addition, fractions) and "Little Bits" (subtraction) in *You Read to Me, I'll Read to You.* Illus. by Edward Gorey. Lippincott/Harper, 1961.

———. "A Divided Opinion" in *Mummy Took Cooking Lessons.* Illus. by Merle Nacht. Houghton, 1990. (division)

De Regniers, Beatrice Schenk. *So Many Cats!* Illus. by Ellen Weiss. Clarion/Ticknor and Fields, 1988. (addition)

Gag, Wanda. *Millions of Cats.* Putnam, 1928. (fiction)

Hoberman, Mary Ann. "One Half of the Giraffe" in *A Fine Fat Pig*. Illus. by Malcah Zeldis. Harper, 1991. (fractions)

Hulme, Joy N. *Sea Squares*. Illus. by Carol Schwartz. Hyperion/Disney, 1991. (multiplication)

Kuskin, Karla. "Is Six Times One a Lot of Fun?" in *Near the Window Tree*. Harper, 1975. (multiplication)

Lee, Dennis. "Nine Black Cats" in *The Ice Cream Store*. Illus. by David McPhail. Scholastic, 1992. (addition)

Lewin, Betsy. *Cat Count*. Putnam, 1981. (addition)

McCord, David. "Dividing" (division), "Exit X" (algebra), "Rhyme" (multiplication), and "Who Hasn't Played Gazinta?" (all) in *One at a Time*. Little, 1986.

Merriam, Eve. "Gazinta" in *Chortles: New and Selected Word Play Poems*. Illus. by Sheila Hamanaka. Morrow, 1989. (division)

Pomerantz, Charlotte. "The Half Lullaby" in *All Asleep*. Illus. by Nancy Tafuri. Puffin, 1986. (fractions)

Prelutsky, Jack. "A Microscopic Topic" in *The New Kid on the Block*. Illus. by James Stevenson. Greenwillow, 1984. (all)

Reeves, James. "A Pig Tale" in De Regniers, Beatrice Schenk. *Sing a Song of Popcorn: Every Child's Book of Poems*. Scholastic, 1988. (subtraction)

*Roll Over!: A Counting Song*. Illus. by Merle Peek. Clarion/Houghton, 1981. (subtraction)

*Ten in a Bed*. Illus. by Mary Rees. Joy Street/Little, 1988. (subtraction)

Watson, Clyde. "Mister Lister" in *Father Fox's Pennyrhymes*. Illus. by Wendy Watson. Harper, 1971. (multiplication)

# TIME

Time is a complex subject with rich poetic implications. Young children study the terminology of time and learn to use the instruments that measure it. They may wonder how much time Max spent with the Wild Things in *Where the Wild Things Are* or wish for a day of magic time when peculiar things can happen as in David Wiesner's *Tuesday*. Older students may struggle with the more abstract aspects of time as they read Natalie Babbitt's *Tuck Everlasting* or Madeleine L'Engle's *A Wrinkle in Time* and other novels that deal with relativity, eternal life, or the possibility of moving through time and space.

Time has its own large and complex vocabulary. We might begin a unit on time by webbing or listing all of the "time" words we know or wonder about. Some words such as "clock," "watch," "year," and "day" come quickly. Other words or questions may come up as we read and discuss. Why, for example, does the word "quarters" mean a particular fraction, a period of time, a school term, and also a piece of money? What is a fortnight, a term that appears in many British books students read? What is a score in Lincoln's "Gettysburg Address" and in Whittier's poem "Barbara Frietchie"? What is a centennial? An octogenarian? Is biweekly twice a week or every two weeks?

As we read time fantasy and factual material and experiment with measurement of time, we can collect poems for this unit. Some poems are about particular elements of time: hours, days, and weeks. Nursery rhymes, for example, sometimes use a convention of days as a form, such as "Monday's child is fair of face" and "Solomon Grundy, born on a Monday." Poetry books such as Lucille Clifton's *Everett Anderson's Christmas Coming* or Josette Frank's *Snow towards Evening: A Year in a River Valley* use time as an organizing device, with a poem for each day of the week or month of the year.

Some poems discuss the differences in time around the world. "The Sun's Travel" by Robert Louis Stevenson tells of the child in India who is going to bed just as the child in the West is arising. Marilyn Singer's poetic *Nine O'Clock Lullaby* follows the sun around the world in a similar manner. This poem echoes the simple prose of Ellen Kandoian's picture book *Under the Sun* and together these three writings can introduce children to the concept of time zones. Lillian Morrison's "The Sun" describes the sun's journey around the planet and our greetings to it as it grows taller and brighter in the sky.

Sometimes "clock" time is compared with the changes of the seasons. Aileen Fisher's "On Time" tells us to set our watches "half a tick to spring!" This poem makes a nice pairing with Eve Merriam's "Is It Robin O'Clock?" in which she compares waiting for spring to clock time.

## Time Poems

Aylesworth, Jim. *The Completed Hickory Dickory Dock*. Illus. by Eileen Christelow. New York: Atheneum, 1990. (hours)

Babbitt, Natalie. *Tuck Everlasting*. Farrar, 1975. (fiction)

"Bell Horses, Bell Horses," "A Dillar A Dollar," "Hickory Dickory Dock," and "Wee Willie Winkie" in Provensen, Alice and Martin. *The Mother Goose Book*. Random, 1976. (hours and minutes)

Bruchac, Joseph, and Jonathon London. *Thirteen Moons on a Turtle's Back*. Illus. by Thomas Locker. Philomel/Putnam, 1992. (months in Native American calendar)

Carlstrom, Nancy White. *How Do You Say It, Jesse Bear?* Illus. by Bruce Degen. Macmillan, 1992. (months)

Ciardi, John. "At Night" (minutes), "How Time Goes" (years) in *Doodle Soup*. Illus. by Merle Nacht. Houghton, 1986.

———. "Well, Welcome Now That You're Here" and "I Hate to Wait" in *Fast and Slow*. Illus. by Becky Gaven. Houghton, 1978.

Clifton, Lucille. *Everett Anderson's Christmas Coming*. Illus. by Jan Spivey Gilchrist. New York: Holt, 1991. (days before Christmas)

———. *Everett Anderson's Nine Month Long*. Illus. by Ann Grifalconi. Holt, 1978. (months)

Coleridge, Sara. "A Calendar" in Wolman, Bernice. *Taking Turns*. Atheneum/ Macmillan, 1992. (months)

De Regniers, Beatrice Schenk. "The Churlish Child's Week/The Cheerful Child's Week" in *The Way I Feel...Sometimes*. Illus. by Susan Meddagh. Clarion/Ticknor and Fields, 1988. (days)

Fisher, Aileen. "On Time" in *Always Wondering*. Illus. by Joan Sandin. Harper, 1991.

Frank, Josette, sel. *Snow towards Evening: A Year in a River Valley*. Illus. by Thomas Locker. Dial, 1990. (months)

Kandoian, Ellen. *Under the Sun*. Philomel/Putnam, 1987.

Kitching, John. "Ways of the Week" in Foster, John. *A Very First Poetry Book*. Oxford, 1987. (days)

L'Engle, Madeleine. *A Wrinkle in Time*. Farrar, 1962. (fiction)

"Lesson from a Sundial" in Harrison, Michael. *Splinters*. Oxford, 1988. (hours)

Lewis, J. Patrick. "The White Wind" in *Earth Verses and Water Rhymes*. Illus. by Robert Sabuda. Atheneum/Macmillan, 1991. (days)

Lobel, Arnold. "I Married a Wife on Sunday" in *Whiskers and Rhymes*. Greenwillow, 1985. (days)

McGinley, Phyllis. "Daylight Saving Time" in Prelutsky, Jack. *Random House Book of Poetry for Children*. Random, 1983.

McNaughton, Colin. "Monday's Child Is Red and Spotty" in Prelutsky, Jack. *For Laughing Out Loud*. Knopf, 1991. (days)

Merriam, Eve. "The Clock Ticks" in *A Sky Full of Poems*. Illus. by Walter Geffney-Kessell. Dell, 1986.

———. "Is It Robin O'Clock?" in *Blackberry Ink*. Illus. by Hans Wilhelm. Morrow, 1985.

———. *Train Leaves the Station*. Illus. by Dale Gottlieb. Holt, 1992. (minutes and hours)

"Monday's Child" and "Solomon Grundy" in Briggs, Raymond. *The Mother Goose Treasury*. Coward/Putnam, 1966. (days)

Moore, Lilian. "Telling Time" in *Something New Begins*. Illus. by Mary Jane Dunton. Atheneum/Macmillan, 1982.

Morrison, Lillian. "The Sun" in *Whistling the Morning In*. Illus. by Joel Cook. Wordsong/Boyds Mills, 1992.

Nims, Bonnie. "How to Get There" in Prelutsky, Jack. *Random House Book of Poetry for Children*. Random, 1983. (days)

Sendak, Maurice. *Where the Wild Things Are*. Harper, 1988. (fiction)

Sheridan, Richard B. "The Months" in Wolman, Bernice. *Taking Turns*. Atheneum/Macmillan, 1982.

Singer, Marilyn. *Nine O'Clock Lullaby*. Illus. by Frane Lessac. Harper, 1991.

*Solomon Grundy*. Illus. by Susan Ramsay Hoguet. Dutton, 1986. (days)

Stevenson, Robert Louis. "The Sun's Travel" in *A Child's Garden of Verses*. Illus. by Michael Foreman. Delacorte, 1985. (time zones)

"Thirty Days Hath September" in Briggs, Raymond. *The Mother Goose Treasury*. Coward/Putnam, 1966. (months)

Thurman, Judith. "Clockface" in Harrison, Michael. *Splinters*. Oxford, 1988.

Wiesner, David. *Tuesday*. Clarion/Houghton, 1991. (fiction)

## Time Relativity

Some "time" poems discuss the theory of relativity in simple terms. In "Cliché," Eve Merriam discusses how time can pass very quickly when we are happily engaged and moves slowly when things are not going so well. Phyllis McGinley's poem "Lengths of Time" discusses this feeling as well, giving examples of events that cause time to fly and those, like being sick with a cold, that cause it to slow down. Other poems talk about how time seems long for the very young and short for the old and how long a lifetime can seem when you are small. The May fly's whole life takes place in just one day. Mary Ann Hoberman's "May Fly" in her now out-of-print collection, *Bugs*, and Paul Fleischman's "Mayflies" show this little piece of relative time.

Brooks, Gwendolyn. "Marie Lucille" in *Bronzeville Boys and Girls*. Illus. by Ronni Solbert. Harper, 1967.

Fleischman, Paul. "Mayflies" in *Joyful Noise*. Illus. by Eric Beddows. Harper, 1988.

Hoberman, Mary Ann. "May Fly" in *Bugs*. Illus. by Victoria Chess. Viking, 1976.

McCord, David. "No Present Like the Time" in *One at a Time*. Little, 1986.

McGinley, Phyllis. "Lengths of Time" in De Regniers, Beatrice Schenk. *Sing a Song of Popcorn*. Scholastic, 1988.

Merriam Eve. "A Cliché" and "The Time Is" in *A Sky Full of Poems*. Illus. by Walter Gaffney-Kessell. Dell, 1986.

Sullivan, A. M. "Measurement" in Prelutsky, Jack. *The Random House Book of Poetry for Children*. Random, 1983.

## Measuring Time

Other poems are about the instruments that measure time: clocks, watches, and calendars. Sometimes poems look at old timepieces: family heirlooms and reminders of past times. Lessie Jones Little and Myra Cohn Livingston have both written about grandfather clocks and their connection to an older family member. Some poems play with the sounds of clocks and watches. Eve Merriam has written a poem that lists ways of winding a watch. X.J. Kennedy has even written a poem about using a clock to open a lid in "Clockwise."

Ciardi, John. "Do You Suppose?" and "The Mechanic" in *Mummy Took Cooking Lessons*. Illus. by Merle Nacht. Houghton, 1990.

Cole, William. "Time Piece" in Janeczko, Paul. *Pocket Poems*. Bradbury/Macmillan, 1985.

Esbensen, Barbara Juster. "Time" in *Who Shrank My Grandmother's House?* Illus. by Eric Beddows. Harper, 1992.

Kennedy, X.J. "Lines for Remembering about Lids" in *The Kite That Braved Old Orchard Beach*. Illus. by Marion Young. M.K. McElderry/Macmillan, 1991.

———. "A Quick Hush" in *The Forgetful Wishing Well*. Illus. by Monica Incisa. M.K. McElderry/Macmillan, 1985.

Little, Lessie Jones. "Mama's Grandpa Clock" in *Children of Long Ago*. Illus. by Jan Spivey Gilchrist. Philomel/Putnam, 1988.

Livingston, Myra Cohn. "Grandfather Clock" in *Worlds I Know*. Illus. by Tim Arnold. M.K. McElderry/Macmillan, 1985.

McCord, David. "Tick Tock Talk" in *One at a Time*. Little, 1986.

Merriam, Eve. "Ways of Winding a Watch" in *A Sky Full of Poems*. Illus. by Walter Gaffney-Kessell. Dell, 1986.

Prelutsky, Jack. "Tick Tock Clock" in *Rainy Rainy Saturday*. Illus. by Marylin Hafner. Greenwillow, 1980.

Wallace, Robert. "The Gold Nest" in Janeczko, Paul. *Pocket Poems*. Bradbury/Macmillan, 1985.

Worth, Valerie. "Clock" in *All the Small Poems*. Illus. by Natalie Babbitt. Farrar, 1987.

## Aeons and Ages

All of us have trouble imagining vast periods of time. The vast spans of time that were involved in the formation of fossils and high deserts and moraines left after the receding of the glaciers are difficult to imagine. Children younger than about age nine will tell me that dinosaurs lived shortly before the first Thanksgiving or, sometimes, just before their own parents were born. Eve Merriam's poem "Forever" comments on this, with a child accepting the notion of aeons but also believing that somehow her father has always been here, too. Poets have attempted to address the ages, and their poems, when displayed for contemplation, may help students grasp this concept more clearly.

Baylor, Byrd. *If You Are a Hunter of Fossils*. Illus. by Peter Parnell. Scribner/Macmillan, 1980.

Mitchell, Adrian. "A Speck Speaks" in Harrison, Michael. *The Oxford Book of Story Poems*. Oxford, 1990.

Moore, Lilian. "Fossils" in *Something New Begins*. Illus. by Mary Jane Dunton. Atheneum/Macmillan, 1982.

Prelutsky, Jack. "Long Gone" in Prelutsky, Jack. *Random House Book of Poetry for Children*. Random, 1983.

Raine, Kathleen. "From "Rock"" in Plotz, Helen. *Imagination's Other Place*. Crowell/Harper, 1987.

Worth, Valerie. "Dinosaurs" in *All the Small Poems*. Illus. by Natalie Babbitt. Farrar, 1987.

Young, Andrew. "The Fairy Ring" in Harrison, Michael. *Splinters*. Oxford, 1988.

## COINS AND MONEY

Poems can discuss simple coinage and money, use money as a symbol for something else, and look at using money wisely and what it can and cannot buy. Shel Silverstein's "Smart," in which the young narrator doesn't know he's being shortchanged, is popular with readers and makes an important point about knowing how money works. Carl Sandburg ruminates on the idea that "money is power" in a section of the poem "The People, Yes." Gary Soto worries about economics in "How Things Work."

Bodecker, N. M. "Water Pennies" in *Water Pennies*. M.K. McElderry/Macmillan, 1991.

Merriam, Eve. "A Poem for a Pickle" in *A Poem for a Pickle*. Illus. by Sheila Hamanaka. Morrow, 1989.

Milne, A. A. "Market Square" in *When We Were Very Young*. Illus. by Ernest H. Shepard. Dutton, 1988.

Sandburg, Carl. "The People, Yes" in Hopkins, Lee Bennett. *Rainbows Are Made*. Harcourt, 1982.

Silverstein, Shel. "Smart" in *Where the Sidewalk Ends*. Harper, 1974.

Soto, Gary. "How Things Work" in *A Fire in My Hands*. Scholastic, 1991.

Worth, Valerie. "Coins" in *All the Small Poems*. Illus. by Natalie Babbitt. Farrar, 1987.

## MEASUREMENT

Poems tend to use abstract measuring systems such as the measurement used by inchworms or frogs, as Mildred Luton does in "Bullfrog Communique." This poem records the water measurements frogs call out to each other and would make a delightful choral reading. Students might want to consider other "natural" measures from the perspective of an animal. How would an ant measure distance? How would an elephant measure the same distance?

Sometimes poets look at phrases and terms used in measurement. Eloise Greenfield's poem "Weights" looks at what is behind the expression "weight of the world on your shoulders." Students might want to look at other expressions such as "arm's length," "keeping your distance," or "pound for pound." Some poets try to figure out the meaning of terms of measurement such as John Ciardi does in "What Is a Gross?" We might investigate or write poems about other measurement terms such as "bushel" and "peck." Students may be surprised to find that "mark twain" is actually a measurement term. Occasionally poems are written about the instruments of measurement, such as rulers, yardsticks, scales, or thermometers.

Adoff, Arnold. "Mathematical Metric Conversion Version" in *Chocolate Dreams*. Illus. by Turie MacCombie. Lothrop, 1989.

Aldis, Dorothy. "Inch-worm" in Hopkins, Lee Bennett. *Flit, Flutter, Fly*. Illus. by Peter Palagonia. Doubleday, 1992.

Bodecker, N. M. "Inchworm" and "Keeping in Step" in *Water Pennies*. Illus. by Eric Blegvad. M.K. McElderry/Macmillan, 1991.

Ciardi, John. "How Much Is a Gross?" in *Doodle Soup*. Illus. by Merle Nacht. Houghton, 1986.

———. "Rain Sizes" in Booth, David. *Voices on the Wind*. Morrow, 1990.

Greenfield, Eloise. "Weights" in *Nathaniel Talking*. Illus. by Jan Spivey Gilchrist. Black Butterfly/Writers and Readers, 1988.

Luton, Mildred. "Bullfrog Communique" in Cole, William. *An Arkful of Animals*. Houghton, 1978.

McCord, David. "How Tall?" in *One at a Time*. Little, 1986.

Milne, A.A. "Halfway Down" in *When We Were Very Young*. Illus. by Ernest H. Shepard. Dutton, 1988.

## GEOMETRY

Some poets describe shapes, lines, dots, and angles or use them as ways to describe other things. Circles are sometimes used to show completeness and inclusion. Myra Cohn Livingston's poem "Circles" shows how painful a broken family circle can be. Carl Sandburg has used the circle to show the limits of human knowledge and human pride in "The White Man Drew a Small Circle in the Sand." Florence Grossman suggests that students might try to write a poem to a geometric figure and gives examples of poems that have been written to a circle, a cube, and an ellipsis in *Getting from Here to There: Writing and Reading Poetry*.

Cohen, Marya. "Circle" in Grossman, Florence. *Getting from Here to There*. Boynton/ Cook, 1982.

Crews, Donald. *Ten Black Dots*. Greenwillow, 1986.

Kuskin, Karla. "Square as a House" in *Dogs and Dragons, Trees and Dreams*. Harper, 1980.

Livingston, Myra Cohn. "Circles" in *There Was a Place*. M.K. McElderry/Macmillan, 1988.

Milne, A. A. "Lines and Squares" in *When We Were Very Young*. Illus. by Ernest H. Shepard. Dutton, 1988.

Riss, Wendy. "Ellipsis" in Grossman, Florence. *Getting from Here to There*. Boynton/ Cook, 1982.

Sandburg, Carl. "The White Man Drew a Small Circle in the Sand" from "The People, Yes" in Hopkins, Lee Bennett. *Rainbows Are Made*. Harcourt, 1982.

Schlossberg, Lili. "Cube" in Grossman, Florence. *Getting from Here to There*. Boynton/Cook, 1982.

Silverstein, Shel. "Shapes" in *A Light in the Attic*. Harper, 1981.

Testa, Fulvio. *If You Look around You*. Dial, 1987.

Weil, Zaro. "A Walk" in *Mud, Moon, and Me*. Illus. by Jo Burroughs. Houghton, 1992.

## PATTERNS

Children need to be able to recognize patterns of objects to understand the complexities of multiplication and number systems. The simplest pattern is a series in which objects are placed in some kind of order. This order might be from smallest to largest, like the Russian nesting dolls, or a range of height, length, or width. It might be a series from light to heavy or from narrow to wide. A nursery rhyme using the "nesting" pattern is "This Is the Key to My Kingdom," in which the kingdom contains a city, which contains a town, and so on until the reader finds some flowers in a basket on a bed. In two picture book versions of this poem, artists Lydia Dabcovich in *These Are the Keys to My Kingdom* and Diane Worfolk Allison in *This Is the Key to the Kingdom* visualize this simple pattern poem very differently. Versions of the poem also appear in nursery rhyme collections without illustrations. Karla Kuskin's "Around and Around" uses this nesting pattern, starting with a bee on a flower and ending with herself sitting on the world, spinning around the sun.

Another pattern in poems is the cumulative pattern in which the number of objects increases or diminishes as the poem progresses. Some counting rhymes start with some characters and descend through the order of numbers until one is reached. Molly Bang uses this countdown pattern in *Ten, Nine, Eight,* ending with one child ready for bed. Other rhymes listed in the "Counting" section of this chapter also use the countdown pattern. Teachers who have accompanied children on long bus trips are familiar with a popular countdown in the seemingly endless "One hundred bottles of pop on the wall." A well-known example of a cumulative pattern with increasing numbers is the Christmas song, "The Twelve Days of Christmas." Elizabeth Lee O'Donnell has played with this pattern in her picture book poem, *The Twelve Days of Summer,* using summer activities and objects.

Poems and chants often encourage a pattern of movements and choruses. Patterned activities are common in young children's fingerplays and hand plays. Older children may participate in rhythmic clapping games or chants that include elaborate patterns of physical and verbal play. Examples of these patterned rhythmic activities and poems are included in Chapter 7.

The simple question-and-answer pattern of Bill Martin's *Brown Bear, Brown Bear, What Do You See?* is repeated in his sequel, *Polar Bear, Polar Bear, What Do You Hear?* Repeated readings of one favorite poem or of two poems that follow the same pattern can help children to begin to recognize patterns in the forms of the poems they enjoy. Many poems use the recognizable patterns and structures that we call literary forms. Examples of these patterns are included in Chapter 5.

Another way poets show patterns is through the use of concrete poetry (or what X.J. Kennedy calls "show and spell poems") in which the poem actually takes the shape of the object that it is about. Judith Viorst has written a poem called "Sometimes Poems" about the shapes of poems and arranged it so that it oozes down to the bottom of the page. Karla Kuskin's description of a tree in "If You Stood with Your Feet in the Earth" is shaped like a tree and William Jay Smith's undulating poem "Seal" is shaped like a seal. Sometimes you have to imagine the shape. In "You Must Read This Word under Water," Barbara Juster Esbensen asks the reader to imagine the pattern of the word "seahorse" as it would look through water.

Poets often see patterns in nature. One object will be compared to another object that has a similar pattern. Photographer Tana Hoban's *Take Another Look* and *Look Again* use pictures with peep holes in them to show how patterns and textures in nature can be deceiving; some things look like other things. Her photograph of a fish's scales, for example, could be a snake's skin. Ruth Heller's series of small rhymed books on camouflage describe the ways animals hide themselves by matching their patterns to those of something else. Mary Ann Hoberman humorously looks at the striped pattern of the zebra in "Abracadabra." Students can collect examples of poems that show camouflage or comparisons of objects to animals or animals to objects for a "Patterns" unit.

Bang, Molly. *Ten, Nine, Eight*. Greenwillow, 1983.

Esbensen, Barbara Juster. "You Must Read This Word under Water" in *Words with Wrinkled Knees*. Illus. by John Stadler. Crowell/Harper, 1987.

Heller, Ruth. *How to Hide a Butterfly and Other Insects*. Grosset, 1985.

———. *How to Hide a Crocodile*. Putnam, 1986.

———. *How to Hide a Gray Tree Frog*. Putnam, 1986.

———. *How to Hide an Octopus and Other Sea Creatures*. Putnam, 1986.

———. *How to Hide a Polar Bear and Other Mammals*. Putnam, 1986.

———. *How to Hide a Whippoorwill*. Putnam, 1986.

Hoban, Tana. *Look Again*. Macmillan, 1971. (nonfiction)

———. *Take Another Look*. Greenwillow, 1981. (nonfiction)

Hoberman, Mary Ann. "Abracadabra" in *A Fine Fat Pig*. Illus. by Malcah Zeldis. Harper, 1991.

Kennedy, X. J., and Dorothy Kennedy. "Show and Spell Poems" section, *Knock at a Star*. Illus. by Karen Ann Weinhaus. Little, 1985.

Kuskin, Karla. "Around and Around" and "If You Stood with Your Feet in the Earth" in *Dogs and Dragons, Trees and Dreams*. Harper, 1980.

Martin, Bill, Jr. *Brown Bear, Brown Bear, What Do You See?* Illus. by Eric Carle. Holt, 1983.

———. *Polar Bear, Polar Bear, What Do You Hear?* Illus. by Eric Carle. Holt, 1991.

O'Donnell, Elizabeth. *The Twelve Days of Summer*. Illus. by Karen Lee Schmidt. Morrow, 1991.

Smith, William Jay. "Seal" in Dunning, Stephen. *Reflections on a Gift of Watermelon Pickle*. Lothrop, 1966.

*These Are the Keys to My Kingdom: A Poem in Three Languages*. Illus. by Lydia Dabcovich. Lothrop, 1992.

*This Is the Key to My Kingdom*. Illus. by Diane Worfolk Allison. Little, 1992.

*The Twelve Days of Christmas*. Illus. by Jan Brett. Dodd, 1986.

Viorst, Judith. "Sometimes Poems" in *If I Were in Charge of the World and Other Worries*. Illus. by Lynn Cherry. Atheneum/Macmillan, 1984.

## RELATIONSHIPS AMONG THINGS

Mathematics asks us not only to see patterns but also to understand relationships among the items within the pattern. We can describe these items as more or less, bigger or smaller, wider or narrower, older or younger, or in other ways. Often a poem compares shapes and sizes of objects and animals to each other. A classic poem that does this is A. A. Milne's "Four Friends," which is about four creatures that range from Ernest the large elephant to James who is "only a snail." A group of poems that explore the relationships of big and little and our changing perceptions as we ourselves get bigger and older are included here.

Bangs, John Kendricks. "The Little Elfman" in Corrin, Sara. *Once upon a Rhyme.* Faber, 1982.

Behn, Harry. "Growing Up" in Prelutsky, Jack. *Random House Book of Poetry for Children.* Random, 1983.

De la Mare, Walter. "The Fly" in Corrin, Sara. *Once upon a Rhyme.* Faber, 1982.

Esbensen, Barbara Juster "The Visit" in *Who Shrank My Grandmother's House?: Poems of Discovery.* Illus. by Eric Beddows. Harper, 1992.

Fisher, Aileen. "Little Talk" in *Always Wondering.* Illus. by Joan Sandin. Harper, 1991.

Frost, Robert. "Fireflies in the Garden" in *You Come Too.* Illus. by Thomas W. Nason. Holt, 1959.

Hoban, Russell. "Small, Smaller" in Moore, Lilian. *Go with the Poem.* McGraw, 1979.

Kennedy, X. J. "Tear" in *The Forgetful Wishing Well.* M.K. McElderry/Macmillan, 1985.

Kuskin, Karla. "All My Legs Are Very Tired" in *Any Me I Want to Be.* Harper, 1972.

———. "Okay, Everybody, Listen to This" in *Near the Window Tree.* Harper, 1975.

Levy, Constance. "Big and Little" in *I'm Going to Pet a Worm Today.* M.K. McElderry/Macmillan, 1991.

Merriam, Eve. "Big Little Boy" in De Regniers, Beatrice Schenk. *Sing a Song of Popcorn.* Scholastic, 1988.

———. "Mr. Tall and Mr. Small" in *Jamboree.* Dell, 1984.

Milne, A. A. "The Four Friends" in *When We Were Very Young.* Illus. by Ernest H. Shepard. Dutton, 1988.

Prelutsky, Jack. "I Am Tired of Being Little" and "Something Big Has Been Here" in *Something Big Has Been Here.* Illus. by James Stevenson. Greenwillow, 1990.

———. "A Microscopic Topic" in *The New Kid on the Block.* Illus. by James Stevenson. Greenwillow, 1984.

Richards, Laura E. "The Snail and the Mouse" in Prelutsky, Jack. *Read Aloud Rhymes for the Very Young.* Knopf, 1986.

Rowe, Albert. "Fieldmouse" in Foster, John. *A Third Poetry Book.* Oxford, 1987.

Silverstein, Shel. "Me and My Giant" and "One Inch Tall" in *Where the Sidewalk Ends.* Harper, 1974.

## ATTITUDES TOWARD MATHEMATICS

One final set of poems reveals attitudes toward mathematics. A classic poem, "When I Heard the Learn'd Astronomer," by Walt Whitman, wonders how the astronomer can be so caught up with numbers when it is so much more edifying to go out and simply enjoy the stars. Carl Sandburg's "Arithmetic" is enjoyed by upper elementary children who have struggled to figure out speculative math problems, or story problems. Arnold Adoff echoes Sandburg's poem in his "The Old Math: One," which is a story problem involving chocolate. Dennis Lee's story problem, "Nine Black Cats," mocks the traditional rhyme about St. Ives.

Helen Plotz collected poems of science and mathematics in *Imagination's Other Place*. This book is worth looking for in libraries because it contains many poems that show the imaginative and creative side of mathematics. Aliki Barnstone says she both likes and hates math in "Numbers," a poem that might be a good beginning point for a discussion about attitudes toward mathematics. Kalli Dakos includes three poems in her collection of school poems about the difficulties and boredom that may come with math instruction.

Adoff, Arnold. "The Old Math: One" in *Chocolate Dreams*. Illus. by Turie MacCombie. Lothrop, 1989.

Barnstone, Aliki. "Numbers" in Lueders, Edward. *Zero Makes Me Hungry*. Scott, Foresman, 1976.

Dakos, Kalli. "Math Is Brewing and I'm in Trouble," "They Don't Do Math in Texas," and "The Wind Is Calling Me Away" in *If You're Not Here, Please Raise Your Hand*. Illus. by G. Brian Karas. Four Winds/ Macmillan, 1990.

Lee, Dennis. "Nine Black Cats" in *The Ice Cream Store*. Illus. by David McPhail. Scholastic, 1991.

McCord, David. "Exit X" in *One at a Time*. Little, 1986.

Plotz, Helen. *Imagination's Other Place: Poems of Science and Mathematics*. Illus. by Clare Leighton. Crowell/Harper, 1955.

Sandburg, Carl. "Arithmetic" in Hopkins, Lee Bennett. *Rainbows Are Made*. Harcourt, 1982.

Ulrich, George. "Tigers Don't Scare Me" in *The Spook Matinee*. Delacorte, 1992.

Whitman, Walt. "When I Heard the Learn'd Astronomer" in Hopkins, Lee Bennett. *Voyages: Poems by Walt Whitman*. Harcourt, 1988.

## REFERENCES

Burton, G. M. (1985). *Towards a Good Beginning: Teaching Early Childhood Mathematics*. Menlo Park, CA: Addison-Wesley.

Carroll, L. ( 1960). *The Annotated Alice*. Introduction and notes by Martin Gardner. Illus. by John Tenniel. New York: Bramhall House.

Chatton, B. (1992). Journal entry. Laramie, WY.

Gensler, K., and N. Nyhart. (1978). "The Shape of a Poem" in *The Poetry Connection: An Anthology of Contemporary Poems with Ideas to Stimulate Children's Writing*. New York: Teachers and Writers.

Griffiths, R., and M. Clyne. (1988). *Books You Can Count On: Linking Mathematics and Literature*. Portsmouth, NH: Heinemann.

Grossman, F. (1982.). *"Signs": Getting from Here to There*. Montclair, NJ: Boynton/ Cook.

Hurst, C.O. ( 1992). "That's Not Math, Is It?" *Teaching K-8* (January).

Kennedy, X.J. and Dorothy Kennedy. (1982). "Show-And-Spell Poems" in *Knock at a Star*. Boston: Little.

Phelan, C. (1991). "Classroom Connections: Math: More Than Numbers." *Book Links 1* (November): 32-37

Roberts, P. (1990). *Counting Books Are More Than Numbers: An Annotated Action Bibliography*. Hamden, CT: Library Professional Publications.

Whitin, D.J., and S. Wilde. (1992). *Read Any Good Math Lately? Children's Books for Mathematical Learning, K-6*. Portsmouth, NH: Heinemann.

# Chapter 4:
# Poetry and Social Studies

Social studies encompass material about the self, family, community, and society. They help children develop their identity, kinship with others, respect for their heritage, and values. Social studies provide experiences with research skills, social skills, problem solving, and decision-making skills within the context of social interactions. Poetry describing human feelings and events can easily be incorporated into the social studies curriculum.

## SELF, FAMILY, AND FRIENDS

Children in kindergarten, first grade, and second grade begin their social studies with aspects of the world closest to them: studies of self, family, and friends. The curriculum might include discovering who we are and what we like; thinking about daily activities such as getting up, eating, doing chores, going to school, and going to bed; and learning about families and neighborhoods.

Classic poems by A.A. Milne, Dorothy Aldis, and Robert Louis Stevenson are filled with the activities, thoughts, and feelings of young children. Several more recently published collections of poetry have focused on young children. Jack Prelutsky's *Read-Aloud Rhymes for the Very Young* includes poems on the activities and concerns of young children. Shirley Hughes' *Out and About* is a collection of poems about the activities of a young sister and brother as they explore their neighborhood over the course of the seasons.

Although poems about "ourselves" are used in the curriculum in the primary grades, they remain popular with students across the grade levels. Students enjoy poems about experiences that are familiar to them. Popular poets such as Shel Silverstein, Jack Prelutsky, and Judith Viorst know how we like to see ourselves reflected in the poems we read and write mostly lighthearted poems about the joys and difficulties of childhood. Other poets, recognizing that childhood is filled with painful events, have written more serious poems. Myra Cohn Livingston's *There Was a Place and Other*

*Poems* allows young readers to empathize with children who come from broken or mending families. Brenda Seabrook's *Judy Scuppernong*, a collection of poems about a young girl, shows readers a unique child who is suffering from family difficulties but who brings her strength and imagination to the lives of her friends.

Some poets write about childhood, filling their poems with nostalgia for an earlier time, which the child reader does not feel. A good poem about childhood is not an adult poet's comment on childhood but a thought or feeling that comes directly from the experience of being a child. Not all poets can capture this well and not all adult readers can sense the difference. The best way to judge which poems are authentic childhood experiences is to let students read and decide for themselves. Interesting critical discussions can result when children disagree about the "authenticity" of a poem. Sometimes the sheer joy in the language and silliness of a poem will allow students to set aside its "truth" and just enjoy it, whether it is authentic or not.

It is difficult to study the children's lives without studying their families and relationships with others. Units on the self usually overlap with units on family and friends. Poetry anthologies about the self generally include poems on parents, siblings, and extended families as well. Units on families can introduce children to different kinds of families. Picture books and poems for primary children should reflect this diversity, including families with one, two, or more parents; extended families in which grandparents, aunts, and uncles play significant roles; and families from different places and with different customs and traditions. As students and teachers compile collections of family poems, they will find categories of poems within this broad grouping. One category might be poems on particular members of the family such as brothers or grandmothers. Another group might include poems on chores or about going to bed. Another might be poems about special activities that parents and children do together such as going owling as the family in Jane Yolen's *Owl Moon* does.

Poems for children are sometimes about learning to make and keep friends. These poems talk about the pleasures of friendship but also about feelings of being left out, losing friends, or making new ones. Like the poems about families, poems about friendship can be grouped into such categories as new kids, best friends, or bullies.

## Poetry Anthologies about Self, Family, and Friends

De Paola, Tomie, sel. *Tomie De Paola's Book of Poems*. Putnam, 1988.
De Regniers, Beatrice Schenk, et al., sels. *Sing a Song of Popcorn*. Illus. by Caldecott Medal artists. Scholastic, 1988.

Ferris, Helen, sel. *Favorite Poems Old and New*. Illus. by Leonard Weisgard. Doubleday, 1957.

Hopkins, Lee Bennett, sel. *Best Friends*. Illus. by James Watts. Harper, 1986.

———. *Through Our Eyes: Poems and Pictures about Growing Up*. Illus. by Jeffrey Dunn. Little, 1992.

Kennedy, X.J. *Talking Like the Rain: A First Book of Poems*. Illus. by Jane Dyer. Little, 1992.

Prelutsky, Jack, sel. *The Random House Book of Poetry*. Illus. by Arnold Lobel. Random, 1983.

———. *Read-Aloud Rhymes for the Very Young*. Illus. by Marc Brown. Knopf, 1986.

# Picture Books and Poetry Collections about Self, Family, and Friends

Adoff, Arnold. *All the Colors of the Race*. Illus. by John Steptoe. Lothrop, 1982.

———. *Black Is Brown Is Tan*. Illus. by Emily Arnold McCully. Harper, 1973.

———. *In for Winter, Out for Spring*. Illus. by Jerry Pinkney. Harcourt, 1991.

Anholt, Catherine. *Good Days, Bad Days*. Putnam, 1991.

Baylor, Byrd. *Guess Who My Favorite Person Is*. Illus. by Robert Andrew Parker. Scribners, 1977.

Bennett, Jill, sel. *Tiny Tim: Verses for Children*. Illus. by Helen Oxenbury. Delacorte, 1981.

Brooks, Gwendolyn. *Bronzeville Boys and Girls*. Illus. by Ronni Solbert. Harper, 1967.

Carlstrom, Nancy White. *It's About Time, Jesse Bear and Other Rhymes*. Illus. by Bruce Degen. Macmillan, 1990.

———. *Jesse Bear, What Will You Wear?* Illus. by Bruce Degen. Macmillan, 1986.

Clifton, Lucille. *Everett Anderson's Nine Month Long*. Illus. by Ann Grifalconi. Holt, 1978.

———. *Some of the Days of Everett Anderson*. Illus. by Evaline Ness. Holt, 1970.

De Regniers, Beatrice Schenk. *A Week in the Life of Best Friends*. Illus. by Nancy Doyle. Atheneum/Macmillan, 1986.

———. *The Way I Feel . . . Sometimes*. Illus. by Susan Meddaugh. Clarion/Ticknor and Fields, 1988.

Giovanni, Nikki. *Vacation Time: Poems for Children*. Illus. by Marisabina Russo. Morrow, 1981.

Greenfield, Eloise. *Daydreamers*. Illus. by Tom Feelings. Dial, 1981.

———. *Honey, I Love*. Illus. by Leo and Diane Dillon. Crowell/Harper, 1978.

———. *Nathaniel Talking*. Illus. by Jan Spivey Gilchrist. Black Butterfly/ Writers and Readers, 1988.

———. *Night on Neighborhood Street*. Illus. by Jan Spivey Gilchrist. Dial, 1991.

Grimes, Nikki. *Something on My Mind*. Illus. by Tom Feelings. Dial, 1978.

Hoberman, Mary Ann. *Fathers, Mothers, Sisters, Brothers: A Collection of Family Poems*. Illus. by Marylin Hafner. Little, 1991.

Hopkins, Lee Bennett. *Morning, Noon, and Nighttime, Too*. Illus. by Nancy Hannans. Harper, 1980.

Hughes, Shirley. *Out and About*. Lothrop, 1988.

Joseph, Lynn. *Coconut Kind of Day*. Illus. by Sandra Speidel. Lothrop, 1990.

Komaiko, Leah. *Annie Bananie*. Illus. by Laura Cornell. Harper, 1987.

————. *Earl's Too Cool for Me*. Illus. by Laura Cornell. Harper, 1988.

Lewis, Claudia. *Long Ago in Oregon*. Illus. by Joel Fontaine. Harper, 1987.

————. *Up in the Mountains*. Illus. by Joel Fontaine. Harper, 1991.

Little, Jean. *Hey World, Here I Am!* Illus. by Sue Truesdale. Harper, 1989.

Livingston, Myra Cohn, sel. *Birthday Poems*. Illus. by Margot Tomes. Holiday, 1989.

————. *Poems for Brothers, Poems for Sisters*. Illus. by Jean Zollinger. Holiday, 1991.

————. *Poems for Fathers*. Illus. by Robert Casilla. Holiday, 1989.

————. *Poems for Grandmothers*. Illus. by Patricia Cullen-Clark. Holiday, 1990.

————. *Poems for Mothers*. Illus. by Deborah Kogan Ray. Holiday, 1988.

————. *There Was a Place and Other Poems*. M.K. McElderry/Macmillan, 1988.

————. *Worlds I Know and Other Poems*. Illus. by Tim Arnold. M.K. McElderry/Macmillan, 1985.

Milne, A.A. *Now We Are Six*. Illus. by Ernest H. Shepard. Dutton, 1988.

————. *When We Were Very Young*. Illus. by Ernest H. Shepard. Dutton, 1988.

Prelutsky, Jack. *The New Kid on the Block*. Illus. by James Stevenson. Greenwillow, 1984.

————. *Something Big Has Been Here*. Illus. by James Stevenson. Greenwillow, 1990.

Rylant, Cynthia. *Waiting to Waltz: A Childhood*. Illus. by Stephen Gammell. Bradbury/Macmillan, 1984.

Seabrooke, Brenda. *Judy Scuppernong*. Illus. by Ted Lewin. Cobblehill/Dutton, 1990.

Slier, Deborah, sel. *Make a Joyful Sound*. Illus. by Cornelius Van Wright and Ying-Hwa Hu. Checkerboard Press, 1991.

Viorst, Judith. *If I Were in Charge of the World and Other Worries*. Illus. by Lynn Cherry. Atheneum, 1981.

Weil, Zaro. *Mud, Moon, and Me*. Illus. by Jo Burroughs. Houghton, 1992.

Yolen, Jane. *Owl Moon*. Illus. by John Schoenherr. Philomel/Putnam, 1987.

# HOUSES

Many primary teachers use Mary Ann Hoberman's *A House Is a House for Me*, a rhymed and rhythmic introduction to all kinds of houses, as the centerpiece of a unit on houses. After sharing this picture book with second graders several times, one teacher asked them to help her chart the kinds of houses Hoberman listed in the book. One category the children included was "animal houses" and they included nests, barns, and shells. She asked them if they could think of other animal houses. The children thought of dens and lairs. When she asked them where fish live, one bright child said "fish bowl," which led to a discussion of other pet houses including terrariums and aquariums. Other categories the children found in the book included "clothing houses" and "food houses."

The children also charted names for human houses that Hoberman mentioned such as wigwams, castles, and tree houses. Other names they knew for houses included haciendas and "round and square" houses (the children had heard Ann Grifalconi's story, *The Village of Round and Square Houses* not long before) as well as condominiums, apartments, and duplexes. One child noted that some children do not have a house to live in. The teacher brought out Eve Bunting's *Fly Away Home* about a homeless father and son who live at an airport and asked the children what this family's home would be. A child remembered hearing the old phrase "Home is where the heart is" and the class agreed that this was what Bunting's book was about. They added the phrase "where the heart is" to the list of names of people's homes. The teacher then shared several poems from Myra Cohn Livingston's *There Was a Place and Other Poems,* which feature children coping with the loss of a home because of personal tragedies.

The teacher and children began collecting poems about houses of all kinds, those for humans and animals, as well as poems about metaphorical homes. They enjoyed Karen Ackerman's *I Know a Place* and Ruth Yaffe Radin's *A Winter Place*, both free verse texts that give a sense of the warmth and coziness of home. They worked to create their own poems and art work describing their houses.

Joan Blos' *A Seed, A Flower, a Minute, an Hour*, which is about change, contrasts a "house" with a "home." After reading Ackerman's and Radin's books, children might want to think about the meaning of "Home is where the heart is" and discuss the differences between "house" and "home."

Older students might want to read Myra Cohn Livingston's "Garage Apartment" when they read Lois Lowry's *Rabble Starkey,* as both feature garage apartments shared by a mother and daughter during a time of transition. Sometimes, as in this novel, a house is the critical setting for the action of the story. The ramshackle house in Janet Taylor Lisle's *Afternoon of the Elves* and the abandoned house taken over by the group of boys in Felice Holman's *Secret City, U.S.A.* are almost characters in these stories. Students may want to read these and other novels and look at the influence houses have on characters and events.

Historical novels often describe houses of earlier times in some detail. Laura Ingalls Wilder's stories provide particularly detailed descriptions of the construction and living conditions in houses of various types. James S. Tippett's "Old Log House" perfectly describes the log cabin in *Little House in the Big Woods*, the first of these houses. Other historical novels with strong house settings, such as Joan Blos' *Gathering of Days* and Elizabeth George Speare's *Sign of the Beaver*, which features both American Indian and European settlers' houses, provide a springboard to discussions of past houses and living conditions.

Some poems are nostalgic descriptions of a poet's favorite house. Students may want to use Myra Cohn Livingston's poems about favorite houses of relatives in a midwestern town from *Worlds I Know and Other Poems* or Claudia Lewis' poem about saying goodbye to a favorite house, "Moving to Salem," as springboards to writing about or creating works of art describing their favorite houses.

Ackerman, Karen. *I Know a Place*. Illus. by Deborah Kogan Ray. Houghton, 1992.

Adoff, Arnold. "This House Is the Center" in *In for Winter, Out for Spring*. Illus. by Jerry Pinkney. Harcourt, 1991.

Aldis, Dorothy. "No One Heard Him Call" in Kennedy, X.J. *Talking Like the Rain*. Little, 1992.

Blos, Joan W. *Gathering of Days*. Scribner/Macmillan, 1979. (historical fiction)

———. *A Seed, A Flower, a Minute, an Hour*. Illus. by Hans Poppel. Simon, 1992.

Bunting, Eve. *Fly Away Home*. Illus. by Ronald Himler. Houghton, 1991. (fiction)

Esbensen, Barbara Juster. "The Visit" in *Who Shrank My Grandmother's House?* Illus. by Eric Beddows. Harper, 1992.

Giovanni, Nikki. "Houses" in *Vacation Time*. Illus. by Marisabina Russo. Morrow, 1981.

Grifalconi, Ann. *The Village of Round and Square Houses*. Little, 1986. (folk literature)

Hoberman, Mary Ann. *A House Is a House for Me*. Illus. by Betty Fraser. Viking, 1978.

Holman, Felice. *Secret City, U.S.A.* Scribner/Macmillan, 1990. (fiction)

Levy, Constance. "A House" in *I'm Going to Pet a Worm Today*. Illus. by Ronald Himler. M.K.McElderry/Macmillan, 1991.

Lewis, Claudia. "Moving to Salem" in *Long Ago in Oregon*. Illus. by Joel Fontaine. Harper, 1987.

Lisle, Janet Taylor. *Afternoon of the Elves*. Orchard, 1989. (fiction)

Livingston, Myra Cohn. "Aunt Flora (Envoi)," "Big House," and "Fletcher Avenue" in *Worlds I Know and Other Poems*. M.K. McElderry/Macmillan, 1985.

———. "Garage Apartment," "Home," and "Olive Street" in *There Was a Place and Other Poems*. M.K.McElderry/Macmillan, 1988.

Lowry, Lois. *Rabble Starkey*. Houghton, 1987. (fiction)

Miller, Mary Britton. "Houses" in De Regniers, Beatrice Schenk. *Sing a Song of Popcorn*. Scholastic, 1988.

Morley, Christopher. "Song for a Little House" in Ferris, Helen. *Favorite Poems Old and New*. Doubleday, 1957.

Morris, Ann. *Houses and Homes*. Illus. by Ken Heyman. Lothrop, 1992.

O'John, Calvin. "Dancing Teepees" in Sneve, Virginia Driving Hawk. *Dancing Teepees*. Holiday, 1989.

Prelutsky, Jack, sel. *The Random House Book of Poetry for Children* ("Home! You're Where It's Warm Inside" section). Illus. by Arnold Lobel. Random, 1983.

Radin, Ruth Yaffe. *A Winter Place*. Illus. by Mattie Lou O'Kelley. Little, 1982.

Robinson, Edwin Arlington. "The House on the Hill" in Ferris, Helen. *Favorite Poems Old and New*. Doubleday, 1957.

Rosen, Michael J., sel. *Home: A Collaboration of Thirty Distinguished Authors and Illustrators of Children's Books to Aid the Homeless*. Charlotte Zolotow/Harper, 1992.

Seabrooke, Brenda. "Judy's House" in *Judy Scuppernong*. Illus. by Ted Lewin. Cobblehill/ Dutton, 1990.

Simmie, Lois. "Jeremy's House" in Booth, David. *'Til All the Stars Have Fallen*. Viking, 1990.

Speare, Elizabeth George. *Sign of the Beaver*. Houghton, 1983. (historical fiction)
Tippett, James S. "Old Log House" in Ferris, Helen. *Favorite Poems Old and New*. Doubleday, 1957.
Watson, Wendy. *Thanksgiving at Our House*. Clarion/Houghton, 1991.
Wilder, Laura Ingalls. *Little House in the Big Woods*. Illus. by Garth Williams. Harcourt, 1953. (historical fiction)

## SCHOOL

Primary grade units generally contain material about school, although poems about school, especially negative ones, remain popular with children throughout the grades. Poems from Kalli Dakos' *If You're Not Here, Please Raise Your Hand* and poems from various other collections can be added to classroom units on school. Students will find much to identify with in poems about homework, boredom, arithmetic lessons, and other topics. Some poems present schools and teachers in a negative light and might be used to provoke discussions about ways that school could be made more interesting and challenging for students. David McCord's "Chant II" and John Cunliffe's chanted poem "Another Day" use sounds to show the ways that students may dislike and abuse the time they have in school. Nikki Giovanni's poem "Joy" about a child who creates a new verb "to have joy" only to be told this is incorrect is a small but sad lesson on stifled creative language use. Other poems celebrate teachers and teaching. Claudia Lewis in "Not in a Hundred Years" and Kalli Dakos in "Dancing on a Rainbow" celebrate reading teachers.

Some poems help children understand the schoolrooms of earlier times. Claudia Lewis includes several poems on aspects of school in the early twentieth century in *Up in the Mountains* and *Long Ago in Oregon*. Her poem "The Woolen Dress," about making fun of a girl who wears a heavy woolen dress and later finding out she has died, is reminiscent of the emotion and setting of Eleanor Estes' novel *The Hundred Dresses*. A piece from John Greenleaf Whittier's long poem "School Days," titled "In School Days," appears in Helen Ferris' *Favorite Poems Old and New*. Whittier's description of a schoolroom and of a girl who worries about beating a boy in a spelling bee might be used in conjunction with Bette Greene's *Philip Hall Likes Me, I Reckon Maybe,* in which a similar incident occurs. The first four stanzas of this poem, which describe the schoolroom, are echoed in descriptions of classrooms in Carol Ryrie Brink's *Caddie Woodlawn*, Laura Ingalls Wilder's *These Happy Golden Years*, and in Patricia MacLachlan's picture book about a rural school, *Three Names*.

Baer, Edith. *This Is the Way We Go to School: A Book about Children Around the World*. Illus. by Steve Bjorkman. Scholastic, 1990.

Brink, Carol Ryrie. *Caddie Woodlawn*. Macmillan, 1973. (historical fiction)

Cunliffe, John. "Another Day" in Foster, John. *A Very First Poetry Book*. Oxford, 1987.

Dakos, Kalli. *If You're Not Here, Please Raise Your Hand*. Illus. by G. Bryan Karas. Four Winds/Macmillan, 1990.

De Regniers, Beatrice Schenk. "Co-op-er-ate" in *The Way I Feel...Sometimes*. Illus. by Susan Meddaugh. Clarion/Ticknor and Fields, 1988.

Estes, Eleanor. *The Hundred Dresses*. Illus. by Louis Slobodkin. Harcourt, 1944. (fiction)

Farjeon, Eleanor. "School-Bell" in Ferris, Helen. *Favorite Poems Old and New*. Doubleday, 1957.

Finney, Eric. "Mystery Story" in Foster, John. *A Very First Poetry Book*. Oxford, 1987.

Fisher, Aileen. "First Day of School" in *Always Wondering*. Illus. by Joan Sandin. Harper, 1991.

Fufuka, Karama. "Summer Vacation" in Slier, Deborah. *Make a Joyful Sound*. Checkerboard, 1991.

Giovanni, Nikki. "Education" in *Sing a Soft Black Song*. Illus. by George Martins. Hill and Wang, 1985.

————. "Joy" in *Vacation Time*. Illus. by Marisabina Russo. Morrow, 1981.

Greene, Bette. *Philip Hall Likes Me, I Reckon Maybe*. Dial, 1974. (fiction)

Grimes, Nikki. "I Don't Understand" and "My Summer Vacation" in *Something on My Mind*. Illus. by Tom Feelings. Dial, 1986.

Hearn, Michael Patrick. "I Can't Go Back to School" in Janeczko, Paul. *The Place My Words Are Looking For*. Bradbury/Macmillan, 1990.

Hoban, Russell. "Homework" in *Egg Thoughts and Other Frances Songs*. Illus. by Lillian Hoban. Harper, 1972.

Hopkins, Lee Bennett, sel. *Morning, Noon, and Nighttime Too*. (section on school) Illus. by Nancy Hannans. Harper, 1980.

Kennedy, X.J. "Circus Dreams" and "Generation Gap" in *The Kite That Braved Old Orchard Beach*. Illus. by Marion Young. M.K. McElderry/ Macmillan, 1991.

————. "Teacher" in *The Forgetful Wishing Well*. Illus. by Monica Incisa. M.K. McElderry/ Macmillan, 1985.

Lewis, Claudia. "Not in a Hundred Years" in *Long Ago in Oregon*. Illus. by Joel Fontaine. Harper, 1987.

————. "Slap! Slap!" and "The Woolen Dress" in *Up in the Mountains*. Illus. by Joel Fontaine. Harper, 1991.

Little, Jean. "Today" in *Hey World, Here I Am!* Illus. by Sue Truesdell. Harper, 1986.

MacLachlan, Patricia. *Three Names*. Illus. by Alexander Pertzoff. Harper, 1991. (historical fiction)

McCord, David. "Chant II" and "The Adventures of Chris" in *One at a Time*. Little, 1986.

"Now I Lay Me Down to Rest" in Prelutsky, Jack. *Poems of A. Nonny Mouse*. Illus. by Henrik Drescher. Knopf, 1989.

Prelutsky, Jack. "Homework! Oh, Homework!" and "New York Is in North Carolina" in *The New Kid on the Block*. Illus. by James Stevenson. Greenwillow, 1984.

Prince Redcloud. "Now" in Hopkins, Lee Bennett. *The Sky Is Full of Song*. Harper, 1983.

Turner, Ann. "That's Gloria," "Read," and "Teacher Talk" in *Street Talk*. Houghton, 1986.

Ulrich, George. "Take Me to Your Teacher" in *The Spook Matinee*. Delacorte, 1992.
Whittier, John Greenleaf. "In School-Days" in Ferris, Helen. *Favorite Poems Old and New*. Doubleday, 1957.
Wilder, Laura Ingalls. *These Happy Golden Years*. Harper, 1943.
Zolotow, Charlotte. "School Day" in *Everything Glistens and Everything Sings*. Illus. by Margot Tomes. Harcourt, 1987.

## NEIGHBORHOOD AND COMMUNITY

Neighborhood and community are often studied in second and third grade. Poems can show children images of their own neighborhoods or help them imagine a neighborhood very different from their own. Children who grow up in a small town and have not visited a large city may not be able to imagine its traffic, noise, or color. When collecting books and poems for units on cities, be careful to balance positive and negative images. Picture books for children sometimes focus on the negative aspects of city life, such as its poverty, crime, and dreariness. Books such as Virginia Lee Burton's *The Little House* paint the city as a kind of monster that absorbs the country and pollutes it. Others, such as Vera B. Williams' *A Chair for My Mother*, paint a livelier picture of city neighborhoods as warm and friendly places. From ancient times, as Aesop's fable *The City Mouse and the Country Mouse* shows, life in the city was less appealing than life in the country. Lilian Moore's short novels, *I'll Meet You at the Cucumbers* and *Don't Be Afraid, Amanda*, loosely based on this traditional fable, present a more balanced picture, showing country mice coming to appreciate the city and city mice coming to appreciate the country. These books have an added benefit because Adam, the country mouse, is a poet. A separate collection of Adam's poems is also available, *Adam Mouse's Book of Poems*.

Poetry collections about the city give both points of view of city life. Poems in Lucille Clifton's Everett Anderson books and in Eloise Greenfield's *Night on Neighborhood Street* show both the pleasures and the hardships of life in the city. Many of the poems in Lee Bennett Hopkins' collection, *A Song in Stone: City Poems*, focus on the color and excitement of the city.

Just as rural children find it hard to imagine the city, children who grow up in a city may find it difficult to imagine life in a small town. Often, poems and collections that describe life in small towns describe it in the past tense. Byrd Baylor's *Best Town in the World* is set in a small town in Texas early in the twentieth century. Claudia Lewis' two collections of poetry about her own childhood in a small town in Oregon, *Up in the Mountains* and *Long Ago in Oregon*, also provide historical perspective. City children may not realize that small-town life is not exactly like this. Picture books such as Cynthia Rylant's free verse book, *Night in the Country*, give insight into the quiet of small towns compared to the noise of the city, and her poems about her childhood in the town of Beaver in *Waiting to Waltz: A Childhood* reveal other aspects of town life. Myra Cohn Livingston's poem "Kansas Visit" shows the surprise of the narrator who comes to so empty a place. Teachers and students may want to search for and collect poems that reflect small-town life as they know it.

Barracca, Debra and Sal Barracca. *The Adventures of Taxi Dog*. Illus. by Mark Buehner. Dial, 1990.

———. *Maxi the Hero*. Illus. by Mark Buehner. Dial, 1991.

Baylor, Byrd. *The Best Town in the World*. Illus. by Peter Parnall. Scribner/Macmillan, 1983.

Brooks, Gwendolyn. *Bronzeville Boys and Girls*. Illus. by Ronni Solbert. Harper, 1967.

Burton, Virginia Lee. *The Little House*. Houghton, 1942.

Ferris, Helen, sel. *Favorite Poems Old and New*. (section on city and town). Doubleday, 1957.

Greenfield, Eloise. *Night on Neighborhood Street*. Illus. by Jan Spivey Gilchrist. Dial, 1991.

Hopkins, Lee Bennett. *A Song in Stone: City Poems*. Illus. by Anna H. Audette. Crowell/ Harper, 1983.

Hughes, Shirley. *Out and About*. Lothrop, 1988.

*The Keys to My Kingdom: A Poem in Three Languages*. Illus. by Lydia Dabcovich. Lothrop, 1992.

Lewis, Claudia. *Long Ago in Oregon*. Illus. by Joel Fontaine. Harper, 1987.

———. *Up in the Mountains*. Illus. by Joel Fontaine. Harper, 1991.

Livingston, Myra Cohn. "Kansas Visit" in *I Never Told and Other Poems*. M.K. McElderry/ Macmillan, 1992.

Merriam, Eve. "Out of the City" in *The Singing Green*. Illus. by Kathleen Collins Howell. Morrow, 1992.

Moore, Lilian. *Adam Mouse's Book of Poems*. Illus. by Kathleen Garry McCord. Atheneum/Macmillan, 1992.

———. *Don't Be Afraid, Amanda*. Illus. by Kathleen Garry McCord. New York: Atheneum/Macmillan, 1992. (fiction)

———. *I'll Meet You at the Cucumbers*. Illus. by Sharon Wooding. Atheneum/ Macmillan, 1988. (fiction)

———. *Something New Begins*. (includes poems from her *I Thought I Heard the City*). Illus. by Mary Jane Dunton. Atheneum/Macmillan, 1982.

Prelutsky, Jack, sel. "City, Oh City" section in *The Random House Book of Poetry for Children*. Illus. by Arnold Lobel. Random, 1983.

Rylant, Cynthia. *Night in the Country*. Illus. by Mary Szilagyi. Bradbury/Macmillan, 1984.

———. *Waiting to Waltz: A Childhood*. Illus. by Stephen Gammell. Bradbury/ Macmillan, 1984.

Stevenson, Robert Louis. *Block City*. Illus. by Ashley Wolff. Dutton, 1988.

*This is the Key to the Kingdom*. Illus. by Diane Worfolk Allison. Little, 1992.

Turner, Ann. *Street Talk*. Houghton, 1986.

Williams, Vera B. *A Chair for My Mother*. Greenwillow, 1982. (fiction)

## CULTURAL DIVERSITY

As the world seems to get smaller and our "neighborhoods" get closer together, more emphasis is put on understanding people whose cultural background is different from our own. Some poets suggest focusing on our common humanity, not on our differences. In *All the Colors of the Race*, the narrator thinks that "the real color is behind the color;" it is our shared humanity that is important. In "No Difference" Shel Silverstein asks us to remember that we are all the same "when we turn off the light."

Multicultural education is best incorporated throughout the curriculum so that variations in lifestyle and beliefs are perceived as normal and natural. When multicultural understanding is relegated to a "unit" or a holiday it becomes just a topic for study rather than a necessary part of our daily lives in contemporary society. Poetry by poets of many races and cultural traditions should be incorporated into all units.

Some of this poetry is difficult to locate. Fine books by poets from representative cultural traditions have been allowed to go out of print. Many ethnic and cultural groups within the United States are not well represented in poetry for children. What follows is a list of books and poems to help children expand their understanding of others. This selection of titles includes picture books and collections of poems by poets from various cultural groups in the United States so that teachers and librarians can make a concerted effort to include these books in all units of study.

Because so few works by Asian-American, Hispanic-American, and other ethnic poets are available for children, it is particularly important to look for accessible poems in adult collections. Collections of works by American Indian poets or from their oral traditions in adult collections are valuable additions to schools. Two collections of poems by Chinese-American poets are particularly valuable because of their connections to American history. *Island: Poems and History of Chinese Immigrants on Angel Island, 1910–1940* includes poems found written and carved on the walls of the detention barracks of Chinese immigrants. *Songs of Gold Mountain* includes poems from the same period from San Francisco's Chinatown. The poems in both books are in both Chinese and English.

Not all poetic portraits of members of racial and ethnic groups are positive. Any classic or historical poem should be read in the context of the time in which it was written and not as an explanation of a people or a culture. Teachers can help children understand that the messages in some poems may not be as acceptable today. Rosemary and Stephen Vincent Benet's classic, *A Book of Americans* contains poems about Christopher Columbus, Crazy

Horse, and Pocahontas that reflect attitudes of other eras. These poems might be compared to more recent poems and biographies.

Contemporary presentations that have come under fire can also be thoughtfully explored with children. Susan Jeffers' presentation of Chief Seattle's poetic speech, *Brother Eagle, Sister Sky,* has been controversial for a number of reasons, including illustrations that do not accurately reflect the Chief's culture and the fact that the speech is a rewritten version produced for an environmental film. Teachers and librarians can present these arguments to children who read this book as a starting point for discussions about how we portray cultures and individuals in the books and poems we share.

Sometimes an artist broadens our interpretation of a poem by choosing to portray people of a particular ethnic or cultural tradition in the illustrations for a picture book poem. Ed Young shows an Asian-American child asleep on the cover of Mary Calhoun's *While I Sleep* and an Asian-American family in Barbara Savadge Horton's *What Comes in Spring?* Brian Pinkney portrays an African-American child exploring the trail to the ocean in Burton Albert's *Where Does the Trail Lead?*

## Portrayals of Different Cultures

Adoff, Arnold. "I Think the Real Color Is Behind the Color" in *All the Colors of the Race*. Illus. by John Steptoe. Lothrop, 1982.

Benet, Rosemary and Stephen Vincent Benet. *A Book of Americans*. Illus. by Charles Child. Holt, 1984.

Seattle, Chief. *Brother Eagle, Sister Sky: A Message from Chief Seattle*. Illus. by Susan Jeffers. Dial, 1991.

Silverstein, Shel. "No Difference" in *Where the Sidewalk Ends*. Harper, 1974.

## Poems By and About African Americans

Adoff, Arnold. *All the Colors of the Race*. Illus. by John Steptoe. Lothrop, 1982.

———. *Black Is Brown Is Tan*. Illus. by Emily Arnold McCully. Harper, 1973.

———. sel. *I am the Darker Brother: An Anthology of Modern Poems by Black Americans*. Macmillan, 1970.

———. *In for Winter, Out for Spring*. Illus. by Jerry Pinkney, Harcourt, 1991.

———. sel. *My Black Me: A Beginning Book of Black Poetry*. New York: Dutton, 1974.

Albert, Burton. *Where Does the Trail Lead?* Illus. by Brian Pinkney. Simon, 1991.

Bang, Molly. *Ten, Nine, Eight*. Greenwillow, 1983.

———. *Yellow Ball*. Morrow, 1991.

Brooks, Gwendolyn. *Bronzeville Boys and Girls*. Illus. by Ronni Solbert. Harper, 1956.

Bryan, Ashley, sel. *All Night, All Day: A Child's First Book of African-American Spirituals*. Atheneum/Macmillan, 1991.

———. *Sing to the Sun.* Harper, 1992.

Clifton, Lucille. *Everett Anderson's Christmas Coming.* Illus. by Jan Spivey Gilchrist. Holt, 1991.

———. *Everett Anderson's Goodbye.* Illus. by Ann Grifalconi. Holt, 1983.

———. *Everett Anderson's Nine Month Long.* Illus. by Ann Grifalconi. Holt, 1978.

———. *Some of the Days of Everett Anderson.* Illus. by Evaline Ness. Holt, 1970.

Giovanni, Nikki. *Ego Tripping.* Illus. by George Ford. Hill, 1974.

———. *Spin a Soft Black Song.* Illus. by George Martins. Farrar, 1985.

———. *Vacation Time.* Illus. by Marisabina Russo. Morrow, 1980.

Greenfield, Eloise. *Daydreamers.* Illus. by Tom Feelings. Dial, 1981.

———. *Honey, I Love* Illus. by Leo and Diane Dillon. Crowell/Harper, 1978.

———. *Nathaniel Talking.* Illus. by Jan Spivey Gilchrist. Black Butterfly/Writers and Readers, 1988.

———. *Night on Neighborhood Street.* Illus. by Jan Spivey Gilchrist. Dial, 1991.

Grimes, Nikki. *Something on My Mind.* Illus. by Tom Feelings. Dial, 1978.

Hughes, Langston. *Dream Keeper.* Illus. by Helen Sewell. Knopf, 1962.

Little, Lessie Jones. *Children of Long Ago.* Illus. by Jan Spivey Gilchrist. Philomel/ Putnam, 1988.

Slier, Deborah, sel. *Make a Joyful Sound.* Illus. by Cornelius Van Wright and Ying-Hwa Hu. Checkerboard Press, 1991.

Strickland, Dorothy S., sel. *Listen Children: An Anthology of Black Literature.* Illus. by Leo and Diane Dillon. Bantam, 1982.

Sullivan, Charles, sel. *Children of Promise.* Abrams, 1991.

*This Is the Key to the Kingdom.* Illus. by Diane Worfolk Allison. Little, 1992.

## Poems By and About American Indians

Baylor, Byrd. *The Desert Is Theirs.* Illus. by Peter Parnell. MacMillan, 1975.

———. *Hawk, I'm Your Brother.* Illus. by Peter Parnell. Macmillan, 1976.

Bierhorst, John, sel. *In the Trail of the Wind: American Indian Poems and Ritual Orations.* Farrar, 1971.

Bruchac, Joseph and Jonathon London. *Thirteen Moons on a Turtle's Back: A Native American Year of Moons.* Illus. by Thomas Locker. Philomel/Putnam, 1992.

Carlstrom, Nancy White. *Northern Lullaby.* Illus. by Leo and Diane Dillon. Philomel/ Putnam, 1992.

Clark, Ann Nolan. *In My Mother's House.* Illus. by Velino Herrara. Viking, 1991.

Goble, Paul. *I Sing for the Animals.* Bradbury/Macmillan, 1991.

Grossman, Virginia. *Ten Little Rabbits.* Illus. by Sylvia Long. Chronicle Books, 1991.

Hirschfelder, Arlene B., and Beverly Singer, sels. *Rising Voices: Writings of Young Native Americans.* Scribners, 1992.

Longfellow, Henry Wadsworth. *Hiawatha.* Illus. by Keith Mosely. Philomel/Putnam, 1988.

———. *Hiawatha.* Illus. by Susan Jeffers. Dutton, 1983.

———. *Hiawatha's Childhood.* Illus. by Errol LeCain. Farrar, 1984.

Mederis, Angela Shelf. *Dancing with the Indians.* Illus. by Samuel Byrd. Holiday, 1991.

Ortiz, Simon. *The People Shall Continue.* Illus. by Sharol Graves. Children's, 1988.

Seattle, Chief. *Brother Eagle, Sister Sky: A Message from Chief Seattle.* Illus. by Susan Jeffers. Dial, 1991.

Sneve, Virginia Driving Hawk, sel. *Dancing Teepees.* Illus. by Stephen Gammell. Holiday, 1989.

Wood, Nancy. *Many Winters: Prose and Poetry of the Pueblos.* Illus. by Frank Howell. Doubleday, 1974.

## Poems By and About Asian Americans

Calhoun, Mary. *While I Sleep.* Illus. by Ed Young. Morrow, 1992.

Hom, Marlon K. *Songs of Gold Mountain: Cantonese Rhymes from San Francisco Chinatown.* University of California, 1987.

Horton, Barbara Savadge. *What Comes in Spring?* Illus. by Ed Young. Knopf, 1992.

Lai, Him Mark, Genny Lim, and Judy Young. *Island: Poetry and History of Chinese Immigrants on Angel Island, 1910–1940.* University of Washington Press, 1980.

## Poems By and About Hispanic Americans

Pena, Sylvia Cavazos. *Kikiriki: Stories and Poems in English and Spanish for Children.* Arte Publico, 1989.

———. *Tun-Ta-Ca-Tun: More Stories and Poems in English and Spanish for Children.* Arte Publico, 1985.

Soto, Gary. *A Fire in My Hands.* Illus. by James M. Cardillo. Scholastic, 1990.

———. *Neighborhood Odes.* Illus. by David Diaz. Harcourt, 1992.

*The Zebra-Riding Cowboy: A Folk Song from the Old West.* Illus. by Maria Christina Brusca. Holt, 1992.

# TRANSPORTATION: TRAINS

Transportation is often covered in social studies programs, and poetry about various modes of transportation is fairly easy to locate. Students may want to create their own collections of poems about particular forms of transportation such as automobiles or boats. Many poems have been written about airplanes, the sensation of flying, and even about fears of flying. Examples of these are included in the unit on flight in Chapter 2. For me, the most "moving" poetry written about transportation is about trains, perhaps because the rhythms and sounds of trains seem inherently poetic. Poems about trains lend themselves naturally to choral presentations, which stress their onomatopoetic and rhythmic qualities through use of voices, rhythm sticks, clapping, or drums. David McCord's classic "Song of the Train," with its clickety-clack rhythms and Eloise Greenfield's "Riding on the Train," with its flitting descriptions of things seen from the train window as it moves, are good examples of poems that can be presented dramatically.

Other poems about trains look at the romance of this form of transportation. "Casey Jones," from folk song tradition, tells of the exploits of a courageous engineer. In her classic poem about trains, "Travel," Edna Saint Vincent Millay says there isn't a train she wouldn't take "no matter where it's going." Still other poems are silly or metaphorical or look at the impact of the train on U.S. settlement. An anonymous poem, "The Railroad Cars Are Coming," shows the excitement that people felt when the lines were built through their small towns. This poem could be contrasted with Paul Yee's short story, "Spirits of the Railway," which is about Chinese laborers who died building the railroad, or with Paul Goble's retelling of the American Indian legend in *The Death of the Iron Horse*, in which Plains Indians "killed" an early locomotive, not knowing that thousands more trains would follow.

Bennett, Rowena. "A Modern Dragon" in Prelutsky, Jack. *Read-Aloud Rhymes for the Very Young*. Knopf, 1986.

Bogan, Louise. "Train Tune" in Morrison, Lillian. *Rhythm Road*. Lothrop, 1988.

*Casey Jones*. Illus. by Carol York. Troll, 1980.

Dickinson, Emily. "The Locomotive" in Ferris, Helen. *Favorite Poems Old and New*. Doubleday, 1957.

Ferris, Helen, sel. *Favorite Poems Old and New*. (section on transportation). Doubleday, 1957.

Goble, Paul. *Death of the Iron Horse*. Bradbury/Macmillan, 1987. (traditional story)

Greenfield, Eloise. "Riding on the Train" in *Honey, I Love*. Illus. by Leo and Diane Dillon. Crowell/ Harper, 1978.

Hopkins, Lee Bennett. *Click, Rumble, Roar*. Illus. by Anna H. Audette. Crowell/ Harper, 1987.

McCord, David. "Song of the Train" in *One at a Time*. Little, 1986.

Merriam, Eve. *Train Leaves the Station*. Illus. by Dale Gottlieb. Holt, 1992.

———. "Traveling" in *The Singing Green*. Illus. by Kathleen Collins Howell. Morrow, 1992.

Millay, Edna St. Vincent. "Travel" in *Edna St. Vincent Millay's Poems Selected for Young People*. Illus. by Ronald Keller. Harper, 1979.

"The Railroad Cars Are Coming" in Brewton, Sara and John. *America Forever New*. Crowell/Harper, 1989.

Riddell, Elizabeth. "The Train in the Night" in Larrick, Nancy. *When the Dark Comes Dancing*. Philomel/Putnam, 1983.

Siebert, Diane. *Train Song*. Illus. by Mike Wimmer. Harper, 1990.

Stevenson, Robert Louis. "From a Railway Carriage" in *A Child's Garden of Verses*. Illus. by Michael Foreman. Delacorte, 1985.

Tippett, James S. "Trains" in Ferris, Helen. *Favorite Poems Old and New*. Doubleday, 1957.

Yee, Paul "Spirits of the Railway" in *Tales from Gold Mountain*. Illus. by Simon Ng. Macmillan, 1990. (fiction)

Zolotow, Charlotte. "The Train" and "The Train Melody" in *Everything Glistens and Everything Sings*. Illus. by Margot Tomes. Harcourt, 1987.

## GEOGRAPHY: PLACE NAMES

People have always had the opportunity to be poets in naming the places they live. I live in Wyoming in the shade of the Snowy Range, but I like to visit the Neversummer Range in Colorado. While both names indicate that there is snow on these great Rocky Mountain peaks all year around, "Snowy" is merely descriptive and "Neversummer" explains it poetically. A friend has a photograph he took of the sign for the ghost town of Difficulty, Wyoming, in the Freezeout Mountains. These two names tell us why Difficulty might be a ghost town. Students may enjoy exploring the names on the land around them and selecting and recording those they consider to be poetic. They may want to create a poetic name for a place near their school such as a local park, pond, or hill.

Poets, too, have played with the geography of names. Some have simply used geographic names to create rhymes. Edward Lear's classic limericks rely on the use of a place name to establish their rhyme ("There was a young lady of..."). Arnold Lobel has mimicked Lear's limericks in his *Pigericks*, each of which is also set in a geographic locale. Jack Prelutsky creates a nonsense rhyme for many of the states in *Ride a Purple Pelican* and adds city names to many poems in *Beneath a Blue Umbrella*. Eve Merriam's poem "Schenectady" plays with the lovely sound of its name. One classic children's game uses geographic names as part of an alliterative exercise, as the child chants, "A my name is Alice and my husband's name is Alex. We come from Alaska and we sell ants...." This is modeled in Jane Bayer's picture book, *A My Name Is Alice*.

Sometimes poets play with geography in their poems for other reasons. Jack Prelutsky's "New York Is in North Carolina" is a list of some of the answers he gave when "I flunked the geography test." Samuel Marshak's *Hail to Mail* follows the course of a letter from geographic locale to geographic locale. Eve Merriam's "Traveling" plays with the sounds of the names of places and the words with which they rhyme ("Flip a coin in Des Moines"). In her poem "Geography" she creates rhymes for the abbreviations for the states and leaves 17 undone so that children can try their own rhymes.

Other poets have dealt with more serious aspects of naming. M.B. Goffstein's small book, *The School of Names*, is a free verse poem to the beauties of naming. Goffstein wants "to go to the School of Names" to learn the names of all of the lakes, rivers, stars, and creatures, enjoying the sounds of their beauty. Several poets have celebrated American Indian place names. Lydia Huntley Sigourney's "Indian Names" comments on the tragic loss of native people whose names live on. Meguido Zola has written "Canadian Indian Place Names" using the onomatopoetic names of Canadian Indian peoples and Myra Cohn Livingston includes the names of the tribes of Indians of the prairies in "Indians of the Plains." Stephen Vincent Benet's poem "American Names" about the ethnic mixture of American names appears in *America Forever New* with several other geographic poems, such as John Holmes' "Map of My Country."

Bayer, Jane. *A, My Name Is Alice.* Illus. by Steven Kellogg. Dial, 1984.

Benet, Stephen Vincent. "American Names" in Brewton, Sara and John E. *America Forever New.* Crowell/Harper, 1989.

Goffstein, M.B. *The School of Names.* Harper, 1986.

Holmes, John. "Map of My Country" in Brewton, Sara and John E. *America Forever New.* Crowell/ Harper, 1989.

Lear, Edward. *The Nonsense Poems of Edward Lear.* Illus. by Leslie Brooke. Clarion/ Houghton, 1991.

Livingston, Myra Cohn. "Indians of the Plains" in *Worlds I Know and Other Poems.* Illus. by Tim Arnold. M.K. McElderry/ Macmillan, 1985.

Lobel, Arnold. *The Book of Pigericks.* Harper, 1973.

Marshak, Samuel. *Hail to Mail.* Illus. by Vladimir Radunsky. Holt, 1990.

Merriam, Eve. "Geography," "Schenectady," and "Traveling" in *The Singing Green.* Illus. by Kathleen Collins Howell. Morrow, 1992.

Prelutsky, Jack. *Beneath a Blue Umbrella.* Illus. by Garth Williams. Greenwillow, 1990.

———. "New York Is in North Carolina" in *The New Kid on the Block.* Illus. by James Stevenson. Greenwillow, 1984.

———. *Ride a Purple Pelican.* Illus. by Garth Williams. Greenwillow, 1986.

Sigourney, Lydia Huntley. "Indian Names" in Brewton, Sara and John E. *America Forever New.* Crowell/ Harper, 1989.

Zola, Meguido. "Canadian Indian Place Names" in Booth, David. *Til All the Stars Have Fallen.* Viking, 1990.

## AMERICAN HISTORY

When incorporated into the study of history poetry provides insights into past events and the feelings of people who lived through them. Because American society seems relentlessly fixed in the present, children may not understand how past and present are woven together. Many think history is dry and boring. Poetry helps children to see that history is full of drama and emotion. Visits to sites that show the imprints of ancient creatures on rocks and stones, the wagon ruts of those who crossed the prairies, and reconstructed villages and farms, as well as picture books and stories, help children feel something for the past. Poems shared during these experiences often reinforce the connections. Barbara Juster Esbensen describes in "Campsite" the sense that "something wants us here" as she sits at the site of an ancient campfire. Shirley Graham describes hearing the beat of drums from the past, a beat that will continue to be heard long into the future, in "Drums of My Father." Eloise Greenfield explains in "Tradition" that what we do connects us to our past. She says that when the people of the Bahamas carry fruits and other items on their heads, they are doing something that connects them to their African past, they "also carry history."

Two general collections contain many poems that can be used with studies of U.S. history. Sara and John E. Brewton's *America Forever New* includes poems about historic events, poems about regions and states of the United States, and biographical poems about historical figures. Rosemary and Stephen Vincent Benet's *A Book of Americans* is a collection of biographical poems.

One way to include poetry in the study of history is to let students read examples of poems that were popular in the time periods they study. Students are surprised at the rigid propriety in poetry for children in the New England colonies or at the treacly sweet instruction in nineteenth-century poems. These poems can give them a new understanding of childhood in the periods they study and often can be linked effectively with works of historical fiction. Donald Hall's *Oxford Book of Children's Verse in America* is useful for this kind of assignment because it is arranged chronologically. Selections from the *New England Primer* and "John Rogers' Exhortation to His Children" reinforce a sense of the rigid Puritan childhood for readers of Elizabeth George Speare's *The Witch of Blackbird Pond*.

Walt Whitman wrote poems about slavery, the Civil War, and the death of Abraham Lincoln based on his own experiences and feelings. These poems can help students experience the war firsthand. A selection of Whitman's poems on these subjects is included in a section titled "I mourned, and yet shall mourn" in Lee Bennett Hopkins" collection *Voyages: Poems by Walt Whitman*.

Children who are curious about early books used by schoolchildren might want to look at the Puritan alphabets in *The Oxford Book of Children's Verse in America*. Two picture books also present the alphabet as it was or might have been shared with children in other times. Alice and Martin Provensen's illustrated version of *A Peaceable Kingdom: A Shaker Abecedarius* was part of the Shaker Manifesto of 1882. Jim Aylesworth's *Folks in the Valley: A Pennsylvania Dutch ABC* has rhymed text and illustrations by Stefano Vitale that show traditional activities and dress of the Pennsylvania Dutch.

Sometimes a poem about a historical incident adds poignancy to children's reading of a historical novel. Students who read Carol Ryrie Brink's *Caddie Woodlawn* may be aware when they read that the mass killings of the passenger pigeons described in the novel caused their extinction, just as Caddie fears. Paul Fleishman's "Passenger Pigeon" in his *I Am Phoenix: Poems for Two Voices* can be performed after reading the novel to highlight this incident. The poem shows, through the use of large numbers and an echoing quality of many wings, what the population was like in Caddie's time and ends quietly with the voice of the last surviving pigeon.

Helen Plotz's *Saturday's Children: Poems of Work* (now out of print) contains several poems, both nineteenth-century and more modern ones, that tell of the virtual enslavement of factory girls. When used with Katherine Paterson's novel *Lyddie*, these poems echo the harsh conditions described in the book. Lessie Jones Little's "Children of Long Ago," which describes the lives of children in "little country towns," although describing towns of the South, echoes the activities and feelings of the Ingalls children in Laura Ingalls Wilder's *Little Town on the Prairie*. Students may want to try to locate other poems that describe the events, characters, or settings of the historical novels they read.

Picture book versions of classic poems about historic events such as Henry Wadsworth Longfellow's *Paul Revere's Ride* and John Greenleaf Whittier's *Barbara Frietschie* provide both the poem's text and illustrations which can help children visualize history. Picture book versions of poems set within a historical context can also do this. Donald Hall, for example, has written two free verse poems that have been issued in picture book format. His *Ox-Cart Man*, a Caldecott Medal winner, is a circular story of an eighteenth-century New Hampshire farmer's annual trips to market and the preparations for the trip. In *The Man Who Lived Alone* Hall describes the solitary life of a New England farmer from childhood to old age.

## Poems about American History

Brink, Carol Ryrie. *Caddie Woodlawn*. Macmillan, 1973. (fiction)

Esbensen, Barbara Juster. "Campsite" in *Cold Stars and Fireflies*. Illus. by Susan Bonners. Harper, 1991.

Fleischman, Paul. "The Passenger Pigeon" in *I Am Phoenix*. Illus. by Ken Nutt. Dutton, 1991.

Graham, Shirley. "Drums of My Father" in Booth, David. *Til All the Stars Have Fallen*. Viking, 1989.

Greenfield, Eloise. "Tradition" in *Under the Sunday Tree*. Illus. by Amos Ferguson. Harper, 1988.

Paterson, Katherine. *Lyddie*. Dutton, 1991. (fiction)

Speare, Elizabeth George. *The Witch of Blackbird Pond*. Houghton, 1958. (fiction)

Wilder, Laura Ingalls. *Little Town on the Prairie*. Illus. by Garth Williams. Harper, 1953. (fiction)

## Collections of Poems about U.S. History and Geography

Adoff, Arnold, sel. *I Am the Darker Brother: An Anthology of Modern Poems by Black Americans*. Macmillan, 1968.

Benet, Rosemary and Stephen Vincent Benet, sels. *A Book of Americans.* Illus. by Charles Child. Holt, 1933.

Brewton, Sara and John E., sels. *America Forever New* Illus. by Ann Grifalconi. Crowell/Harper, 1989.

Ferris, Helen. sel. *Favorite Poems Old and New.* Illus. by Leonard Weisgard. Doubleday, 1957.

Hall, Donald, sel. *Oxford Book of Children's Verse in America.* Oxford, 1985.

Lewis, Claudia. *Long Ago in Oregon.* Illus. by Joel Fontaine. Harper, 1987.

Little, Lessie Jones. *Children of Long Ago.* Illus. by Jan Spivey Gilchrist. Philomel/ Putnam, 1988.

Plotz, Helen, sel. *Saturday's Children* Greenwillow, 1982.

Sullivan, Charles, sel. *Children of Promise.* Abrams, 1991.

Whitman, Walt. "I mourned, and yet shall mourn" section in Hopkins, Lee Bennett. *Voyages: Poems by Walt Whitman.* Illus. by Charles Mikolaycak. Harcourt, 1988.

## Poem Picture Books about U.S. History

Aylesworth, Jim. *The Folks in the Valley: A Pennsylvania Dutch ABC.* Illus. by Stefano Vitale. Harper, 1992.

Field, Rachel. *General Store.* Illus. by Nancy Winslow Parker. Greenwillow, 1988.

Hale, Sarah Josepha. *Mary Had a Little Lamb.* Illus. by Tomie De Paola. Holiday, 1984.

Hall, Donald. *The Man Who Lived Alone.* Illus. by Mary Azarian. Godine, 1984.

———. *The Ox-Cart Man.* Illus. by Barbara Cooney. Viking, 1979.

Hoguet, Susan Ramsay. *Solomon Grundy.* Dutton, 1986.

Lindbergh, Reeve. *Johnny Appleseed.* Illus. by Kathy Jakobsen. Little, 1990.

Longfellow, Henry Wadsworth. *Paul Revere's Ride.* Illus. by Nancy Winslow Parker. Greenwillow, 1985.

Medearis, Angela Shelf. *Dancing with the Indians.* Illus. by Samuel Byrd. Holiday House, 1991.

Ortiz, Simon. *The People Shall Continue.* Illus. by Sharol Graves. Children's Book Press, 1988.

*A Peaceable Kingdom: The Shaker Abecedarius.* Illus. by Alice and Martin Provensen. Viking, 1971.

Service, Robert. *The Cremation of Sam McGee.* Illus. by Ted Harrison. Greenwillow, 1987.

———.*The Shooting of Dan McGrew.* Illus. by Ted Harrison. Godine, 1988.

Whitman, Walt. *I Hear America Singing.* Illus. by Robert Sabuda. Philomel/Putnam, 1991.

Whittier, John Greenleaf. *Barbara Frietchie.* Illus. by Nancy Winslow Parker. Greenwillow, 1992.

## BIOGRAPHY

In "When I Read the Book," Walt Whitman speculates on how well the author has told the story of a person's life and wonders if a biographer will ever write of him and his life. Many poets write biographical poems about people they admire, which may be narrative poems that tell a story about either the whole of or an incident from an individual's life or descriptive poems which describe an individual's character and personality. Poems have been written about well-known people from history, art, music, and sports and are in poetry collections on these subjects in the various chapters of this book. Most anthologies of poems for children include a section of poems about people.

Picture book versions of some biographical poems give the poem's text and background illustration that tell about life in a particular period. Sometimes poems take a legendary figure and give that figure poetic life as in Reeve Lindbergh's version of the story of Johnny Appleseed and Susan Ramsay Hoguet's illustrated *Solomon Grundy,* which fleshes out the life and times of this imaginary nursery rhyme figure.

## Biographical Poems

Blos, Joan. *The Heroine of the Titanic.* Illus. by Tennessee Dixon. Morrow, 1991.

Gerrard, Roy. *Sir Francis Drake, His Daring Deeds.* Farrar, 1988.

Hoguet, Susan Ramsay. *Solomon Grundy.* Dutton, 1986.

Lindbergh, Reeve. *Johnny Appleseed.* Illus. by Kathy Jakobsen. Little, 1990.

———. *View from the Air: Charles Lindbergh's Earth and Sky.* Illus. by Richard Brown. Viking, 1992.

Livingston, Myra Cohn. *Let Freedom Ring: A Ballad of Martin Luther King, Jr.* Illus. by Samuel Byrd. Holiday House, 1992.

Longfellow, Henry Wadsworth. *Paul Revere's Ride.* Illus. by Nancy Winslow Parker. Greenwillow, 1985.

Whitman, Walt. "When I Read the Book" in Hopkins, Lee Bennett. *Voyages: Poems by Walt Whitman.* Harcourt, 1988.

Whittier, John Greenleaf. *Barbara Frietchie.* Illus. by Nancy Winslow Parker. Greenwillow, 1992.

Willard, Nancy. *The Voyage of the Ludgate Hill: Travels with Robert Louis Stevenson.* Illus. by Alice and Martin Provensen. Harcourt, 1987.

## Martin Luther King, Jr.

When students are reading biographies, they may find poems that describe the person about whom they are reading. If they don't find specific poems, they can look for poems that describe the person's qualities. They might look for poems that describe, for example, a fighter for freedom or a person who takes risks. Instead of comparing a book and a poem, they might compare two poems about a person. Martin Luther King, Jr., for example, has been the subject of several poems. Students could compare poems to try to answer some questions: How does the poet portray Dr. King? What aspects of his life and character are included in the poem? What events are mentioned? Why do you think the poet wrote this poem?

Cornish, Sam. "Death of Dr. King #1" in Adoff, Arnold. *My Black Me.* Dutton, 1974.

Giovanni, Nikki. "The Funeral of Martin Luther King, Jr." in Sullivan, Charles. *Children of Promise.* Abrams, 1991.

Jackson, Mae. "I Remember." in Adoff, Arnold. *My Black Me.* Dutton, 1974.

Kennedy, X.J. "Martin Luther King Day" in *The Kite That Braved Old Orchard Beach.* Illus. by Marion Young. M.K. McElderry/Macmillan, 1991.

Livingston, Myra Cohn. *Let Freedom Ring: A Ballad of Martin Luther King, Jr.* Illus. by Samuel Byrd. Holiday House, 1992.

———. "Martin Luther King" in Prelutsky, Jack. *Random House Book of Poetry for Children.* Random, 1983.

———. "Martin Luther King Day" in *Celebrations.* Illus. by Leonard Everett Fisher. Holiday, 1985.

Merriam, Eve. "Keep to the March" from *I Am a Man: Ode to Martin Luther King, Jr.* in Larrick, Nancy. *Bring Me All of Your Dreams.* Evans, 1988.

Perkins, Useni Eugene. "Martin Luther King, Jr." in Slier, Deborah. *Make a Joyful Sound.* Checkerboard, 1991.

## MEMORIES

Memories are an aspect of autobiography. Some are a poet's actual memories and others are created. A unit titled "Memories" can include material from social studies, poetry and other literature, and language arts. *Wilfred Gordon MacDonald Partridge* by Mem Fox could introduce such a unit. In this simple picture book, a small boy helps an older friend, Miss Nancy Alison Delacourt Cooper, to "find" her memory by encouraging her to tell stories about her life. David McCord's poem, "Forget It," presents the issue of memory from Miss Nancy's point of view, saying that what has been forgotten is not so important as what is remembered when someone really listens to us share it.

Once children begin to think about what a memory is they might look at books and poems that describe memories and talk with older people who can share memories about particular events. Some poets share childhood memories. Students might want to read poetry by Paul Janeczko, Claudia Lewis, Cynthia Rylant, and Gary Soto, who write about their own child-hoods in their poems.

Fox, Mem. *Wilfred Gordon MacDonald Partridge.* Illus. by Julie Vivas. Kane/Miller, 1985. (fiction)

Janeczko, Paul. *Brickyard Summer.* Illus. by Ken Rush. Orchard, 1989.

Lewis, Claudia. *Long Ago in Oregon.* Illus. by Joel Fontaine. Harper, 1987.

———. *Up in the Mountains.* Illus. by Joel Fontaine. Harper, 1991.

Little, Lessie Jones. *Children of Long Ago.* Illus. by Jan Spivey Gilchrist. Philomel/Putnam, 1988.

Livingston, Myra Cohn. *Worlds I Know and Other Poems.* Illus. by Tim Arnold. M.K. McElderry/Macmillan, 1985.

McCord, David. "Forget It" in *All Small.* Illus. by Madelaine Gill Linden. Little, 1986.

Medearis, Angela Shelf. *Dancing with the Indians*. Illus. by Samuel Byrd. Holiday, 1991.

Rylant, Cynthia. *Waiting to Waltz: A Childhood*. Illus. by Stephen Gammell. Bradbury/Macmillan, 1984.

Soto, Gary. *A Fire in My Hands*. Scholastic, 1990.

# WORLD CULTURES

With changes in international politics and concern for the global environment, more emphasis is being put on a world view that sees all nations and peoples as interdependent. Some books of poetry for children have this holistic world view in that they give a glimpse of the ways people around the world do things differently and yet are in many ways the same. Byrd Baylor's *Way to Start a Day*, for example, briefly describes the ways people around the earth rise and welcome the new day. Edith Baer's *This Is the Way We Go to School: A Book about Children around the World* shows children taking various modes of transportation as they head to school in many places. Nancy Larrick's collection of bedtime poems, *When the Dark Comes Dancing*, helps us end the day on the same note by including lullabies from several different countries in Africa as well as a Russian night poem. Jane Yolen's *Street Rhymes around the World* presents traditional rhymes from many places. Naomi Shihab Nye has collected poems from contemporary poets around the world in *This Same Sky*, with an introduction encouraging us to see the larger world around us.

Some classic poems about children of other countries, on the other hand, give uncomfortable messages. "Foreign Children" continues to appear in reprints of Robert Louis Stevenson's *A Child's Garden of Verses*. This poem suggests that his English childhood is the only good one to have, ending in the line, "O! Don't you wish that you were me?" T.S. Eliot's "Growltiger's Last Stand," although ostensibly about cats, uses inaccurate references to the people of Thailand, such as having them ride in junks and sampans and calling them a "fierce Mongolian horde" and "Chinks." While the Siamese are cheered as the victors in this melee, their image is not positive by contemporary standards and teachers may want to use this poem in discussions about stereotyping.

The social studies curriculum often condenses so much information about other countries and cultures into such a short time that trying to sort out individual cultural or national experiences is difficult. As a result, teachers and schools have chosen to focus on one or two countries or continents in the course of a year and have attempted to do more in-depth study of these areas. Some geographic areas are well represented in the literature for children while others are sadly lacking, resulting in more difficult research tasks for teachers and students.

This is reflected in poetry as well. Most collections of poetry for children contain poems from other English-speaking countries. The poems found in Oxford Books of poetry for children as well as selections by such poets as Canadian Dennis Lee and English poets Kit Wright and Paul Rosen show children that though there may be small differences, life in these countries is similar to theirs. Children's poetry from other cultures has not been translated and is not so easily available as English-language poetry. Several anthologists have made a concerted effort to include representative selections from a variety of national and cultural groups in their collections. These poems do not so much reveal a great deal about the country of the poet as they help children understand that poets and poems thrive in all cultures and languages. Teachers may have to use adult poetry collections to find poems to include with some units.

Picture books with poetic texts and collections of poems that reflect national and cultural experiences are listed with the name of the country or culture in parentheses. Teachers and librarians should encourage children from all cultural groups to share poetry and songs from their own backgrounds. Folk rhymes, songs, serious poems, and light verse in other languages and translations can be copied for display or bound for classroom or library collections and children can teach the words and music to others.

## Poems for Discussion of Cultural Stereotyping

> Eliot, T.S. "Growltiger's Last Stand" in *Growltiger's Last Stand and Other Poems.* Illus. by Errol Le Cain. Farrar, 1986.
> Stevenson, Robert Louis. "Foreign Children" in *A Child's Garden of Verses*. Illus. by Michael Foreman. Delacorte, 1985.

## Books and Collections with an International Focus

> Baer, Edith. *This Is the Way We Go to School: A Book about Children around the World.* Illus. by Steve Bjorkman. Scholastic, 1990.
> Baylor, Byrd. *The Way to Start a Day.* Illus. by Peter Parnell. Macmillan, 1978.
> Elledge, Scott, sel. *Wider than the Sky.* Harper, 1990.
> Gordon, Ruth. *Time Is the Longest Distance.* Harper, 1991.
> Higginson, William J., sel. *Wind in the Long Grass.* Illus. by Sandra Speidel. Simon, 1991.
> Koch, Kenneth, and Kate Farrell, sels. *Talking to the Sun.* Holt/The Metropolitan Museum of Art, 1985.
> Larrick, Nancy, sel. *When the Dark Comes Dancing.* Illus. by John Wallner. Philomel/ Putnam, 1983.
> LeTord, Bijou, sel. *Peace on Earth.* Doubleday, 1992.

Nye, Naomi Shihab. *This Same Sky*. Four Winds/Macmillan, 1992.

Slier, Deborah, sel. *Make a Joyful Sound*. Checkerboard, 1991.

Whipple, Laura. *Animals, Animals*. Illus. by Eric Carle. Philomel/Putnam, 1989.

———. *Dragons, Dragons and Other Creatures That Never Were*. Illus. by Eric Carle. Philomel/Putnam, 1991.

Yolen, Jane, sel. *Street Rhymes around the World*. Illus. by Jeanette Winter and 17 international artists. Wordsong/Boyds Mills, 1992.

## Poems About or From Specific Places

Adoff, Arnold. *Flamboyan*. Illus. by Karen Barbour. Harcourt, 1988. (Puerto Rico)

Belting, Natalia M., sel. *Moon Was Tired of Walking on Air*. Illus. by Will Hillenbrand. Houghton, 1992. (South America)

Bodecker, N.M., sel. *It's Raining Said John Twaining: Danish Nursery Rhymes*. M.K. McElderry/Macmillan, 1973. (Denmark)

Brebeuf, Jean de. *The Huron Carol*. Illus. by Frances Tyrrell. Dutton, 1990. (Canada)

Carlstrom, Nancy White. *Baby-O*. Illus. by Sucie Stevenson. Little, 1992. (West Indies)

Cassedy, Sylvia, and Kunihiro Suetake, sels. *Red Dragonfly on My Shoulder*. Illus. by Molly Bang. Harper, 1992. (Japan)

Delacre, Lulu, sel. *Arroz Con Leche: Popular Songs and Rhymes from Latin America*. Scholastic, 1989. (Latin America)

Fox, Mem. *Shoes from Grandpa*. Illus. by Patrick Mullins. Orchard, 1990. (Australia)

Garne, S.T. *One White Sail: A Caribbean Counting Book*. Illus. by Lisa Etre. Green Tiger, 1992. (Caribbean)

Greenfield, Eloise. *Africa Dream*. Illus. by Carole Byard. Harper, 1977. (Africa)

———. *Under the Sunday Tree*. Illus. by Amos Ferguson. Harper, 1988. (The Bahamas)

Griego, Margot C., Betsy L. Bucks, and Laurel H. Kimball, sels. *Tortillitas Para Mama and Other Nursery Rhymes*. Illus. by Barbara Cooney. Holt, 1981. (Mexico)

*The House That Jack Built*. Illus. by Jenny Snow. Dial, 1992. (Antigua)

Joseph, Lynn. *Coconut Kind of Day: Island Poems*. Illus. by Sandra Speidel. Lothrop, 1990. (Trinidad)

———. *An Island Christmas*. Illus. by Catherine Stock. Clarion/Houghton, 1992. (Trinidad/Tobago)

Lessac, Frane, sel. *Caribbean Canvas*. Harper, 1989. (Caribbean)

Lewis, Richard. *All of You Was Singing*. Illus. by Ed Young. Atheneum/Macmillan, 1991. (Aztec/Mexico)

———. *In a Spring Garden*. Illus. by Ezra Jack Keats. Dial, 1965. (Japan)

———. *In the Night Still Dark*. Illus. by Ed Young. Atheneum/Macmillan, 1988. (Polynesian)

Linden, Anne Marie. *One Smiling Grandma: A Caribbean Counting Book*. Illus. by Lynne Russell. Dial, 1992. (Caribbean)

Mado, Michio. *The Animals*. Illus. by Mitsumasa Anno. M.K. McElderry/Macmillan, 1992. (Japan)

Nichols, Grace. *Come on into My Tropical Garden*. Lippincott/Harper, 1988. (Guyana)

Trinca, Rod. *One Wooly Wombat.* Illus. by Kerry Argent. Kane/Miller, 1985. (Australia)

Wyndham, Robert, sel. *Chinese Mother Goose Rhymes.* Illus. by Ed Young. Philomel/Putnam, 1989. (China)

# REFERENCES

"Celebrating Liberty." *The Web* 10 (Summer, 1986): 8–16.

Chatton, B. "Dateline U.S.A." Column, *Booklinks Magazine.*

Ensler, K., and N. Nyhart. (1978). "Persona Poems." *The Poetry Connection: An Anthology of Contemporary Poems with Ideas to Stimulate Children's Writing.* New York: Teachers and Writers Press, 29–32.

Grossman, F. (1982). "People" and "Persona." *Getting from Here to There: Writing and Reading Poetry.* Montclair, NJ: Boynton/Cook, 74–96, 129–144.

Harris, V. J. (1992). *Teaching Multicultural Literature in Grades K-8.* Norwood, MA: Christopher-Gordon.

"Houses." *The Web* 5 (Fall, 1980):12–23.

Kettel, R. (1992). "Children and the Homeless." *Booklinks* 1 (May): 51–55.

James, M., and J. Zarrillo. (1989). Teaching history with children's literature: A concept-based interdisciplinary approach. *Social Studies* 80 (July–August): 153–8.

Jarolimek, J. (1986). *Social Studies in Elementary Education.* 7th ed. New York: Macmillan.

"Reading the World." Column, *Booklinks Magazine.*

"Who's News." *USA Weekend* (July 3–5, 1992): 2.

# Chapter 5:
# Poetry and Language Arts

## WRITING POETRY

Those who are interested in teaching children to write poetry will find many manuals available on the subject. Some of these manuals use models to help children see the possible forms for poetry and include sections on haiku, limericks, cinquains, and so on. Others believe that these models limit creativity and lead to unconscious plagiarism. Some include classical examples, and others, believing these are deadly, include poems created by young people. Some books provide worksheets to teach "poetry skills" while others provide only suggestions on broad themes or topics that might be popular. Some believe that children should avoid rhyme and encourage free verse, while others give suggestions for using rhyme. Some believe that poetry writing should be noisy and collaborative work, while others believe that it is a solitary business.

Most of the methods suggested in manuals on teaching poetry emerge from the short-term experiences of poets-in-residence. The writing programs are suggested by poets who come periodically or occasionally to the classroom to "do" poetry with children and who must create activities and ideas that can be generated quickly and completed within a prescribed time frame. If a poet is to work with children for two hours once a week, the use of a model to start discussion and to provide a form for a "product" is necessary. Though poets-in-residence have done a great deal of good, especially in schools where poetry has not been taught, they are operating under rigid time constraints and are likely to have only a short-term effect. Poetry writing and poetry sharing make a bigger difference when they are done consistently. When presented only infrequently as a special event, poetry loses its power to transform students.

Two books explore the use of poetry across the curriculum and the school day in whole language classrooms. Robert Hull's *Behind the Poem: A Teacher's View of Children Writing* (1988) is a description of Hull's own classroom and his attempts to put poetry in the center of his students' experiences. He decries the use of formulas, saying that good teaching of any subject is a process of interactions among human beings and, as such, emerges from their questions, concerns, and ideas. He then carefully describes his struggle with his own role, showing the questions he asks himself and his students, his struggles with intervention as opposed to interference, and his care not to assume cause and effect in his work.

Amy McClure (1990) has written *Sunrises and Songs: Reading and Writing Poetry in the Elementary School* with Peggy Harrison and Sheryl Reed, two classroom teachers who integrate poetry in their classrooms. They also say that there are no absolute do's and don'ts for teaching poetry. Poetry writing is a process that emerges over time in a language-rich environment in which reading and sharing poems, experimentation with many forms, and honesty and feedback are honored. McClure's descriptions of the ways these teachers work to create this environment each year with new groups of students, the problems that emerge, and the fear that this just might be the year this open-endness won't work will ring true to many teachers.

## THE POWER OF LANGUAGE

Poetry writing occurs naturally in whole language classrooms in response to poems, classroom events, and readings. Writing a poem is one of the many ways students can express themselves. Aside from writing and presenting poems, part of the "language arts" experience of poetry is the way it teaches how language works. Poems reveal the power of language. Students who know the playground rhyme "Sticks and stones can break my bones but names will never hurt me" use this chant to ward off one of the most powerful weapons: language. Poems about the power of words can be used to help students realize how carefully they need to speak and write. Edward Field has translated a poem of Netsilik Eskimo origin, "Magic Words," that suggests that the power of words is an ancient one. In that magic time, thinking about something in words could cause it to happen. In "Old Mountains Want to Turn to Sand," Tommy Olofsson suggests that the power of words is like water on rock; words can move mountains. "From Prison," by Osip Mandelstam, says very simply that words have power even when they are not allowed to be spoken. William Carlos Williams' "Fragment" shares the heartbreak of words written in a letter by someone who does not know how powerful words can be. Carl Sandburg's two classic poems on the power of language, "Little Girl, Be Careful What You Say" and "Primer Lesson," also assert this power. In a sense, every well-written poem asserts the power of language. The poet concentrates and selects language so that the reader or listener will be moved and understand.

Field, Edward. "Magic Words" in Lueders, Edward. *Zero Makes Me Hungry*. Scott Foresman, 1976.

Mandelstam, Osip. "From Prison" in Harrison, Michael. *Splinters*. Oxford, 1988.

Olofsson, Tommy. "Old Mountains Want to Turn to Sand" in Nye, Naomi Shihab. *This Same Sky*. Four Winds/ Macmillan, 1992.

Sandburg, Carl. "Little Girl, Be Careful What You Say" and "Primer Lesson" in Hopkins, Lee Bennett. *Rainbows Are Made*. Harcourt, 1982.

Williams, William Carlos. "Fragment" in Harrison, Michael. *Splinters*. Oxford, 1988.

## THE ALPHABET

Poetry not only describes the power of language, it plays with the elements of language—letters, words, phrases, and the ways we put them together. Poetry can teach the alphabet or play with letters. Poems talk about grammar, parts of speech, vocabulary, spelling, and punctuation. Poetry takes many forms, each of which may express a particular idea or emotion. Some poets even write about a form using the form itself. Poetry can introduce the devices that poets use, such as metaphor and imagery. Poetry encompasses the richness of the sound of language and the ways those sounds affect us.

The alphabet provides one of the first forms of language children play with, and poets and artists have played with it as well. Some poets create a rhymed story using the letters of the alphabet as a framework. Others provide an alliterative phrase or sentence for each letter of the alphabet, and still others use a bit of alphabetical nonsense for each letter. Some poets have used the convention of the alphabet to organize poetry collections for older readers, with a poem about an object or person for each letter of the alphabet. Some alphabet books can serve as "primers" for learning the alphabet because the use of rhyme and rhythm can help children learn letters in order and connect them with a particular sound. But many authors and illustrators have used the alphabet for more sophisticated purposes, and these books are enjoyed by all ages. The convention of poetry used in each of the following books is indicated in parentheses.

Aylesworth, Jim. *The Folks in the Valley: A Pennsylvania Dutch ABC*. Illus. by Stefano Vitale. Harper, 1992. (rhyme)

———. *Old Black Fly*. Illus. by Stephen Gammell. Holt, 1992. (rhyme)

Base, Graeme. *Animalia*. Abrams, 1987. (alliteration)

Bayer, Jane. *A, My Name Is Alice*. Illus. by Steven Kellogg. Dial, 1984. (alliteration)

Bragg, Ruth Gembicki. *Alphabet Out Loud*. Picture Book Studio, 1991. (alliteration)

Cassedy, Sylvia. *Roomrimes*. Illus. by Michele Chessare. Harper, 1987. (room poem for each letter)

Chess, Victoria. *Alfred's Alphabet Walk.* Greenwillow, 1979. (alliteration)

Dragonwagon, Crescent. *Alligator Arrived with Apples.* Illus. by Jose Aruego and Ariane Dewey. Macmillan, 1987. (alliteration, rhyme)

Eichenberg, Fritz. *Ape in a Cape.* Harcourt, 1952. (rhyme)

Elliot, David. *An Alphabet of Rotten Kids!* Illus. by Oscar de Mejo. Philomel/Putnam, 1991. (poems for children named for each letter of the alphabet)

Farber, Norma. *As I Was Crossing Boston Common.* Illus. by Arnold Lobel. Dutton, 1992, 1975. (rhyme)

Gag, Wanda. *The ABC Bunny.* Coward/Putnam, 1978. (rhyme)

Gardner, Beau. *Have You Ever Seen...? An ABC Book.* Putnam, 1986. (nonsense alliteration)

Geringer, Laura. *The Cow Is Mooing Anyhow: A Scrambled Alphabet Book to Be Read at Breakfast.* Illus. by Dirk Zimmer. Harper, 1991. (rhyme)

Hague, Kathleen. *Alphabears.* Illus. by Michael Hague. Holt, 1984. (rhyme)

King-Smith, Dick. *Alphabeasts.* Illus. by Quentin Blake. Macmillan, 1992. (animal poem for each letter of the alphabet)

Lear, Edward. *A Was Once an Apple Pie.* Illus. by Julie Lacome. Candlewick, 1992. (nonsense)

————. *An Edward Lear Alphabet.* Illus. by Carole Newsom. Lothrop, 1983. (interior rhyme, nonsense)

LeCourt, Nancy. *Abracadabra to Zigzag.* Illus. by Barbara Lehman. Morrow, 1991. (ricochet words)

Leedy, Loreen. *The Dragon ABC Hunt.* Holiday, 1986. (starts and ends with rhyme)

Lobel, Anita. *Alison's Zinnia.* Greenwillow, 1990. (alliteration)

Lobel, Arnold. *On Market Street.* Illus. by Anita Lobel. Greenwillow, 1981. (alliteration)

Merriam, Eve. *Good Night to Annie.* Illus. by Carol Schwartz. Hyperion, 1992. (alliteration, onomatopoeia, assonance)

————. *Halloween ABC.* Illus. by Lane Smith. Macmillan, 1987. (poem for each letter)

————. *Where Is Everybody? An Animal Alphabet.* Illus. by Diane De Groat. Simon, 1989. (alliteration)

*A Peaceable Kingdom: The Shaker Abecedarius.* Illus. by Alice and Martin Provensen. Viking, 1978. (rhyme)

Piatti, Celestino. *Celestino Piatti's Animal ABC.* Atheneum, 1966. (rhyme)

Purviance, Susan, and Marcia O'Shell. *Alphabet Annie Announces an All-American Album.* Illus. by Ruth Brunner-Strosser. Houghton, 1988. (alliteration)

Reeves, James. *Ragged Robin: Poems from A-Z.* Illus. by Emma Chichester Clark. Little, 1990. (poems titled in alphabetical order)

Sendak, Maurice. *Alligators All Around.* Harper, 1962. (alliteration)

Seuss, Dr. *Dr. Seuss's ABC.* Random, 1963. (alliteration)

Steig, Jeanne. *Alpha Beta Chowder.* Illus. by William Steig. Harper, 1992. (poem for each letter)

Thornhill, Jan. *The Wildlife ABC.* Simon, 1988. (rhyme)

Van Allsburg, Chris. *The Z Was Zapped.* Houghton, 1987. (alliteration)

Watson, Clyde. *Applebet.* Illus. by Wendy Watson. Farrar, 1982. (rhyme)

Yolen, Jane. *All in the Woodland Early.* Illus. by Jane Breskin Zalben. Caroline/Boyds Mills, 1991.

————. *Elfabet.* Illus. by Lauren Mills. Little, 1990. (alliteration)

## POEMS ABOUT LANGUAGE

Besides playing with the alphabet, poets have written poems about individual letters. Eve Merriam, for example, has a "quibble" with the letter "Q" having to be used with "U." Dr. Seuss has even imagined that the letters go "On Beyond Zebra" and invented a series of additional letters.

Other poets have written poems that play with words and their meanings. David McCord has written many poems using word play. Jeanne Steig fills each poem in *Alpha Beta Chowder* with long and wonderful-sounding words. Charlotte Pomerantz's "Where Do These Words Come From?" lists words derived from languages spoken by Native Americans. Eve Merriam loves the English language. All of her collections contain poems about spelling, punctuation, homonyms, unusual words, word origins, and other interesting aspects of language. Ruth Heller has written picture book poems to explain the parts of speech.

A number of poets agree with school children that spelling is not their favorite subject. In *The Best Town in the World*, Byrd Baylor would like to have grown up spelling any way she wanted. Cynthia Rylant remembers with chagrin her spelling of "woke" in "Spelling Bee." Various folk and street rhymes try to help spellers by giving them rhymed tips on "i before e" and other spelling problems. Other poems about grammar, spelling, words, and punctuation are included here. If the topic of the poem is not clear from the title, it is included in parentheses.

### Poems that Play with Language

Baylor, Byrd. *The Best Town in the World.* Illus. by Ronald Himler. Scribner/Macmillan, 1983.

Cole, Joanna, and Stephanie Calmenson. "Spelling Rhymes" in Cole, Joanna. *Miss Mary Mack and Other Children's Street Rhymes.* Morrow, 1990.

Dakos, Kalli. "Call the Periods, Call the Commas" in *If You're Not Here, Please Raise Your Hand.* Illus. by G. Brian Karas. Four Winds/Macmillan, 1990.

Emin, Gevorg. "The Question Mark" in Nye, Naomi Shihab. *This Same Sky.* Four Winds/Macmillan, 1992.

Fisher, Aileen. "Comma in the Sky" in *Always Wondering.* Illus. by Joan Sandin. Harper, 1991.

Heller, Ruth. *Kites Sail High.* Grosset, 1988.

———. *Merry-Go-Round.* Grosset, 1990.

———. *Up, Up, and Away.* Grosset, 1991.

Hymes, Lucia, and James L. Hymes, Jr. "My Favorite Word" in De Regniers, Beatrice Schenk. *Sing A Song of Popcorn.* Scholastic, 1988.

Livingston, Myra Cohn. "S: Silent Shark" in *I Never Told and Other Poems.* M.K. McElderry/Macmillan, 1992.

McCord, David. "Alphabet (Eta Z)," "LMNTL," "The Likes and Looks of Letters," "Spelling Bee," "X and Y," and "Z" in *One at a Time*. Little, 1986.

――――. "Pome" in *All Small*. Illus. by Madelaine Gill Linden. Little, 1986.

――――. "W" in De Regniers, Beatrice Schenk. *Sing a Song of Popcorn*. Scholastic, 1988.

Merriam, Eve. "By the Shores of Pago Pago" (repeated syllables), "Ditto Marks, or How Do You Amuse a Muse?" "Parenthesis," and "Unfinished" ("kn" sounds) in *Chortles*. Illus. by Sheila Hamanaka. Morrow, 1989.

――――. "Can a Can?" in *A Poem for a Pickle*. Illus. by Sheila Hamanaka. Morrow, 1989.

――――. "Latch, Catch" in *Blackberry Ink*. Illus. by Hans Wilhelm. Morrow, 1985. (uses of word "catch")

――――. "A Jamboree for J" and "Quibble" in *The Singing Green*. Illus. by Kathleen Collins Howell. Morrow, 1992.

――――. "Markings" (punctuation), "Nym and Graph" (homonyms), "One, Two, Three-Gough!" (homonyms), "Showers, Clearing Later in the Day" (punctuation), "Why I Did Not Reign" (spelling) in *A Sky Full of Poems*. Illus. by Walter Gaffney-Kessell. Dell, 1986.

――――. "A Nanny for a Goat" in *You Be Good and I'll be Night*. Illus. by Karen Lee Schmidt. Morrow, 1988. (compound words)

Moore, Lilian. "Winter Dark" in *Something New Begins*. Illus. by Mary Jane Dunton. Atheneum/Macmillan, 1982. (punctuation)

Noll, Sally. *Jiggle Wiggle Prance*. Greenwillow, 1987. (Verbs)

Pomerantz, Charlotte. "Where Do These Words Come From?" in De Regniers, Beatrice Schenk. *Sing a Song of Popcorn*. Scholastic, 1988.

Prelutsky, Jack. "The Flotz" (punctuation) and "An Unassuming Owl" (who and whom) in *The New Kid on the Block*. Illus. by James Stevenson. Greenwillow, 1984.

Rylant, Cynthia. "Spelling Bee" in *Waiting to Waltz: A Childhood*. Illus. by Stephen Gammell. Bradbury/Macmillan, 1984.

Seuss, Dr. *On Beyond Zebra*. Random, 1955.

Steig, Jeanne. *Alpha Beta Chowder*. Illus. by William Steig. Harper, 1992.

Withers, Carl, sel. "Spelling Rhymes" in *A Rocket in My Pocket*. Illus. by Sussanne Suba. Holt, 1988.

Worth, Valerie. "Water Lily" in *All the Small Poems*. Illus. by Natalie Babbitt. Farrar, 1987. (punctuation)

Yolen, Jane. "The Grammatical Witch" in *Best Witches*. Illus. by Elise Primavera. Putnam, 1989.

## Collective Nouns

The collective noun has received particular attention by language lovers. Brian Wildsmith created three picture books of collective nouns, *Brian Wildsmith's Birds, Brian Wildsmith's Fishes,* and *Brian Wildsmith's Wild Animals*. Peter and Connie Roop use a series of collective nouns to link the actions of animals in *One Earth, A Multitude of Creatures*. Jim Arnosky's *A Kettle of Hawks and Other Wildlife Groups* lists other collective nouns for animals. Patricia Hooper has expanded on the collective noun by providing poems about various groups of animals in her collection, *A Bundle of Beasts.*

Bruce McMillan's photo essay, *The Baby Zoo,* uses the terms for the baby animals of several zoo species. An appendix in the back of the book features a chart that includes names for males and females and collective terms for some animals. If children are interested in finding out more about these collective terms and in creating some of their own for animals, *An Exhaltation of Larks* by James Lipton is a valuable reference. This book contains lists of well-known terms, a history of the creation of these words, and lists of actual and made-up terms for other "collections" besides animals. Other good collective poems are Eve Merriam's "Parking Lot Full" and Ruth Heller's *A Cache of Jewels.* Students might try to write collective terms for people in their schools. What would a group of kindergartners be called? A group of teachers? A group of principals?

Arnosky, Jim. *A Kettle of Hawks and Other Wildlife Groups.* Lothrop, 1990.
Heller, Ruth. *A Cache of Jewels and Other Collective Nouns.* Grosset, 1987.
Hooper, Patricia. *A Bundle of Beasts.* Illus. by Marck Steele. Houghton, 1987.
Lipton, Robert. *An Exhaltation of Larks.* Penguin, 1977. (nonfiction)
McMillan, Bruce. *The Baby Zoo.* Scholastic, 1992.
Merriam, Eve. "Parking Lot Full" in *Chortles.* Illus. by Sheila Hamanaka. Morrow, 1989.
Roop, Peter, and Connie Roop. *One Earth, a Multitude of Creatures.* Illus. by Valerie A. Kells. Walker, 1992.
Wildsmith, Brian. *Brian Wildsmith's Birds.* Oxford, 1967.
———. *Brian Wildsmith's Fishes.* Watts, 1968.
———. *Brian Wildsmith's Wild Animals.* Oxford, 1967.

## NATURAL POETRY

All language is in some ways poetic. Young children learning to express themselves orally often use language in slightly offbeat ways, making small errors that provide their adult listeners with insights into the beauty of language. Kornei Chukovsky (1968) calls this language "the melodic speech of children." Children use aspects of poetry in their play as they pass traditional rhymes, rhythmic games, alliterative phrases, riddles, and other language play from one generation of children to the next. X.J. Kennedy even suggests that there is a poetic quality in the language of signs, warnings, and short messages we may send to each other. He calls the search for this poetry and those poems we find in this way "finders-keepers" poems (Kennedy, 1982).

Recently these untutored or "folk" aspects of language are being taken more seriously as poetry. Collections of children's folk rhymes formerly reserved for folklorists to study are now being published for children. These include collections of jump rope rhymes, clapping games, schoolyard taunts, and books of verse from autograph albums.

Geringer, Laura. *Yours 'Til the Ice Cracks: A Book of Valentines.* Illus. by Andrea Baruffi. Harper, 1992.

Milnes, Gerald. *Granny Will Your Dog Bite.* Illus. by Kimberly Bulcken Root. Knopf, 1990.

Morrison, Lillian. *Remember Me When This You See: A New Compilation of Autograph Verses.* Illus. by Marjorie Bauernschmidt. Crowell, 1961.

———. *Yours Till Niagara Falls: A Book of Autograph Verses.* Illus. by Sylvie Wickstrom. Crowell, 1990, 1950.

Opie, Iona, and Peter Opie, sels. *I Saw Esau: The Schoolchild's Pocket Book.* Illus. by Maurice Sendak. Candlewick, 1992.

Schwartz, Alvin. *And the Green Grass Grew All Around.* Illus. by Sue Truesdell. Harper, 1992.

Yolen, Jane, sel. *Street Rhymes around the World.* Illus. by Jeanette Winter and 17 international artists. Wordsong/Boyds Mill, 1992.

## ELEMENTS OF POETRY

The basic elements of poetry include rhythm, imagery, sound devices, and figurative language. Poems that feature rhythm are included in Chapter 7. Those that use imagery are included in Chapter 2. Sound qualities of poetry including rhyme, alliteration, onomatopoeia, repetition, and use of dialect, as well as aspects of figurative language, including similes and metaphors, are considered here.

## Rhyme

Rhyme is such a commonly used device in verse written for children that many students consider unrhymed poetry not "real" poetry. Children are attracted to the sound qualities of rhyme and easily memorize favorite rhymed poems. When children begin to write poetry, they may write nonsense poems that are lists of sentences or phrases all of which have the same end rhyme (e.g., "When I was green, I went to the Queen, I was feeling lean, I was feeling mean . . . "). As we share rhymed poems with children, we can help them see that there must be sense as well as sound in a good poem. David McCord suggests a form for rhymed lists so that they are much more interesting to read in "Jamboree." Each line of his list poem begins with "A rhyme for . . ." with the name of a food and then supplies a rhyme. Children might try this with a topic they are studying such as frogs or numbers. Children who like to play with rhyme will like Nancy Shaw's *Sheep in a Jeep* and its sequels. In these simple books, Shaw uses end rhyme, internal rhyme, and onomatopoeia to create humorous stories. In *Tommy at the Grocery Store*, Bill Grossman uses many repetitions of the rhyming of "Tommy" and "mommy" to create a silly story. Bill Martin, Jr., and John Archambault's *Chicka Chicka Boom Boom* uses rhyme and rhythm in a cumulative piece.

We do not want to stop sharing rhyme with children but instead expand their ideas about how rhyme can be used in poems. We should introduce children to a variety of rhyme schemes by sharing poems using rhymed couplets, rhyme every other line, every third line, or limericks with their distinctive rhymed pattern. We might collect poems that use internal rhyme in which the next-to-the-last word in each line rhymes. In Ffrida Wolfe's classic "Choosing Shoes," the last word of many lines is "shoes," and the internal rhymes include "new" and "blue" and "you." Catherine Anholt's picture book of poems, *Good Days, Bad Days*, also uses internal rhyme. Betsy Lewin in *Cat Count* and Beatrice Schenk de Regniers in *So Many Cats!* use internal rhyme.

Some poets have even written poems in rhyme about people who use rhyme. John Ciardi's "I Met a Man That Was Playing Games" and Karla Kuskin's "Alexander Soames: His Poems" are both about rhymers.

Anholt, Catherine. *Good Days, Bad Days*. Putnam, 1991.
Ciardi, John. "I Met a Man That Was Playing Games" in *I Met a Man*. Illus. by Robert Osborn. Houghton, 1973.
De Regniers, Beatrice Schenk. *So Many Cats*. Illus. by Ellen Weiss. Clarion/Ticknor and Fields, 1988.
Grossman, Bill. *Tommy at the Grocery Store*. Illus. by Victoria Chess. Harper, 1989.
Kuskin, Karla. "Alexander Soames: His Poems" in *Dogs and Dragons, Trees and Dreams*. Harper, 1980.
Lewin, Betsy. *Cat Count*. Putnam, 1981.
McCord, David. "Jamboree" in *One at a Time*. Little, 1986.
Martin, Bill, Jr., and John Archambault. *Chicka Chicka Boom Boom*. Illus. by Lois Ehlert. Simon, 1989.
Shaw, Nancy. *Sheep in a Jeep*. Illus. by Margot Apple. Houghton, 1986.
———. *Sheep in a Ship*. Illus. by Margot Apple. Houghton, 1992.
———. *Sheep in a Shop*. Illus. by Margot Apple. Houghton, 1991.
———. *Sheep out to Eat*. Illus. by Margot Apple. Houghton, 1992.
Wolfe, Ffrida. "Choosing Shoes" in Bennett, Jill. *Tiny Tim*. Delacorte, 1982.

## Alliteration/Tongue Twisters

Individual skills in poetry and prose writing can be explored through poetry. As children enjoy alphabet and other books that use alliteration, they may discover that this poetic quality is actually similar to the childhood game of "tongue twisters." As they practice traditional tongue twisters and try to say out loud some of the tongue-twisting alliterations of alphabet books, they can have fun with this kind of language. Poems such as Karla Kuskin's "Thistles" and Jeanne Steig's poems in *Alpha Beta Chowder* help them see the more subtle ways poets use repetition.

Barrett, Judi. *A Snake Is Totally Tail*. Illus. by L.S. Johnson. Macmillan, 1983.

Base, Graeme. *Animalia*. Abrams, 1987.

Bayer, Jane. *A, My Name Is Alice*. Illus. by Steven Kellogg. Dial, 1984.

Bragg, Ruth Gembicki. *Alphabet Out Loud*. Picture Book Studio, 1991.

Chess, Victoria. *Alfred's Alphabet Walk*. Greenwillow, 1979.

Dragonwagon, Crescent. *Alligator Arrived with Apples*. Illus. by Jose Aruego and Ariane Dewey. Macmillan, 1987.

Enderle, Judith Ross, and Stephanie Gordon Tessler. *Six Creepy Sheep*. Illus. by John O'Brien. Caroline/Boyds Mills, 1992.

Gackenbach, Dick. *Timid Timothy's Tongue Twisters*. New York: Holiday, 1986.

Kellogg, Steven. *Aster Aardvark's Alphabet Adventures*. Morrow, 1987.

Kuskin, Karla. "Thistles" in *Dogs and Dragons, Trees and Dreams*. Harper, 1980.

Lobel, Anita. *Alison's Zinnia*. Greenwillow, 1990.

Merriam, Eve. *Where Is Everybody?* Illus. by Diane de Groat. Simon, 1989.

Obligado, Lillian. *Faint Frogs Feeling Feverish and Other Terrifically Tantalizing Tongue Twisters*. Viking, 1983.

Purviance, Susan, and Marcia O'Shell. *Alphabet Annie Announces an All-American Album*. Illus. by Ruth Brunner-Strosser. Houghton, 1988.

Schwartz, Alvin. *Busy Buzzing Bumblebees and Other Tongue Twisters*. Illus. by Paul Meisel. Harper, 1992, 1982.

―――. *A Twister of Twists, a Tangler of Tongues*. Illus. by Glen Rounds. Lippincott/ Harper, 1972.

Sendak, Maurice. *Alligators All Around*. Harper, 1962.

Seuss, Dr. *Dr. Seuss's ABC*. Random, 1963.

Steig, Jeanne. *Alpha Beta Chowder*. Illus. by William Steig. Harper, 1992.

Van Allsburg, Chris. *The Z Was Zapped*. Houghton, 1987.

Yolen, Jane. *Elfabet*. Illus. by Lauren Mills. Little, 1990.

## Onomatopoeia/Sound Effects

Classroom activities and events can be created around the poetic concept of onomatopoeia and "sound" words in conjunction with units on listening and hearing or simply as an exercise in exploring language. Children might brainstorm a "sound effects" web with words that "sound like themselves." Books such as Peter Spier's *Crash, Bang, Boom,* and *Gobble, Growl, Grunt* and Michelle Koch's *Hoot, Howl, Hiss* can be the starting point for this webbing activity in primary grades; older students may be able to generate more ideas on their own. Many children have a large repertoire of "sound effect" words from watching cartoons and fantasy and science fiction movies. One group of older students kept a record of the sound effect words they heard other children using on the playground during recess and added them to the web.

Poets have commented in their poems about the natural and pleasing sounds of words. In his poem "Take Sky," David McCord asks why the word sky "sounds so well out loud" and then mentions other words that sound like what they represent. In his poem "The Look and Sound of Words," he suggests that the sound of a word matters. Mary O'Neill explores the sounds of words in her poem "Feelings about Words," saying that some words actually sound like the shape and size of the object or action they represent. Karla Kuskin has written two poems, "Cow Sounds Heavy" and "Worm," which show how names for creatures are appropriate for their size, shape, and abilities. Barbara Juster Esbensen's collection of animal poems, *Words with Wrinkled Knees*, focuses on the sounds of animal names.

Blake, Quentin. *All Join In*. Little, 1991.

Calmenson, Stephanie. *Zip, Whiz, Zoom!* Illus. by Dorothy Scott. Joy Street/Little, 1992.

Cummings, E.E. *Hist Whist*. Illus. by Deborah Kogan Ray. Crown, 1989.

Dodds, Ann. *Do Bunnies Talk?* Illus. by A. Dubanevich. Harper, 1992.

———. *Wheel Away!* Illus. by Thatcher Hurd. Harper, 1989.

Esbensen, Barbara Juster. *Words with Wrinkled Knees*. Illus. by John Stadler. Crowell/Harper, 1987.

Fleming, Denise. *In the Tall, Tall Grass*. Holt, 1991.

Hindley, Judy. *Soft and Noisy*. Illus. by Patrice Aggs. Hyperion, 1992.

Koch, Michelle. *Hoot, Howl, Hiss*. Greenwillow, 1991.

Kuskin, Karla. "Cow Sounds Heavy" and "Worm" in *Near the Window Tree*. Harper, 1975.

McCord, David. "The Look and Sound of Words," "The Pickety Fence," "Song of the Train," and "Take Sky" in *One at a Time*. Little, 1986.

Merriam, Eve. "Bam, Bam, Bam" in *Jamboree*. Illus. by Walter Gaffney-Kessell. Dell, 1984.

O'Neill, Mary. "Feelings about Words" in Prelutsky, Jack. *The Random House Book of Poetry for Children*. Random, 1983.

Schott, Penelope Scrambly. "Chimera" in Whipple, Laura. *Dragons, Dragons*. Philomel/Putnam, 1991.

Spier, Peter. *Crash, Bang, Boom*. Doubleday, 1972.

———. *Gobble, Growl, Grunt*. Doubleday, 1971.

Wilson, Sarah. *Garage Song*. Illus. by Bernie Karlin. Simon, 1991.

## Repetition/Cumulation

Repetition is an aspect of sound used so frequently in poetry that students will find it easy to collect poems that feature different kinds of repetition. In Margaret Wise Brown's classic *Goodnight Moon*, for example, the child/bunny repeats "goodnight" to all of the objects in its bedroom. Nancy White Carlstrom's *Northern Lullaby* echoes this repetition of the word "goodnight" as the child in this book says goodnight to stars, trees, and animals on an Alaskan winter night. Other poems also repeat the initial word in each line to form a list or a litany.

Children are most familiar with song refrains and recognize a similar use of refrains in classic poems and ballads. Children enjoy the refrain "Perhaps she'll die" in *I Know an Old Lady Who Swallowed a Fly*. The repeated refrain in Mary Ann Hoberman's *House Is a House for Me* adds to the bouncy rhythms of this poem picture book, and children often will join in the chorus as they listen to it. Some poems use a refrain to build a scary mood, as Laura Gerringer does in *Look Out, Look Out, It's Coming!* and Jack Prelutsky does in "The Bogeyman."

Older children may want to consider why a poet chooses to repeat a line in a poem. One of the classic repetitions is "and miles to go before I sleep" in Robert Frost's *Stopping by Woods on a Snowy Evening*. One fifth grader told me it made the poem seem more "dutiful." This child understood the feeling of having to go home after a day in the woods.

Brown, Margaret Wise. *Goodnight Moon.* Illus. by Clement Hurd. Harper, 1947.
Carlstrom, Nancy White. *Northern Lullaby.* Illus. by Leo and Diane Dillon. Philomel/Putnam, 1992.
Frost, Robert. *Stopping by Woods on a Snowy Evening.* Illus. by Susan Jeffers. Dutton, 1978.
Geringer, Laura. *Look Out, Look Out, It's Coming!* Illus. by Sue Truesdell. Harper, 1992.
Hoberman, Mary Ann. *A House Is a House for Me.* Illus. by Betty Fraser. Viking, 1978.
*I Know an Old Lady Who Swallowed a Fly.* Illus. by Glen Rounds. Holiday, 1990.
Prelutsky, Jack. "The Bogeyman" in *Nightmares.* Illus. by Arnold Lobel. Greenwillow, 1976.

## Dialect and Multilingual Poems

Another way that poets try to capture the beauty of language is to use dialect or more than one language in their poems. Lucille Clifton and Eloise Greenfield have included conventions of African-American speech in their poetry. Lynn Joseph and Grace Nichols use Caribbean dialect in their poems. Gary Soto includes the Spanish language conversations of Mexican-American young people of California. In *Granny Will Your Dog Bite*, which comes with an audiotape so children can hear the language spoken, Gerald Milnes shares the unique language of people of southern Appalachia. These poets treat dialect as an integral part of the way people express themselves with a natural beauty to be admired and respected.

Some poems are presented in several languages. Lulu Delacre's collections include poems in both Spanish and English, Tomie De Paola includes several poems by Frederico Garcia Lorca in both languages in his collection of poems. We can also share poems written in a language other than English.

Students, parents, librarians, or principals who speak the language can share poems they may know so that the sounds and inflections of poetry in another language can be enjoyed.

Some poems feature more than one language, such as Lydia Dabcovich's *Keys to My Kingdom*, which appears in Spanish, French, and English. Eve Merriam's "Conversation" is in four languages. Sometimes the appeal to multiple languages is more playful. Jack Prelutsky's "The Multilingual Mynah Bird" praises this bird who "can say most any word he's heard."

Adoff, Arnold, sel. *I Am the Darker Brother*. Macmillan, 1970. (African-American dialects)

——. *My Black Me*. Dutton, 1974. (African-American dialects)

——. "Trilingual" in *All the Colors of the Race*. Illus. by John Steptoe. Lothrop, 1982. (on using dialect)

Delacre, Lulu. *Arroz Con Leche: Popular Songs and Rhymes from Latin America*. Scholastic, 1989.

——. *Kikiriki: Stories and Poems in English and Spanish for Children*. Houston: Arte Publico, 1987.

——. *Las Navidades: Popular Christmas Songs from Latin America*. Scholastic, 1990.

——. *Tun-Ta-Ca-Tun: More Stories and Poems in English and Spanish for Children*. Arte Publico, 1986.

Joseph, Lynn. *Coconut Kind of Day*. Illus. by Sandra Speidel. Lothrop, 1990. (dialect of Caribbean-Trinidad)

——. *An Island Christmas*. Illus. by Catherine Stock. Houghton, 1992. (dialect of Caribbean-Trinidad)

*Keys to My Kingdom: A Poem in Three Languages*. Lothrop, 1992.

Lorca, Frederico Garcia. "Cancion Tonta/Silly Song" and "Caracola/Snail" in De Paola, Tomic. *Tomie De Paola's Book of Poems*. Putnam, 1988. (Spanish and English)

McCord, David. "Innuendo" in *All Small*. Illus. by Madelaine Gill Linden. Little, 1986. (French and English)

——. "Japanese Lesson" in *One at a Time*. Little, 1986. (Japanese and English)

Merriam, Eve. "Conversation" in *Jamboree*. Illus. by Walter Gaffney-Kessell. Dell, 1984. (Spanish-French-Italian-English)

Milnes, Gerald. *Granny Will Your Dog Bite*. Illus. by Kimberly Bulcken Root. Knopf, 1990.

Nichols, Grace. *Come on into My Tropical Garden*. Illus. by Caroline Binch. Lippincott/Harper, 1990. (Caribbean-Guyana)

Pomerantz, Charlotte. "Lulu, Lulu, I've a Lilo" (Samoan words) and "Where Do These Words Come From?" in De Regniers, Beatrice Schenk. *Sing a Song of Popcorn*. Scholastic, 1988. (words with Native American origins)

——. *The Tamarindo Puppy*. Illus. by Byron Barton. Greenwillow, 1980.

Prelutsky, Jack. "The Multilingual Mynah Bird" in *Zoo Doings*. Illus. by Paul O. Zelinsky. Greenwillow, 1983.

Riley, James Whitcomb. *The Gobble-Uns'll Git You Ef You Don't Watch Out!* Illus. by Joel Schick. Lippincott/Harper, 1991.

——. *When the Frost Is on the Punkin'*. Illus. by Glenna Lang. Godine, 1992.

Slier, Deborah, sel. *Make a Joyful Sound*. Checkerboard, 1991. (African-American dialects)

Soto, Gary. *Neighborhood Odes.* Illus. by David Diaz. Harcourt, 1992. (Mexican-American/California dialect)

Sullivan, Charles, sel. *Children of Promise.* Abrams, 1991. (African-American dialects)

Yolen, Jane. *Street Rhymes around the World.* Illus. by Jeannette Winter and 17 international artists. Wordsong/Boyds Mills, 1992. (all in original language and in English)

## Similes/Clichés

Figurative language, the use of comparisons to describe one thing in terms of another, is not only essential to poetry but to all language in which we strive to communicate effectively. Most of us use comparisons when we describe how we feel or what something looks like. We frequently use similes, which are sometimes clichés. As Eve Merriam points out in "Cliché," a cliché is a lazy way to make a comparison. She wonders if a mouse is actually quiet as she thinks about the cliché "quiet as a mouse." Instead of fresh language, we borrow a trite, old phrase that may not even be accurate. Children do not necessarily recognize these heavily used similes as clichés. Audrey Wood points this out in her picture book, *Quick as a Cricket.* About half of the self-descriptions given by the child narrator of the book are clichés and the other half are newly created by the book's author. Young readers may not be able to tell which of these similes are commonly used and which are invented. They may be comfortable with using clichés in poems they create. Time spent looking at Merriam's poem and webbing or listing other clichés can help children focus on the use of clichés on television, in readings, and by the adults around them.

A class of fourth graders created a list of clichés, starting with the ones found in Merriam's poem. From her poem they gathered "warm as toast," "quiet as a mouse," "slow as molasses," and "quick as a wink." The students thought of "red as a beet," "silly as a goose," "sly as a fox," and two they had heard but didn't understand, "clean as a whistle" and "dead as a doorknob." After such a list has been posted for a while and added to, children may want to do as Merriam did in the poem and think of better things to use as comparisons. We could then add a second part to our list. One side would list "clichés we've heard," the other, "some better ways to say this." The students may, at some point, choose their favorite comparisons.

In this activity children have the opportunity to create similes as they play with clichés outside of the context of a whole poem. Sometimes the use of similes comes up as children read and discuss novels. In a discussion group, some third graders noticed how often Eleanor Coerr uses comparisons in *Sadako and the Thousand Paper Cranes,* and they decided to make a list of those they found in one chapter. The teacher had them write one or two comparisons themselves, using things they knew about, and they shared their best ones with one another. She later told them that these comparisons had a name, "similes." Several weeks later a child commented on the "similars" she was finding in a book she was currently reading. "Similars" describes quite well what these phrases do.

Coerr, Eleanor. *Sadako and the Thousand Paper Cranes.* Putnam, 1977. (fiction)

Juster, Norman. *As: A Surfeit of Similes.* Illus. by David Small. Morrow, 1989.

Merriam, Eve. "Cliché" and "Simile: Willow and Ginko" in *A Sky Full of Poems.* Illus. by Walter Gaffney-Kessell. Dell, 1986.

Wood, Audrey. *Quick as a Cricket.* Illus. by Don Wood. Child's Play, 1982.

Yolen, Jane. "The Witch's Cauldron" in *Best Witches.* Illus. by Elise Primavera. Putnam, 1989.

## Metaphors/Riddles

Riddles, a much-loved word game, are a form of language play that relies on homonyms. Riddles are also metaphors, in which one thing is described as if it is another. Several poets have written riddle poems and several collections of these are available. Some poets, as Karla Kuskin does in *Any Me I Want to Be,* write poems that describe objects and animals in human terms for the reader to figure out. Many short poems for children are like riddles. Valerie Worth's "Safety Pin," for example, in which she describes a closed safety pin as if it were a shrimp and an opened one as a small fish, can be read or shared without the title as a perfect little riddle. Riddle poems can be copied onto pieces of paper on a "riddle board" for children to read and try to guess the answer. Children may want to try writing their own riddle poems.

Ciardi, John. "Have You Met This Man?" "I Met a Man I Could Not See," "I Met a Man with Three Eyes," "Then I Met Another Man I Could Not See," and "This Man Went Away" in *I Met a Man.* Illus. by Robert Osborne. Houghton, 1961.

―――. "Riddle" in *Fast and Slow.* Illus. by Becky Gaver. Houghton, 1978.

Frost, Robert. "One Guess" in *You Come Too.* Illus. by Thomas Nason. Holt, 1959.

Gibson, Douglas. "Cat in Moonlight" in Larrick, Nancy. *Cats Are Cats.* Philomel/ Putnam, 1988. (without title)

Hoberman, Mary Ann. "One Two" in *A Fine Fat Pig.* Illus. by Malcah Zeldis. Harper, 1991.

Kuskin, Karla. *Any Me I Want to Be.* Harper, 1972.

Livingston, Myra Cohn. *My Head Is Red and Other Riddle Rhymes.* Illus. by Tere LoPrete. Holiday, 1990.

―――. "Satellites" in *Space Songs.* Illus. by Leonard Everett Fisher. Holiday, 1988. (without title)

McCord, David. "Look: What Am I?" in *One at a Time.* Little, 1986.

Magee, Wes. "The Mystery Creatures" in Foster, John. *A Third Poetry Book*. Oxford, 1987. (without last lines)

Marzollo, Jean. *I Spy: A Book of Picture Riddles*. Illus. by Walter Wick. Scholastic, 1992.

Merriam, Eve. "Riddle-Go-Round" in *A Poem for a Pickle*. Illus. by Sheila Hammond. Morrow, 1989.

————. "Metaphor" and "Metaphor Man" in *A Sky Full of Poems*. Illus. by Walter Gaffney-Kessell. Dell, 1986.

Nichols, Grace. "Riddle" in *Come on into My Tropical Garden*. Illus. by Caroline Binch. Lippincott/Harper, 1990.

Nims, Bonnie Larkin. *Just Beyond Reach and Other Riddle Poems*. Illus. by George Ancona. Scholastic, 1992.

Parker, Nancy Winslow, and Joan Richards Wright. *Bugs*. Greenwillow, 1987.

"Riddling Song" and "Riddles" in *Tail Feathers from Mother Goose*. Little, 1988.

Roethke, Theodore. "The Sloth" in Elledge, Scott. *Wider Than the Sky*. Harper, 1990. (without title)

Schwartz, Alvin, sel. "Riddles" in *And the Green Grass Grew All Around*. Illus. by Sue Truesdell. Harper, 1992.

Smith, William Jay, and Carol Ra, sels. *Behind the King's Kitchen: A Roster of Rhyming Riddles*. Wordsong/Boyds Mills, 1992.

Swenson, May. "Living Tenderly" in Wolman, Bernice. *Taking Turns*. Atheneum/ Macmillan, 1992.

Swift, Jonathan. "AEIOU" in Blishen, Edward. *The Oxford Book of Poetry for Children*. Oxford, 1984.

Withers, Carl. "Riddles" in *A Rocket in My Pocket*. Illus. by Sussanne Suba. Holt, 1988.

Worth, Valerie. "Safety Pin" in *All the Small Poems*. Illus. by Natalie Babbitt. Farrar, 1987.

## FORMS OF POETRY

Writing a poem from a particular model is done so frequently in schools that students have developed an aversion to such commonly assigned forms as haiku, cinquains, or acrostic poems. Reading examples of a form and attempting to create poems in that form should emerge naturally from events in the classroom, not as isolated language arts lessons. One sixth-grade class studying Japan looked at the origins of and the famous poets who created haiku in Japan and read many to discover what might be common themes and topics of these poems. They then read haiku that originated in other countries to see if these poets had been true to the Japanese tradition. A few children chose to write haiku after they had done this assignment.

Fourth graders who were enjoying Dick King-Smith's novels with pig characters began collecting pigs in picture books and discovered Arnold Lobel's *Pigericks* in the process. They became interested in the limerick through Lobel's book and went on to read limericks by Edward Lear. Some of them tried their hand at writing limericks.

Some forms of poetry are not recognized in literary texts, such as questions or lists. One form of poetry that students discovered when sorting through books was the "short poem." In this category they included collections of terse verse, such as Bruce McMillan's *One Sun*, limerick collections, and collections of short poems such as *Splinters*. Some poets use a form borrowed from other writings. Jane Yolen, for example, writes "Letter from a Witch Named Flo"; Arnold Adoff includes poems in the forms of recipes in *Eats*; and Carmen Bernos de Gasztold writes poems in the forms of prayers. Eloise Greenfield has written two poems using the structure of twelve bar blues in her collection *Nathaniel Talking*. Examples of poems in these and in more traditional forms and lists of books about writing forms of poetry are included at the end of this chapter.

## Questions

Many poems are arranged as sets of questions or questions and answers. Lee Bennett Hopkins' recent anthology, *Questions,* includes poems grouped by the five questions: who, what, where, when, and why. Question poems take many forms. Some questions are rhetorical, such as Langston Hughes' "What happens to a dream deferred?" in "Harlem." Some poems ask accusing questions. Karla Kuskin's "Where Have You Been, Dear?" which includes a litany of questions from a parent figure followed by a brief, doleful answer from the child, is an example of this form. Some poems are conversational questions and answers between a child and an adult, as in Nancy White Carlstrom's *Goodbye Geese*. Other examples of conversations that involve questions and answers are included in the "Conversations" unit in Chapter 1.

Sometimes the list of questions is speculative. Beatrice Schenk de Regniers asks questions such as, "What if my cat could talk?" in her poem "What If." At other times, the poem contains questions that ask the reader to speculate about the nature of life and the ways things work, the questions of the scientist. Aileen Fisher includes many questions about nature in her collection of poems, *Always Wondering*. Myra Cohn Livingston's poem "Secrets" asks questions about space and suggests that the important thing about questions is that we continue to ask them. In her poem "Moon," she speculates on the changing faces of the moon and wonders about the figure that we see on its surface.

Sometimes poems focus on nonsensical or silly questions. Jane Yolen's "Silly Questions" provides the questions and answers for four truly awful Halloween puns. David McCord suggests in "Owls Talking" that somewhere perhaps owls don't ask "who" but "which," "why," or "what" instead.

After reading poems that use questions, children may want to write their own poems in which questions play a prominent role or simply write one powerful, carefully worded thought in the form of a question.

Bodecker, N. M. "Why Do Weeping Willows Weep?" in *Snowman Sniffles*. M.K. McElderry/Macmillan, 1983.

Carlstrom, Nancy White. *Goodbye Geese*. Illus. by Ed Young. Philomel/Putnam, 1991.

Ciardi, John. "Questions! Questions! Questions" in *Fast and Slow*. Illus. by Becky Gaven. Houghton, 1978.

De Regniers, Beatrice Schenk. "What If" in *The Way I Feel...Sometimes*. Illus. by Susan Meddaugh. Clarion/Ticknor and Fields, 1988.

Esbensen, Barbara Juster. "A Question" and "Tell Me" in *Who Shrank My Grandmother's House?* Illus. by Eric Beddows. Harper, 1992.

―――. "Questions for September" in *Cold Stars and Fireflies*. Illus. by Susan Bonners. Harper, 1991.

Farjeon, Eleanor. "Poetry" in Elledge, Scott. *Wider Than the Sky*. Harper, 1990.

Fisher, Aileen. *Always Wondering*. Illus. by Joan Sandin. Harper, 1991.

Hirschi, Ron. *What Is a Bird?* Illus. by Galen Burrell. Walker, 1987.

Holder, Julie. "Sad Things," "Mad Things," "Scary Things," and "Glad Things" in Foster, John. *A Very First Poetry Book*. Oxford, 1987.

Hopkins, Lee Bennett, sel. *Questions*. Illus. by Carolyn Croll. Harper, 1992.

Hubbell, Patrica. "The World Turned Horses" in *A Green Grass Gallop*. Illus. by Ronald Himler. Atheneum/Macmillan, 1990.

Hughes, Langston. "Harlem" in Larrick, Nancy. *Bring Me All of Your Dreams*. M. Evans, 1988.

Kuskin, Karla. "The Question," "Square as a House," "Where Have You Been, Dear?" and "Where Would You Be?" in *Dogs and Dragons, Trees and Dreams*. Harper, 1980.

Levy, Constance. "Questions to Ask a Butterfly" in *I'm Going to Pet Worm Today*. Illus. by Ronald Himler. M.K. McElderry/Macmillan, 1991.

Livingston, M.C. "Moon" in *Sky Songs*. Illus. by Leonard Everett Fisher. Holiday, 1984.

―――. "Secrets" in *Space Songs*. Illus. by Leonard Everett Fisher. Holiday, 1988.

McCord, David. "Owls Talking" and "Question" in *One at a Time*. Little, 1986.

Merriam, Eve. "Talking to the Sun" in *The Singing Green*. Illus. by Kathleen Collins Howell. Morrow, 1992.

Moore, Lilian. "Lost" and "Yellow Weed" in *Something New Begins*. Illus. by Mary Jane Dunton. Atheneum/Macmillan, 1982.

Prelutsky, Jack. "Do Oysters Sneeze?" in *The New Kid on the Block*. Illus. by James Stevenson. Greenwillow, 1984.

Rossetti, Christina. *Color*. Illus. by Mary Teichman. Harper, 1992.

―――. "What Are Heavy?" in Elledge, Scott. *Wider Than the Sky*. Harper, 1990.

―――. "Who Has Seen the Wind?" in Blishen, Edward. *Oxford Book of Poetry for Children*. Oxford, 1984.

Ryder, Joanne. *Under Your Feet*. Illus. by Dennis Nolan. Four Winds/Macmillan, 1990.

Silverstein, Shel. "How Many, How Much" and "Whatif" in *A Light in the Attic*. Harper, 1981.

Singer, Marilyn. "March Bear" and "Canada Goose" in *Turtle in July*. Illus. by Jerry Pinkney. Macmillan, 1989.

Weil, Zaro. "Questions and Answers" in *Mud, Moon, and Me*. Illus. by Jo Burroughs. Houghton, 1992.

Yolen, Jane. "Silly Questions" in *Best Witches*. Illus. by Elise Primavera. Putnam, 1989.

## Lists/Litanies

Some poems are lists. At times a poet tries to define or explain a difficult subject with a list. Lines from Carl Sandburg's list of qualities of poems from "Tentative (First Model) Definitions of Poetry" appear as the section headings in *Rainbows Are Made*. Sandburg also listed the qualities of arithmetic in his poem "Arithmetic." Mary Ann Hoberman lists things that are "houses" in *A House Is a House for Me* and items that are "cozy" in *The Cozy Book*.

Florence Grossman, in *Getting from Here to There*, suggests that children may want to try to draft beautiful lists of more abstract items, such as "coldnesses" or "things I leave behind" (Grossman, 1982).

Sometimes lists have a particular number of items. Eve Merriam creates "throws" of threes: short lists of three items that represent a concept or idea to her, such as "cures for melancholy" or "locked doors." Similarly, X.J. Kennedy's "Ten Little Likenesses" contains ten brief lists of items with common elements. Patricia Hubbell lists "Ten valentines for a horse" in *A Green Grass Gallop*. In "One, Two, Three, Four, M-O-T-H-E-R" Felice Holman lists four things a child does not like about her mother and four things that she likes.

Even the familiar lists of rules and shopping lists appear in poems. In Jack Prelutsky's "My Mother Says I'm Sickening," his mother provides a list of rules for mannerly eating, and Karla Kuskin provides her list of manners in "Rules." A light hearted list of rules is J. Patrick Lewis' "Rules for the Elephant Parade." Jane Yolen makes a bizarre shopping list in "At the Witch's Drugstore."

The litany is a particular form of list poem in which each line of the poem begins with the same word. Students who have been asked to list things they are thankful for will enjoy Jack Prelutsky's litany, "I'm Thankful." Christopher Smart's "For I Will Consider My Cat Jeoffry" is a litany; each line begins, "For he..." and describes a particular characteristic of his cat. List poems that take the form of litanies are indicated here in parentheses.

Brown, Margaret Wise. *Goodnight Moon*. Harper, 1947. (litany)

———. *The Important Book*. Harper, 1947. (litany)

Ciardi, John. "A Short Checklist of Things to Think about before Being Born" in *You Read to Me, I'll Read to You*. Illus. by Edward Gorey. Lippincott/Harper, 1961.

Edens, Cooper. *If You're Afraid of the Dark, Remember the Night Rainbow*. Green Tiger, 1981. (litany)

Hayes, Sarah. *This Is the Bear and the Scary Night*. Illus. by Helen Craig. Harper, 1986. (litany)

Hoberman, Mary Ann. *The Cozy Book*. Illus. by Tony Chen. Viking, 1982.

————. *A House Is a House for Me*. Illus. by Betty Fraser. Viking, 1978.

Holman, Felice. "One, Two, Three, Four, M-O-T-H-E-R" in Livingston, Myra Cohn. *Poems for Mothers*. Holiday, 1988.

Hubbell, Patricia. "Ten Valentines for a Horse" in *A Green Grass Gallop*. Illus. by Ronald Himler. Atheneum/Macmillan, 1990.

Kennedy, X.J. "Collecting Things" and "Ten Little Likenesses" in *The Kite That Braved Old Orchard Beach*. M.K. McElderry/Macmillan, 1991.

Kuskin, Karla. "Rules" in *Dogs and Dragons, Trees and Dreams*. Harper, 1980.

Lewis, J. Patrick. "Rules for the Elephant Parade" and "A Tomcat Is" in *A Hippopotamustn't*. Illus. by Victoria Chess. Dial, 1990.

Merriam, Eve. "Giving Thanks" and "A Throw of Threes" in *Fresh Paint*. Illus. by David Frampton. Harper, Macmillan, 1986.

————. "Beware, Or Be Yourself," "Miss Hepzibah," and "Ways of Winding a Watch" in *A Sky Full of Poems*. Illus. by Walter Gaffney-Kessell. Dell, 1986.

Prelutsky, Jack. "I'm Thankful" in *The New Kid on the Block*. Illus. by James Stevenson. Greenwillow, 1984.

Sandburg, Carl. "Arithmetic" and "Tentative (First Model) Definitions of Poetry" in Hopkins, Lee Bennett. *Rainbows Are Made*. Harcourt, 1982.

Smart, Christopher. "For I Will Consider My Cat Jeoffry" in Blishen, Edward. *Oxford Book of Poetry for Children*. Bedrick, 1984.

Stevens, Wallace. "Thirteen Ways to Look at a Blackbird" in Elledge, Scott. *Wider Than the Sky*. Harper, 1990.

Yolen, Jane. "At the Witch's Drugstore" in *Best Witches*. Illus. by Elise Primavera. Putnam, 1989.

# POEMS IN VARIOUS FORMS

Recognized forms of poetry such as couplets and haiku as well as "short" poems and poems that use prose forms are included here.

## Couplet

Florian, Douglas. *A Summer Day*. Greenwillow, 1988.

Grossman, Virginia. *Ten Little Rabbits*. Illus. by Sylvia Long. Chronicle, 1991.

McCord, David. "Write Me a Verse: Couplet" in *One at a Time*. Little, 1986.

McMillan, Bruce. *One Sun: A Book of Terse Verse*. Holiday, 1990.

————. *Play Day: A Book of Terse Verse*. Holiday, 1991.

Merriam, Eve. "Couplet Countdown" in *A Sky Full of Poems*. Illus. by Walter Gaffney-Kessell. Dell, 1986.

## Quatrain

McCord, David. "Write Me a Verse: Quatrain" in *One at a Time*. Little, 1986.

Merriam, Eve. "Quatrain" in *A Sky Full of Poems*. Illus. by Walter Gaffney-Kessell. Dell, 1986.

# Cinquain

McCord, David. "The Cinquain" in *One at a Time*. Little, 1986.
Merriam, Eve. "On Being Introduced to You" in *The Singing Green*. Illus. by Kathleen Collins Howell. Morrow, 1992.

# Haiku

Cassedy, Sylvia, and Kunihiro Suetake, sels. *Red Dragonfly on My Shoulder*. Illus. by Molly Bang. Harper, 1992.
Higginson, William, sel. *Wind in the Long Grass*. Illus. by Sandra Speidel. Simon, 1991.
Lewis, Richard, sel. *In a Spring Garden*. Illus. by Ezra Jack Keats. Dial, 1965.
McCord, David. "Haiku" in *One at a Time*. Little, 1986.
Merriam, Eve. "Frame for a Picture" in *Fresh Paint*. Illus. by David Frampton. Macmillan, 1986.
Robertson, Joanne. *Sea Witches*. Illus. by Laszlo Gal. Dial, 1991.

# Limerick

Ciardi, John. *The Hopeful Trout and Other Limericks*. Illus. by Susan Meddaugh. Houghton, 1989.
Lear, Edward. *Of Pelicans and Pussycats*. Illus. by Jill Newton. Dial, 1990.
Livingston, Myra Cohn. *Lots of Limericks*. Illus. by Rebecca Perry. M.K. McElderry/ Macmillan, 1991.
Lobel, Arnold. *The Book of Pigericks*. Harper, 1983.
McCord, David. "Write Me a Verse: Limerick" in *One at a Time*. Little, 1986.
Merriam, Eve. "Leaning on a Limerick" in *A Sky Full of Poems*. Illus. by Walter Gaffney-Kessell. Dell, 1986.

# Short Poems

See also "The Couplet" and "Limerick."

Harrison, Michael, sel. *Splinters*. Illus. by Sue Heap. Oxford, 1988.
Janeczko, Paul B., sel. *Pocket Poems*. Bradbury/Macmillan, 1985.
McCord, David. *All Small*. Illus. by Madelaine Gill Linden. Little, 1986.
Moore, Lilian. "Lost and Found" in *Something New Begins*. Illus. by Mary Jane Dunton. Atheneum/Macmillan, 1982.
Worth, Valerie. *All the Small Poems*. Illus. by Natalie Babbitt. Farrar, 1987.

# Letters, Notes, and Diary Entries

Fleishman, Paul. "Chrysalis Diary" in *Joyful Noise*. Illus. by Eric Beddows. Harper, 1988.
"Letter from a Schoolboy in the Country to his Mother in Town" in Harvey, Anne. *Shades of Green*. Greenwillow, 1992.

Livingston, Myra Cohn. "Letter" in *There Was a Place*. M.K. MacElderry/Macmillan, 1988.

Moore, Lilian. "Letter to a Friend" in *Something New Begins*. Illus. by Mary Jane Dunton. Atheneum/Macmillan, 1982.

Schuyler, James. "I Think" in Harvey, Anne. *Shades of Green*. Greenwillow, 1992.

Viorst, Judith, "Thank-You Note" in *If I Were in Charge of the World and Other Worries*. Illus. by Lynn Cherry. Atheneum/Macmillan, 1981.

Yolen, Jane. "Letter from a Witch Named Flo" in *Best Witches*. Illus. by Elise Primavera. Putnam, 1989.

## Other Poems/Forms

Adoff, Arnold. *Eats*. Illus. by Susan Russo. Lothrop, 1979. (poems in the form of recipes)

De Gasztold, Carmen Bernos. *The Creatures Choir*. French and European, n.d.

———. *Prayers from the Ark*. French and European, n.d.

———. *Prayers from the Ark: Selected Poems*. Illus. by Barry Moser, New York: Viking, 1992. (poems in the form of prayers)

Greenfield, Eloise. "My Daddy" and "Watching the World Go By" in *Nathaniel Talking*. Illus. by Jan Spivey Gilchrist. Black Butterfly/ Writers and Readers, 1988. (twelve bar blues poems)

## POEMS ABOUT POETRY AND WRITING

Poets often write poems about poetry, its forms, or why they write it. Some poets include tips for writers of poetry. Karla Kuskin, for example, suggests ways to be more creative in poems in "Write about a Radish." Students might compare Zaro Weil's ideas for writing in her poem, "How to Get an Idea," with Eve Merriam's "Reply to the Question: 'How Can You Become a Poet?'" as they struggle with their own ideas for poems. Some poems show feelings and thoughts about the act of writing. In "A New Pencil," Eve Merriam talks about what writing can do for a world that "needs stretching or holding together," while in "Notice to Myself" she shows how hard it can be to do that. Barbara Juster Esbensen's "Homework" is a quiet call from "the blank white paper" to the writer about to begin work, and her pencil, like Merriam's, holds words and thoughts.

These poems enrich the language arts program by showing children how and why poets use language and its conventions. Students might post some of these poems for reflection and inspiration. Bobbye S. Goldstein has selected some of her favorite poems on poetry for *Inner Chimes: Poems on Poetry*. Students and teachers may want to follow her lead and create their own collections of poems about poetry.

Clarke, John Henrik. "The Poet Speaks" in Slier, Deborah. *Make a Joyful Sound*. Checkerboard, 1991.

Cullen, Countee. "For a Poet" in Larrick, Nancy. *Bring Me All of Your Dreams*. M. Evans, 1988.

Esbensen, Barbara Juster. "Homework" and "Pencils" in *Who Shrank My Grandmother's House?* Illus. by Eric Beddows. Harper, 1992.

Frost, Robert. "For Allen: Who Wanted to See How I Wrote a Poem" in Hopkins, Lee Bennett. *Side by Side: Poems to Read Together*. Simon, 1988.

Giovanni, Nikki. "Kidnap Poem" in Elledge, Scott. *Wider Than the Sky*. Harper, 1990.

Goldstein, Bobbye S. *Inner Chimes: Poems on Poetry*. Illus. by Jane Breskin Zalben. Wordsong/Boyds Mills, 1992.

Greenfield, Eloise. "Things" in *Honey, I Love*. Illus. by Leo and Diane Dillon. Crowell/Harper, 1978.

Harris, William J. "An Historic Moment" in Kennedy, X.J. *Knock at a Star*. Little, 1985.

Jordan, Norman. "August 8" in Slier, Deborah. *Make a Joyful Sound*. Checkerboard, 1991.

Kennedy, X. J. "Poet" in *The Kite That Braved Old Orchard Beach*. M.K. McElderry/Macmillan, 1991.

Kuskin, Karla. "Take a Word Like Cat," "Thoughts That Were Put into Words," and "Write about a Radish" in *Dogs and Dragons, Trees and Dreams*. Harper, 1980.

———. "Take a Word Like Cat," "Where Do You Get the Idea for a Poem?" and "Write about a Radish" in *Near the Window Tree*. Harper, 1975.

Little, Jean. "About Notebooks," "About Poems, Sort Of," "After English Class," and "Writers" in *Hey World, Here I Am!* Illus. by Sue Truesdell. Harper, 1989.

Merriam, Eve. "Frame for a Picture," "A New Pencil," and "Notice to Myself" in *Fresh Paint*. Illus. by David Frampton. Macmillan, 1986.

———. "Prose and Poetry," "Reply to the Question: 'How Can You Become a Poet?'" "Ways of Composing," and "Where Is a Poem?" in *The Singing Green*. Illus. by Kathleen Collins Howell. Morrow, 1992.

———. "How to Eat a Poem," "'I' Says the Poem," "Leaning on a Limerick," "Some Uses for Poetry," and "Three Birds Flying" in *A Sky Full of Poems*. Illus. by Walter Gaffney-Kessell. Dell, 1986.

Nye, Naomi Shihab. "Valentine for Ernest Mann" in Janeczko, Paul. *The Place My Words Are Looking For*. Bradbury/Macmillan, 1990.

Nye, Naomi Shihab, sel. "Words and Silences" section in *This Same Sky*. Four Winds/Macmillan, 1992.

Sandburg, Carl. "Paper I," "Paper II," "Sketch of a Poet," and "From... Pencils" in Hopkins, Lee Bennett. *Rainbows Are Made*. Harcourt, 1982.

Weil, Zaro. "How to Get an Idea" in *Mud, Moon and Me*. Illus. by Jo Burroughs. Houghton, 1992.

# REFERENCES

Behn, H. (1968). *Chrysalis: Concerning Children and Poetry*. New York: Harcourt.

Carey, M. A. (1989). *Poetry, Starting from Scratch: How to Teach and Write Poetry*. Lincoln, NE: Foundation Books.

Chukovsky, K. (1968). *From Two to Five*. Trans. and ed. by Miriam Morton. Berkeley: University of California, p. xv.

Denham, G. (1988). *When You've Made It Your Own: Teaching Poetry to Young People*. Portsmouth, NH: Heinemann.

Esbensen, B.J. (1975). *A Celebration of Bees: Helping Children Write Poetry.* Minneapolis, MN: Winston.

Gensler, K., and N. Nyhart. (1978). *The Poetry Connection: An Anthology of Contemporary Poems with Ideas to Stimulate Children's Writing.* New York: Teachers and Writers.

Grossman, F. (1982)."Lists," "Signs," and "Images." *Getting from Here to There: Writing and Reading Poetry.* Montclair, NJ: Boynton/Cook.

Heard, G. (1989). *For the Good of Earth and Sun: Teaching Poetry.* Portsmouth, NH: Heinemann.

Hopkins, L.B. (1987). *Pass the Poetry, Please: Using Poetry in Pre-kindergarten-six Classrooms.* 2d ed. New York: Harper.

Hull, Robert. (1988). *Behind the Poem: A Teacher's View of Children Writing.* London: Routledge.

Johnson, D. M. (1990). *Word Weaving: A Creative Approach to Teaching and Writing Poetry.* Urbana, IL: National Council of Teachers of English.

Kennedy, X.J. and D. Kennedy. (1982). *Knock at a Star: A Child's Introduction to Poetry.* Boston: Little.

Lewis, C. (1979). *A Big Bite of the World: Children's Creative Writing.* Englewood Cliffs, NJ: Prentice-Hall.

Lewis, R. (1992). *When Thought is Young: Reflections on Teaching and the Poetry of the Child.* Minneapolis, MN: New Rivers Press.

Livingston, M.C. (1984). *The Child as Poet: Myth or Reality?* Boston: Horn Book.

———. (1990). *Climb into the Bell Tower: Essays on Poetry.* New York: Harper.

———. (1991). *Poem Making: Ways to Begin Writing Poetry.* New York: Harper.

Lopate, P. (1975). *Being with Children.* Garden City, NY: Doubleday.

McClure, A. A., with P. Harrison and S. Reed. (1990). *Sunrises and Songs: Reading and Writing Poetry in the Elementary Classroom.* Portsmouth, NH: Heinemann.

Padgett, R. (1987). *Teachers and Writers Handbook of Poetic Forms.* New York: Teachers and Writers.

# Chapter 6:
# Poetry, Picture Books, and Novels
# in the Literature Program

Poetry is an integral part of the literature program. Poems matched with other poems allow us to see several responses to the same experience. Poems can be shared with picture books and novels about similar topics or themes. Picture books themselves are sometimes poems; they use conventions of poetry such as alliteration and rhyme as well as the spare poetic language that we enjoy in poems themselves.

## POEMS AS TEXTS FOR PICTURE BOOKS

The illustrated picture book in which a poem, often a classic poem, serves as the illustrator's text is becoming increasingly popular, but it is also somewhat controversial. Modern critics say that each person's response to a work of literature is unique, based on development and personal experiences. Nowhere in literature is the range of response as great as it can be to poetry. The spare arrangement of words, the careful word choice, and the spaces between thoughts give the reader room to insert personal feelings and ideas. For this reason, some critics have expressed concern about the growing number of poems appearing in picture book format. When a poem stands alone, without illustration, the reader or listener is free to respond and imagine the meanings and feelings of the words. When the text is accompanied by pictures it is all too easy to see the illustrations as the "right" interpretation of the text of the poem. Susan Jeffers, for example, has been criticized for the sprightly Santa Claus–like figure who visits the woods and leaves food for the animals in her illustrated version of *Stopping by Woods on a Snowy Evening*.

Whenever picture book versions of poems are used with children, the most important thing that teachers and librarians can do is to help students understand that the illustrators are drawing their version of what the poem is about. Their "picture" of the poem is only one response to that poem; ours may be very different.

A group of children who were learning about snow had enjoyed several picture books about snow pleasures including Ruth Yaffe Radin's *Winter Place* and Jane Yolen's *Owl Moon*. Then, their teacher told them about a favorite poem of hers. She told them it was called "Stopping by Woods on a Snowy Evening" by Robert Frost and that she would read it from a collection of his poems. After she announced the poet and title, one child laughed and said that Robert Frost was a good name for someone who wrote about the snow. As the teacher read the poem, the children listened carefully. When she was done, the children asked that she read it again. Then they responded. Some had felt like this when they had to come home after a long day of playing in the mountains; one made a comment about sneaking through fences onto private property; and another wished he had a horse to ride in the snow. When one child commented on the repeated last line of the poem, another said that it was similar to how parents have to keep yelling that it's time to go home except that it was Robert Frost's own head that was yelling at him.

After the children had talked about the poem, the teacher shared Susan Jeffers' illustrated version. She told them that this was what the artist had felt when she read it, and the children thought that she had nice ideas too. These children, authors, poets, and illustrators all had different ideas about snow, and all of them added to the students' understanding of it.

Teachers and librarians can introduce classic poems first through oral readings or on large pieces of chart paper so that they can be read together and wordings relished before they share the illustrated versions with children. Then, as this teacher did, they can share the illustrator's response to the poem. In some cases, particularly the poems by Edward Lear, several illustrated versions of the same poem are available and students might select the one they feel best represents their own feelings about the poem. If none of these versions represents their own ideas, students could create their own illustrated version of the poem. Many editions of Clement Moore's *Night before Christmas* are available, as it seems to be a favorite story for illustrators to use. Because of their numbers and the seasonal nature of this work, they have not been added to this list.

Behn, Harry. *Trees*. Illus. by James Endicott. Holt, 1992.

Belloc, Hilaire. *Jim, Who Ran Away from His Nurse and Was Eaten by a Lion*. Illus. by Victoria Chess. Little, 1987.

———. *Matilda, Who Told Lies and Was Burned to Death*. Illus. by Posy Simmonds. Knopf, 1992.

Browning, Robert. *The Pied Piper of Hamelin*. Retold by Stephen and Sarah Corrin. Illus. by Erroll Le Cain. Harcourt, 1989.

Carroll, Lewis. *Jabberwocky*. Illus. by Disney Archives. Disney, 1992.

―――. *Jabberwocky*. Illus. by Graeme Base. Abrams, 1989.

―――. *Jabberwocky*. Illus. by Kate Buckley. Albert Whitman, 1985.

―――. *The Walrus and the Carpenter*. Illus. by Jane Zalben. Holt, 1986.

Coleridge, Samuel Taylor. *The Rime of the Ancient Mariner*. Illus. by Ed Young. New York: Atheneum, 1992.

Cummings, E.E. *Hist Whist*. Illus. by Deborah Kogan Ray. Crown, 1989.

―――. *In Just Spring*. Illus. by Heidi Goennel. Little, 1988.

―――. *Little Tree*. Illus. by Deborah Kogan Ray. Crown, 1988.

De Paola, Tomie. *The Comic Adventures of Old Mother Hubbard and Her Dog*. Harcourt, 1981.

Eliot, T.S. *Growltiger's Last Stand and Other Poems*. Illus. by Errol Le Cain. Farrar, 1987.

―――. *Mister Mitoffeles with Mungojerrie and Rumpleteazer*. Illus. by Errol Le Cain. Harcourt, 1991.

Emberley, Barbara. *Drummer Hoff*. Illus. by Ed Emberley. Simon, 1985.

Farjeon, Eleanor. *Cats Sleep Anywhere*. Illus. by Mary Price Jenkins. Lippincott/ Harper, 1990.

Field, Eugene. *The Gingham Dog and the Calico Cat*. Illus. by Janet Street. Philomel/ Putnam, 1990.

―――. *Wynken, Blynken, and Nod*. Illus. by Sheilah Beckett. Putnam, 1986.

―――. *Wynken, Blynken, and Nod*. Illus. by Susan Jeffers. Dutton, 1982.

Field, Rachel. *General Store*. Illus. by Nancy Winslow Parker. Greenwillow, 1988.

―――. *General Store*. Illus. by Giles Laroche. Little, 1988.

―――. *Prayer for a Child*. Illus. by Elizabeth Orton Jones. Macmillan, 1984.

Frost, Robert. *Birches*. Illus. by Ed Young. Holt, 1988.

―――. *Christmas Trees*. Illus. by Ted Rand. Holt, 1990.

―――. *Stopping by Woods on a Snowy Evening*. Illus. by Susan Jeffers. Dutton, 1978.

*The Keys to My Kingdom: A Poem in Three Languages*. Illus. by Lydia Dabcovich. New York. Lothrop, 1992.

Kipling, Rudyard. *Gunga Din*. Illus. by Robert Andrew Parker. Harcourt, 1987.

Lear, Edward. *A Was Once an Apple Pie*. Illus. by Julie Lacome. Candlewick, 1992.

―――. *An Edward Lear Alphabet*. Illus. by Carol Newsom. Lothrop, 1983.

―――. *Hilary Knight's the Owl and the Pussycat*. Illus. by Hilary Knight. Macmillan, 1989.

―――. *The Jumblies*. Illus. by Ted Rand. Putnam, 1989.

―――. *The Owl and the Pussycat*. Illus. by Jan Brett. Putnam, 1991.

―――. *The Owl and the Pussycat*. Illus. by Louise Voce. Lothrop, 1991.

―――. *The Owl and the Pussycat*. Illus. by Clare Littlejohn. Harper, 1987.

―――. *The Owl and the Pussycat*. Illus. by Lorinda Bryan Cauley. Putnam, 1986.

―――. *The Owl and the Pussycat*. Illus. by Janet Stevens. Holiday, 1983.

―――. *The Quangle Wangle's Hat*. Illus. by Janet Stevens. Harcourt, 1988.

―――. *The Scroobious Pip*. Illus. by Nancy E. Burkert. Harper, 1987.

Longfellow, Henry Wadsworth. *Hiawatha*. Illus. by Keith Mosely. Philomel/Putnam, 1988.

―――. *Hiawatha*. Illus. by Susan Jeffers. Dial, 1983.

―――. *Hiawatha's Childhood*. Illus. by Errol Le Cain. Farrar, 1984.

―――. *Paul Revere's Ride*. Illus. by Ted Rand. Dutton, 1990.

―――. *Paul Revere's Ride*. Illus. by Nancy Winslow Parker. Greenwillow, 1985.

Millay, Edna St. Vincent. *The Ballad of the Harp Weaver*. Illus. by Beth Peck. Philomel/Putnam, 1991.

Noyes, Alfred. *The Highwayman*. Illus. by Neil Waldman. Harcourt, 1990.

————. *The Highwayman*. Illus. by Charles Keeping. Oxford, 1987.

————. *The Highwayman*. Illus. by Charles Mikolaycak. Lothrop, 1983.

Riley, James Whitcomb. *The Gobble-Uns'll Git You Ef You Don't Watch Out!* Illus. by Joel Schick. Lippincott/Harper, 1975.

————. *Little Orphan Annie*. Illus. by Diane Stanley. Putnam, 1983.

————. *When the Frost Is on the Punkin.'* Illus. by Glenna Lang. Godine, 1992.

Rossetti, Christina. *Color*. Illus. by Mary Teichman. Harper, 1992.

Sendak, Maurice. *Hector Protector and As I Went over the Water*. Harper, 1990.

Service, Robert W. *The Cremation of Sam McGee*. Illus. by Ted Harrison. Greenwillow, 1987.

————. *The Shooting of Dan McGrew*. Illus. by Ted Harrison. Godine, 1988.

Southey, Robert. *The Cataract of Lodore*. Illus. by Mordicai Gerstein. Dial, 1991.

Stevenson, Robert Louis. *Block City*. Illus. by Ashley Wolff. Dutton, 1988.

————. *My Shadow*. Illus. by Glenna Lang. Godine, 1989.

————. *My Shadow*. Illus. by Ted Rand. Putnam, 1990.

Tagore, Rabindranath. *Paper Boats*. Illus. by Grayce Bochak. Caroline House/Boyds Mills, 1992.

Thayer, Ernest L. *Casey at the Bat*. Illus. by Barry Moser. Godine, 1988.

————. *Casey at the Bat: A Ballad of the Republic, Sung in the Year 1888*. Illus. by Wallace Tripp. Coward, 1980.

*This Is the Key to the Kingdom*. Illus. by Diane Worfolk Allison. Little, 1992.

Tolkien, J.R.R. *Bilbo's Last Song (at the Grey Havens)*. Illus. by Pauline Baynes. Houghton, 1990.

Whitman, Walt. *I Hear America Singing*. Illus. by Robert Sabuda. Philomel/Putnam, 1991.

Whittier, John Greenleaf. *Barbara Frietchie*. Illus. by Nancy Winslow Parker. Greenwillow, 1992.

## PICTURE BOOKS WITH RHYMED TEXTS

Rhymed text plays an important role in the reading education of young children as it helps children remember stories and recognize words and word forms. Many books for young children use rhymed text, but not all of them are good poetry. They may neglect the rhythms and sense that are critical to poetry in creating rhyme. They may also get stuck using the most familiar rhyme schemes and meter so that many of these rhymed texts sound alike. Even adults who loved Dr. Seuss as children will find that some of his rhymed stories become exhaustingly repetitious when they are shared again.

Rhymed texts should read well aloud, their rhythms should flow, and they should make sense. Try to share books with a variety of rhythms and rhyme schemes. The list below is selective. I have included some of my favorite stories in rhyme. Some of these books are for young children, some for older students. A list of alphabet books with rhymed texts appears in Chapter 5. A list of counting books with rhymed texts appears in Chapter 3.

Adoff, Arnold. *Black Is Brown Is Tan*. Illus. by Emily Arnold McCully. Harper, 1973.
Ahlberg, Janet, and Allen Ahlberg. *Each Peach Pear Plum*. Viking, 1979.
Alborough, Jez. *Where's My Teddy?* Candlewick, 1992.
Blos, Joan W. *A Seed, a Flower, a Minute, an Hour*. Illus. by Hans Poppel. Simon, 1992.
Burkert, Nancy. *Valentine and Orson*. Farrar, 1989.
Clifton, Lucille. *Everett Anderson's Goodbye*. Holt, 1983.
Coltman, Paul. *Tog the Ribber, or Granny's Tale*. Illus. by Gillian McClure. Farrar, 1985.
De Regniers, Beatrice Schenk. *So Many Cats!* Illus. by Ellen Weiss. Clarion/Ticknor and Fields, 1985.
Ehlert, Lois. *Feathers for Lunch*. Harcourt, 1990.
Fleischman, Paul. *Rondo in C*. Illus. by Janet Wentworth. Harper, 1988.
Geringer, Laura. *Look Out, Look Out, It's Coming!* Illus. by Sue Truesdell. Harper, 1992.
Grossman, Bill. *Tommy at the Grocery Store*. Illus. by Victoria Chess. Harper, 1989.
Hayes, Sarah. *The Grumpalump*. Illus. by Barbara Firth. Clarion/Houghton, 1990.
Hennessy, B. G. *Jake Baked the Cake*. Illus. by Mary Morgan. Viking, 1990.
Hoberman, Mary Ann. *A House Is a House for Me*. Illus. by Betty Fraser. Viking, 1978.
Hoopes, Lyn Littlefield. *Wing a Ding*. Illus. by Stephen Gammell. Little, 1990.
Komaiko, Leah. *Annie Bananie*. Illus. by Laura Cornell. Harper, 1987.
Lindbergh, Reeve. *The Day the Goose Got Loose*. Illus. by Steven Kellogg. Dial, 1990.
Mahy, Margaret. *17 Kings and 42 Elephants*. Illus. by Patricia MacCarthy. Dial, 1987.
Martin, Bill, Jr. *Brown Bear, Brown Bear, What Do You See?* Illus. by Eric Carle. Holt, 1967.
Merriam, Eve. *Train Leaves the Station*. Illus. by Dale Gottlieb. Holt, 1992.
Seuss, Dr. *Horton Hatches the Egg*. Random, 1940.
Shaw, Nancy. *Sheep in a Jeep*. Illus. by Margot Apple. Houghton, 1986.
Siebert, Diane. *Train Song*. Illus. by Mike Wimmer. Harper, 1990.
Temple, Charles. *On the Riverbank*. Illus. by Melanie Hall. Houghton, 1992.
Van Laan, Nancy. *A Mouse in My House*. Illus. by Marjorie Priceman. Knopf, 1990.
Weiss, Nicki. *An Egg Is an Egg*. Putnam, 1990.
Willard, Nancy. *The Voyage of the Ludgate Hill: Travels with Robert Louis Stevenson*. Illus. by Alice and Martin Provensen. Harcourt, 1987.
Zolotow, Charlotte. *Some Things Go Together*. Illus. by Karen Gundersheimer. Crowell/Harper, 1983.

## PICTURE BOOKS WITH FREE VERSE TEXTS

Authors who write the text for picture books must write as poets, using a few carefully selected words to evoke the images an artist then creates for the reader. Picture book authors use the conventions of poetry: rich imagery, sounds of language, and subtle rhythms. Because the book may be laid out with phrases or single lines of text on a page, some picture books take on the qualities of an illustrated poem. Cynthia Rylant's *Night in the Country*, for example, reads like a poem. In some cases the text in the book is set up on the page to look like a poem, as in Byrd Baylor's books. Sometimes books have unusual conventions. Arnold Adoff uses a bright leaf to separate lines of text in *Flamboyan*. If the lines were arranged with a leaf at the beginning of each, the text would resemble a poem. Examples of prose-poem and free verse picture books are included here. Byrd Baylor's books are listed with the web later in this chapter.

Ackerman, Karen. *I Know a Place.* Illus. by Deborah Kogan Ray. Houghton, 1992.

Adoff, Arnold. *Flamboyan.* Illus. by Karen Barbour. Harcourt, 1988.

Arnosky, Jim. *Deer at the Brook.* Lothrop, 1986.

Calhoun, Mary. *While I Sleep.* Illus. by Ed Young. Morrow, 1992.

Carlstrom, Nancy White. *Goodbye Geese.* Illus. by Ed Young. Philomel/Putnam, 1991.

———. *Northern Lullaby.* Illus. by Leo and Diane Dillon. Philomel/Punam, 1992.

Chall, Marsha Wilson. *Up North at the Cabin.* Illus. by Steve Johnson. Lothrop, 1992.

Frasier, Debra. *On the Day You Were Born.* Harcourt, 1991.

Goffstein, M.B. *An Artist.* Harper, 1980.

———. *My Noah's Ark.* Harper, 1978.

———. *The School of Names.* Harper, 1986.

———. *A Writer.* Harper, 1984.

Greenfield, Eloise. *Africa Dream.* Illus. by Carole Byard. Harper, 1977.

———. *Daydreamers.* Illus. by Tom Feelings. Dial, 1981.

Hirschi, Ron. *What Is a Bird?* Illus. by Galen Burrell. Walker, 1987.

Horton, Barbara S. *What Comes in Spring?* Illus. by Ed Young. Knopf, 1992.

Johnston, Tony. *Yonder.* Illus. by Lloyd Bloom. Dial, 1988.

Knutson, Kimberly. *Muddigush.* Macmillan, 1992.

Lewis, Richard. *All of You Was Singing.* Illus. by Ed Young. Atheneum/Macmillan, 1991.

———. *In the Night, Still Dark.* Illus. by Ed Young. Atheneum/Macmillan, 1988.

Luenn, Nancy. *Mother Earth.* Illus. by Neil Waldman. Atheneum/ Macmillan, 1992.

Melville, Herman. *Catskill Eagle.* Illus. by Thomas Locker. Philomel/Putnam, 1991.

Radin, Ruth Yaffe. *A Winter Place.* Illus. by Mattie Lou O'Kelley. Joy Street/Little, 1982.

Ryder, Joanne. *Under Your Feet.* Illus. by Dennis Nolan. Four Winds/Macmillan, 1990.

Rylant, Cynthia. *Night in the Country.* Illus. by Mary Szilagyi. Bradbury/Macmillan, 1986.

———. *This Year's Garden.* Illus. by Mary Szilagyi. Bradbury/Macmillan, 1984.

———. *When I Was Young in the Mountains.* Illus. by Diane Goode. Dutton, 1982.

Shulevitz, Uri. *Dawn.* Farrar, 1974.

———. *Rain Rain Rivers.* Farrar, 1969.

Turner, Ann. *Dakota Dugout.* Illus. by Ronald Himler. Macmillan, 1985.

———. *Heron Street.* Illus, by Lisa Desimini. Harper, 1989.

———. *Rainflowers.* Illus. by Robert J. Blake. Harper, 1992.

Yolen, Jane. *Owl Moon.* Illus. by John Schoenherr. Philomel/Putnam, 1987.

Zolotow, Charlotte. *I Know a Lady.* Illus. by James Stevenson. Greenwillow, 1984.

————. *Say It!* Illus. by James Stevenson. Greenwillow, 1980.
————. *Something Is Going to Happen.* Illus. by Catherine Stock. Harper, 1988.

## POEMS WITH PICTURE BOOKS

Sometimes poems and picture books can be linked. Judith Viorst's *Alexander and the Terrible, Horrible, No Good, Very Bad Day* strikes a universal chord with people who have had "one of those days" and poets agree. In Karla Kuskin's "I Woke Up This Morning" the print grows larger and larger to reflect the narrator's growing anger at a day when nothing seems to be going right. Marchette Chute's poem "The Wrong Start" includes a litany of mishaps, and the narrator decides to go back to start the day over. Jack Prelutsky writes on a similar theme in "I Should Have Stayed in Bed Today." Both Beatrice Schenk de Regniers and Eve Merriam have poems titled "Mean Song." De Regniers' poem includes a beginning note that suggests children read or sing it out loud three times on mornings when they "wake up feeling MEAN!" Merriam's poem seems to hold the kernels for her recent picture book, *Fighting Words*, which also uses words that sound angry.

Sometimes a poem and a picture book share a similar image or idea. Beatrice Schenk de Regniers has a picture book length poem, *So Many Cats!* that describes twelve cats (and maybe more) that come to live with a family. In her book she includes "three/frumpy, fleasy/skinny, sleasy/city cats" and an ugly cat named "Pretty." This picture book can be paired with Eve Merriam's "stray cat" who is a "city cat, not pretty cat," whom she names "Beauty."

Sometimes picture books and poems share a quieter, more thoughtful message. Eloise Greenfield and Tom Feelings' *Daydreamers* is a free verse picture book that describes the growing that children do as they sit quietly and daydream. Gwendolyn Brooks' "Narcissa" describes a child who is "not playing anything at all" but who is daydreaming too. She daydreams of being an ancient queen just as the young girl in Nikki Giovanni's "Poem for Flora" daydreams of being as beautiful as the Queen of Sheba.

Brooks, Gwendolyn. "Narcissa" in *Bronzeville Boys and Girls*. Illus. by Ronni Solbert. Harper, 1967.
Chute, Marchette. "The Wrong Start" in Prelutsky, Jack. *The Random House Book of Poetry for Children*. Random, 1983.
De Regniers, Beatrice Schenk. "Mean Song" in *The Way I Feel...Sometimes*. Illus. by Susan Meddaugh. Clarion/Ticknor and Fields, 1988.
————. *So Many Cats*. Illus. by Ellen Weiss. Clarion/Ticknor and Fields, 1988.
Giovanni, Nikki. "Poem for Flora" in Adoff, Arnold. *My Black Me*. Dutton, 1974.
Greenfield, Eloise. *Daydreamers*. Illus. by Tom Feelings. Dial, 1981.

Kuskin, Karla. "I Woke Up This Morning" in *Dogs and Dragons, Trees and Dreams.* Harper, 1980.

Merriam, Eve. *Fighting Words.* Illus. by David Small. Morrow, 1992.

———. "Mean Song" and "Stray Cat" in *The Singing Green.* Illus. by Kathleen Collins Howell. Morrow, 1992.

Prelutsky, Jack. "I Should Have Stayed in Bed Today" in *Something Big Has Been Here.* Illus. by James Stevenson. Greenwillow, 1990.

Viorst, Judith. *Alexander and the Terrible, Horrible, No Good, Very Bad Day.* Illus. by Ray Cruz. Atheneum/Macmillan, 1972. (fiction)

## PICTURE BOOK UNIT: BYRD BAYLOR

Literature units can develop in many ways. A collection of the books and poems children find on a topic can form the core of a unit. We can also create a unit around the works of a single poet. Byrd Baylor has written several free verse picture books that seem to come from her own life experiences. Several of her books, such as *I'm in Charge of Celebrations,* use a first person narrative. Questions raised by Baylor's books may take students in many directions. They may want to find out about Byrd Baylor's life and why she writes. They may want to try to write in Byrd Baylor's style. While she generally uses the free verse form, one of her books, *One Small Blue Bead,* has rhymed text, and her collection of Pima Indian tales is written in prose. Even within the free verse form each of Baylor's books has a unique style. In *Guess Who My Favorite Person Is*, the text is a series of exchanges about preferences in such things as colors, tastes, and things to dream about, and children may want to write about their own favorites. *Everybody Needs a Rock* is a list of ten "rules" for finding a rock. Students may want to write lists of rules for finding other things, such as a perfect tree to lie under, a perfect catcher's mitt, or a perfect friend. In *I'm in Charge of Celebrations*, Baylor lists special natural events she celebrates, and students may want to create their own calendar or a class calendar of such events.

Students may want to find out more about the Native Americans of the Southwest. Baylor's books include not only the current residents of this region, but references to its ancient cultures and peoples. Other ideas for reading, discussion, and activities are included on the web shown in Figure 6.

Baylor, Byrd. *Amigo.* Illus. by Garth Williams. Macmillan, 1989. (fiction)

———. sel. *And It Is Still That Way: Legends Told by Arizona Indian Children.* Scribner/Macmillan, 1976. (traditional)

———. *Before You Came This Way.* Illus. by Tom Bahti. Dutton, 1969.

———. *The Best Town in the World.* Illus. by Ronald Himler. Scribner/Macmillan, 1982.

———. *Coyote Cry.* Illus. by Symeon Shimin. Lothrop, 1972.

———. *The Desert Is Theirs.* Illus. by Peter Parnell. Scribner/Macmillan, 1975.

## BYRD BAYLOR'S STYLE

Lists: *Everybody Needs a Rock*
*Guess Who My Favorite Person Is*
● Write your own set of rules or list of favorites
Conversation: "It feels like she is talking just to me"
●Tell Byrd Baylor in poetry or prose about yourself and your ideas about her books
Names: Baylor carefully describes and names things
Personification:
● Find examples of descriptions or rocks, plants, and animals. How does she describe them?

## SOLITUDE

*I'm In Charge of Celebrations*
*The Way to Start a Day*
● Is Byrd Baylor lonely? Why or why not?

## ILLUSTRATIONS

Many of Baylor's books are illustrated by Peter Parnell, but she also has books illustrated by Tom Bahti, Ronald Himler, Robert Andrew Parker and with photographs by Marilyn Schweitzer.
Which illustrations do you think best suit Baylor's stories and settings? Why?

## SENSORY EXPERIENCES

*The Other Way to Listen*
● What is the other way to listen? Try it and record what happens.
*Everybody Needs a Rock*
● What senses do you have to use to find the perfect rock?
● Describe how you might use your senses to find the perfect dish of ice cream, the perfect tree, the perfect friend, or anything else you would like to look for.
*Guess Who My Favorite Person Is*
● What's your favorite thing to smell? To touch? Color to see?

## DESERT SOUTH-WEST

*The Desert is Theirs*
*Desert Voices*
*I'm in Charge of Celebrations*
*We Walk in Sandy Places*
● Who are the desert people?
● What do we learn about them in Baylor's books?
● What plants and animals live in the desert of the Southwest?
● What is the desert like?
● How does Byrd Baylor describe it?
● How do the illustrators show it?

# BYRD BAYLOR

## MEMORIES

*The Best Town in the World*
● Describe your "best town in the world"
*I'm in Charge of Celebrations*
● What natural wonders would you like to commemorate so you will remember them?

## WE ARE ALL RELATED

*The Desert is Theirs*
● Baylor says you must treat the land, "The way you treat an old friend" What does she mean?
*Coyote Cry*
*Desert Voices*
*Hawk, I'm Your Brother*
● How are people and animals related?

## REVERENCE FOR OLDNESS

*When Clay Sings*
"Treat it with respect. It is so old."
● Why sould we respect old things?
*Before You Came This Way*
*If You are a Hunter of Fossils*
*One Small Blue Bead*
● How does Baylor help you to picture the ancient past?
● Have you ever found something that was very old, like a fossil, a pottery chip, or arrowhead? How did it make you feel?
*Coyote Cry*
*The Other Way to Listen*
● How does Byrd Baylor describe older people in her books? What roles do they play?

## CELEBRATIONS

*I'm in Charge of Celebrations*
● Keep a class calendar and record celebrations of things that you observe in the classroom, on the playground, and on the way to and from school
*The Best Town in the World*
*The Desert is Theirs*
*The Way to Start a Day*
● What does Byrd Baylor celebrate in these books? Do her other books include celebrations?

## PROFESSIONAL READING

"Byrd Baylor" in Kiefer, Barbara, comp.
*Getting to Know You: Profiles of Children's Authors Featured in Language Arts.* Urbana IL: National Council of Teachers of English, 1991.

**Figure 6. Byrd Baylor Web**

———. *Desert Voices*. Illus. by Peter Parnell. Scribner/Macmillan, 1981.

———. *Everybody Needs a Rock*. Illus. by Peter Parnell. Scribner/Macmillan, 1974.

———. *Guess Who My Favorite Person Is*. Illus. by Robert Andrew Parker. Scribner/ Macmillan, 1977.

———. *Hawk, I'm Your Brother*. Illus. by Peter Parnell. Scribner/Macmillan, 1976.

———. *If You Are a Hunter of Fossils*. Illus. by Peter Parnell. Scribner/Macmillan, 1980.

———. *I'm in Charge of Celebrations*. Illus. by Peter Parnell. Scribner/Macmillan, 1986.

———. *One Small Blue Bead*. Illus. by Symeon Shimin. Macmillan, 1965.

———. *The Way to Start a Day*. Illus. by Peter Parnell. Scribner/Macmillan, 1978.

———. *We Walk in Sandy Places*. Illus. by Marilyn Schweitzer. Scribners, 1976.

———. *When Clay Sings*. Illus. by Tom Bahti. Scribner/Macmillan, 1972.

———. *Your Own Best Secret Place*. Illus. by Peter Parnell. Scribner/Macmillan, 1991.

## USING POETRY WITH NOVELS

Poems can introduce books. They can be shared during or at the end of reading to help summarize or rethink what we have read. Poems can highlight the setting of books, give insight into a character or a theme, and help children understand an aspect of a story that is hard to grasp. Looking for poems to share with other literature is perhaps the most difficult task that the teacher or librarian undertakes. It involves shifting your mindset so that you begin to read poetry with novels in mind and read novels with poems in mind.

The most common strategy when looking for poems to use in the literature program is to find poems on the same topic as the book. This kind of selection works well when the objective is to allow children to see, for example, an animal or an object from several different points of view or to consider what the real animal is like as opposed to a "literary" image of that animal.

In many cases, poems and books about the same subject differ in tone, style, or theme. Finding a poem that fits with a book takes time and thought. Bonnie Robertson, a librarian who was beginning to use poems with books, described this kind of experience as she was looking for poems to be used with Dick King-Smith's humorous fantasy, *The Fox Busters*. She observed that at first she was just pulling out any poems she found on chickens, foxes, or barnyard settings. She discovered that most of the "chicken" poems were light and humorous and showed chickens in a less-than-positive light. The superior breed of "fox buster" chickens were not this kind of chicken at all. They needed to have a chicken hero poem written for them. The closest poem is a short one by John Corben, "In the Eggs," which is a takeoff on the old saying "Don't count your chickens before they're hatched" and suggests that chicks don't count their foxes. She found the traditional poem/song, "A Fox Jumped Up" (also known as "The Fox Went Out on a Chilly Night"), which gives a sense of how foxes operate and is fanciful in the way of the novel. Most poems about foxes did not really capture the sly, unpleasant nature of King-Smith's foxes. Alison Blyler's lyrical *Finding Foxes*, for example, is a too respectful portrait of foxes, more in tune with the theme of Betsy Byars' *Midnight Fox* than with *Fox Busters*. The barnyard settings she found tended to be in short, rhymed verse for younger children and did not effectively capture King-Smith's detailed setting. Robertson (1992) says

> Few poems were found that illustrated the literary qualities I was after for *The Fox Busters*. "Looking for a needle in the haystack" came to mind. Only this time it seemed each needle had a different shape. I didn't know the shapes I was looking for, but would recognize them when I found them....I had to stay open and receptive for a connection. The surface connections can be found rather quickly...I keep finding better and better poems about chickens and foxes and farms and flight.
>
> It's not a failure when you can't put your finger on the "right" poem. You know you have to move on to a deeper level for the "right" poems to connect. I believe in serendipity and that's when I'll find that "right" poem. As Emily Dickinson said in her poem, "'Hope' is the thing with feathers."

Sometimes an educated guess about where to look for poems pays off. Because Joan Blos' *Gathering of Days* is set in rural New Hampshire, Robert Frost's home of many years, you might start by looking through Frost's poems for connections. His poem "Acquainted with the Night" gives insight into the feelings of the runaway slave for whom Catherine leaves the quilt. His poem "Reluctance," which deals with how difficult it is to accept the endings of things, might help us understand Catherine's feelings about her new stepmother and about her friend Cassie's death.

Sometimes we discover poems by accident. While Bonnie Robertson was looking for poems about "finding answers" to use in conjunction with E.L. Konigsburg's *From the Mixed up Files of Mrs. Basil E. Frankweiler*, she happened upon *Talking to the Sun: An Illustrated Anthology of Poems for Young People*. This anthology, compiled by Kenneth Koch and Kate Farrell, features art works displayed in the Metropolitan Museum of Art. These art works and the poems they are linked with might have been enjoyed by Claudia and Jamie (characters in Konigsburg's book) as they resided in the museum.

Blos, Joan. *A Gathering of Days: A New England Girl's Journal*. Scribner/Macmillan, 1979. (fiction)

Blyler, Alison. *Finding Foxes*. Illus. by Robert J. Blake. Philomel/Putnam, 1991. (fiction)

Byars, Betsy. *The Midnight Fox*. Avon, 1975. (fiction)

Corben, John. "In the Eggs" in Harrison, Michael. *Splinters*. Oxford, 1988.

"A Fox Jumped Up" in Clark, Emma C. *I Never Saw a Purple Cow and Other Nonsense Rhymes.* Little, 1990.

Frost, Robert. "Acquainted with the Night" in *You Come Too.* Illus. by Thomas W. Nason. Holt, 1959.

———. "Reluctance" in Bober, Natalie. *A Restless Spirit: The Story of Robert Frost.* Holt, 1991.

King-Smith, Dick. *The Fox-Busters.* Delacorte, 1988. (fiction)

Koch, Kenneth, and Kate Farrell. *Talking to the Sun.* Holt, 1985.

Konigsburg, E.L. *From the Mixed-Up Files of Mrs. Basil E. Frankweiler.* Atheneum/ Macmillan, 1970. (fiction)

## Poems about Setting

When children read or listen to books, the time and place of stories often take a back seat to the plot and characters. A poem that describes the landscape or time period of a story with clear imagery can heighten students' awareness of setting. In *The Desert Is Theirs* and Byrd Baylor's other picture books, for example, she paints an uplifting picture of the southwestern desert, filled with life and beauty. While she enjoys the freedom of the desert, Diane Siebert paints a grimmer picture than Baylor in her picture book *Mojave* with descriptions of the arid land, ghost towns, and sandstorms. The description of the setting often helps to set the tone of a novel, as it does in Baylor's and Siebert's poems. "The Wolf Cry" by Lew Sarett gives a sense of the cold isolation of the Arctic tundra in *Julie of the Wolves.* William H. Moore's "Some Winter Pieces" describes a cold, shadowy setting that could be Susan's Cooper's winter landscape in *The Dark Is Rising.*

Sometimes a poem captures just a "corner" of a place. In Laurence Yep's *Dragonwings*, Moon Shadow is fascinated by the stained glass window in his landlady's house and the way the sunlight streams through the pieces of the western dragon. Myra Cohn Livingston's poem "Fletcher Avenue," in which the child notices the patterns of colored sunlight through the glass in her grandmother's front hall, creates a similar image.

Collections of poems set in homes, neighborhoods, cities, and historical and geographical settings are listed in Chapter 4.

Baylor, Byrd. *The Desert Is Theirs.* Illus. by Peter Parnell. Macmillan, 1975.

Cooper, Susan. *The Dark Is Rising.* M.K. McElderry/Macmillan, 1973. (fiction)

Livingston, Myra Cohn. "Fletcher Avenue" in *Worlds I Know and Other Poems.* Illus. by Tim Arnold. M.K. McElderry/Macmillan, 1985.

Moore, William H. "Some Winter Pieces" in Booth, David. *'Til All the Stars Have Fallen.* Viking, 1990.

Sarett, Lew. "Wolf Cry" in Prelutsky, Jack. *The Random House Book of Poetry for Children.* Random, 1983.

Siebert, Diane. *Mojave.* Illus. by Wendell Minor. Crowell/Harper, 1988.

Yep, Lawrence. *Dragonwings.* Harper, 1975. (fiction)

## Poems about Characters

Good poems to use with characters are those that capture the essence of the character. Certain poems about the elderly, for example, describe them as upbeat, while others focus on illness, aging, and sorrow. Charlotte Zolotow's picture book, *I Know a Lady*, describes a friendly, active older woman and Rose Henderson's "Growing Old" describes an older woman's similarly pleasant existence. In Barbara Cooney's *Miss Rumphius,* the elderly woman has led a full and interesting life and has found something meaningful to do in her later years. Myra Cohn Livingston's "Nanny" has the same sense of adventurousness as Miss Rumphius. Both have ridden on a camel, and both are much admired by a child.

A poem can help readers understand a character's feelings about people and events in a story. Bruce Brooks' *Everywhere* is a short novel about an unhappy boy whose beloved grandfather is ill and who is helped by another boy he hardly knows. John Haislip's poem "At Grandmother's," about a child playing by himself while his grandmother is "dying in quiet that whole season," provides an image of another child in very similar circumstances. In "The Secret," Myra Cohn Livingston describes the feelings of a child who has a family member in prison. This poem can help children better understand how Queenie feels in Robert Burch's *Queenie Peavy.*

The two Sarahs in Patricia MacLachlan's *Sarah Plain and Tall* and Ann Turner's *Third Girl from the Left* are mail-order brides. Myra Cohn Livingston's poem "Lena" describes the feelings these characters have so that children can better understand what this experience might be like. Sometimes a poem creates an image that reflects the feelings of a character without actually describing that character's life. Although "The Rider" by Naomi Shihab Nye is about a rollerskater, the poet could be talking about Maniac, a runner, in Jerry Spinelli's *Maniac Magee* who, like the skater, tries to escape his loneliness through motion.

Sometimes a poem simply evokes something that is important to a character in a book. Bobbi Katz's poem "Grandma's Easter Bonnet," about how important this hat is to her grandmother, could be used to see the importance of the hat in Patricia Polacco's *Chicken Sunday.* In "My Mother," Valerie Worth describes a mother who, like the mother in Patricia MacLachlan's novel, *The Facts and Fictions of Minna Pratt*, prefers reading and writing to housework.

Sometimes a poem describes someone who has had an experience similar to that of a character in a book. Children who read Yoshiko Uchida's *Journey to Topaz* and *Journey Home* find out about how members of Uchida's family survived their internment during World War II and its aftermath. X.J. Kennedy's "Mrs. Morizawa's Morning" shares a look at an elderly woman who remembers both her home in Japan and her experiences during the time of the internment.

Animal characters in fantasies present a particular problem in searching for poems because they often have more human than animal characteristics. When looking for poems for Robert O'Brien's *Mrs. Frisby and the Rats of Nimh*, for example, you might start with collections of poems on mice but only a few of these poems are "matches" to the characters and feelings in the novel. Aileen Fisher's "Timid as a Mouse?" from a collection of her own mouse poems, *The House of a Mouse*, questions the cliché, noting that mice have to do a number of brave things. Fisher's "Careful Mouse" compares two predators, the owl and the cat, both of whom play significant roles in Mrs. Frisby's harrowing quest to move her house. Nancy Larrick's collection, *Mice Are Nice,* includes Lucy Sprague Mitchell's poem, "The House of a Mouse." This poem describes a real mouse home in a meadow that sounds much like Mrs. Frisby's home. Carmen Bernos de Gasztold's "Prayer of the Mouse" could well be one of Mrs. Frisby's prayers when she is feeling a little sorry for herself.

The best place to look for poems on characterization is in collections that contain biographical or "persona" poems. A number of these are listed in the "Biography" section of Chapter 4.

Bernos de Gasztold, Carmen. "Prayer of the Mouse" in Larrick, Nancy. *Mice Are Nice.* Philomel/Putnam, 1990.

Brooks, Bruce. *Everywhere.* Harper, 1990. (fiction)

Burch, Robert. *Queenie Peavy.* Puffin, 1987. (fiction)

Cooney, Barbara. *Miss Rumphius.* Viking, 1982. (fiction)

Fisher, Aileen. "Careful Mouse" and "Timid as a Mouse?" in *The House of a Mouse.* Illus. by Joan Sandin. Harper, 1988.

Haislip, John. "At Grandmother's" in Lueders, Edward. *Zero Makes Me Hungry.* Scott-Foresman, 1976.

Henderson, Rose. "Growing Old" in Prelutsky, Jack. *The Random House Book of Poetry for Children.* Random, 1983.

Katz, Bobbi. "Grandma's Easter Bonnet" in Livingston, Myra Cohn. *Easter Poems.* Holiday, 1985.

Kennedy, X.J. "Mrs. Morizawa's Morning" in *The Kite That Braved Old Orchard Beach.* Illus. by Marion Young. M.K. McElderry/Macmillan, 1981.

Livingston, Myra Cohn. "Lena" and "Nanny" in *Worlds I Know and Other Poems.* Illus. by Tim Arnold. M.K. McElderry/Macmillan, 1985.

———. "The Secret" in *There Was a Place and Other Poems.* M.K. McElderry/ Macmillan, 1988.

MacLachlan, Patricia. *The Facts and Fictions of Minna Pratt.* Harper, 1988. (fiction)

———. *Sarah Plain and Tall.* Harper, 1985. (fiction)

Mitchell, Lucy Sprague. "The House of a Mouse" in Larrick, Nancy. *Mice Are Nice.* Philomel/Putnam, 1990.

Nye, Naomi Shihab. "The Rider" in Janeczko, Paul. *The Place My Words Are Looking For*. Bradbury/Macmillan, 1990.

O'Brien, Robert. *Mrs. Frisby and the Rats of Nimh*. Atheneum/Macmillan, 1971. (fiction)

Polaccho, Patricia. *Chicken Sunday*. Philomel/Putnam, 1991. (fiction)

Spinelli, Jerry. *Maniac Magee*. Little, 1990. (fiction)

Turner, Ann. *Third Girl from the Left*. Macmillan, 1986. (fiction)

Uchida, Yoshiko. *Journey Home*. M.K. McElderry/Macmillan, 1978. (fiction)

————. *Journey to Topaz*. Creative Arts, 1985. (fiction)

Worth, Valerie. "My Mother" in Livingston, Myra Cohn. *Poems for Mothers*. Holiday, 1988.

Zolotow, Charlotte. *I Know a Lady*. Illus. by James Stevenson. Greenwillow, 1984.

## Poems about Themes

Themes can be one of the most troublesome aspects of literature discussions. Traditionally, teachers have expected that a book would have one overarching theme. As more research is done on children's responses to books and poems, it is clear that authors have more than one message in their books and, depending on the individual child, any one of these themes may appear to dominate. Children can easily recognize some themes or messages, but some may be more difficult to understand. Sometimes a carefully selected poem can make a hidden message clear to children. In other cases, children may find poems that reveal a message presented in a book. Themes are very closely connected with the feelings and attitudes of characters. Most of the poems suggested in the section on characters above are also about a theme in the novel. The best place to locate poems on themes is in collections with strong poems about people. Some collections of poems focus on feelings. Although some of these have generally been thought to be for young adults, many of the poems they contain can be understood by elementary school children. Collections with many "theme" poems are included here.

Adoff, Arnold, sel. *I Am the Darker Brother*. Macmillan, 1970.

————. *My Black Me*. Dutton, 1974.

Booth, David, sel. *'Til All the Stars Have Fallen*. Illus. by Kady MacDonald Denton. Viking, 1990.

De Regniers, Beatrice Schenk. *The Way I Feel...Sometimes*. Illus. by Susan Meddaughs. Clarion/Ticknor and Fields, 1988.

Dunning, Stephen, Edward Lueders, and Hugh Smith, sels. *Reflections on a Gift of Watermelon Pickle*. Lothrop, 1966.

Greenfield, Eloise. *Night on Neighborhood Street*. Illus. by Jan Spivey Gilchrist. Dial, 1991.

Hopkins, Lee Bennett, sel. *Through Our Eyes*. Illus. by Jeffrey Dunn. Little, 1992.

Janeczko, Paul, sel. *The Place My Words Are Looking For*. Bradbury/Macmillan, 1990.

————. *Pocket Poems*. Bradbury/Macmillan, 1985.

Lewis, Claudia. *Long Ago in Oregon.* Illus. by Joel Faontaine. Harper, 1987.

———. *Up in the Mountains and Other Poems.* Illus. by Joel Fontaine. Harper, 1991.

Livingston, Myra Cohn. *I Never Told and Other Poems.* M.K. McElderry/Macmillan, 1992.

———. *There Was a Place and Other Poems.* M.K.McElderry/Macmillan, 1988.

———. *Worlds I Know and Other Poems.* Illus. by Tim Arnold. M.K. McElderry/Macmillan, 1985.

## Poetry and Style

Style is the way an author or poet selects or arranges language. Authors and poets use imagery, figurative language, and sound devices to create their own unique style. Some poems have adopted a particular style of telling a story that we associate with prose. Some poems are letters, diary entries, and lists. Some use dialect and language to capture an image, idea, or setting. Examples of all of these types of poems can be found in Chapter 5.

One of the styles of writing in both books and poetry for children is the use of nonsense. Edward Lear's classic nonsense rhymes have been collected in *The Nonsense Poems of Edward Lear. I Never Saw a Purple Cow and Other Nonsense Rhymes* includes many traditional nonsense rhymes as well as those by well-known poets. Students might be interested to know that Lewis Carroll's classic nonsense poem, "Jabberwocky," included nonsense words that have become part of our language. These classic nonsense poets have a worthy successor in Paul Coltman. This poet's picture book, *Tog the Ribber, or Granny's Tale* uses language that, like Carroll's "Jabberwocky," sounds almost correct.

Other authors and poets derive their humor from playing with the inconsistencies in language. Dick King-Smith's fantasy novels and William Steig's picture books and novels make delightful reading to those children who love puns and clever use of words. Some poets love the pun and other forms of word play as well. David McCord and Eve Merriam play with language in many of their poems. John Ciardi and Ogden Nash are beloved for twisting the language to fit the meanings in their poems.

Carroll, Lewis. "Jabberwocky" in Elledge, Scott. *Wider than the Sky.* Random, 1990.

Clark, Emma Chichester, sel. *I Never Saw a Purple Cow and Other Nonsense Rhymes.* Little, 1991.

Coltman, Paul. *Tog the Ribber, or Granny's Tale.* Illus. by Gillian McClure. Farrar, 1985.

Lear, Edward. *The Nonsense Poems of Edward Lear.* Clarion/Houghton, 1991.

## Allusions

Jane Yolen (1981) has said that "Stories lean on stories, art on art"; familiarity with traditional stories is essential to understanding much of literature. Poetry also leans on stories. Poems are full of references to traditional stories, proverbs, songs, retellings of stories, and even parodies of classic works.

Some poems use allusions to stories. They mention a folkloric character or a motif from a well-known story. Paul Coltman's eerie story poem *Witch Watch* is full of references to Baba Yaga, the Russian witch who rides in a mortar and pestle and lives in a house with chicken feet. Constance Levy imagines a butterfly is an enchanted prince who only needs the poet's kiss to be transformed into himself again in "The Kiss." Arnold Adoff makes more modern allusions including one to Raold Dahl's *Charlie and the Chocolate Factory* and even to Kermit from the Muppets.

Adoff, Arnold. "In My Horror Fantasy Chiller" in *Chocolate Dreams*. Illus. by Tori MacCombie. Lothrop, 1989.

———. "One Night" in *Greens*. Illus. by Betsy Lewin. Lothrop, 1988.

Coltman, Paul. *Witch Watch*. Illus. by Gillian McClure. Farrar, 1989.

Corben, John. "In the Eggs" in Harrison, Michael. *Splinters*. Oxford, 1988.

Esbensen, Barbara Juster. "As Soon as You Say This Word" in *Words with Wrinkled Knees*. Illus. by John Stadler. Crowell/Harper, 1987.

Levy, Constance. "The Kiss" in *I'm Going to Pet a Worm Today*. Illus. by Ronald Himler. M.K. McElderry/ Macmillan, 1985.

Livingston, Myra Cohn. "Worlds I Know" in *Worlds I Know and Other Poems*. Illus. by Tim Arnold. M.K. McElderry/Macmillan, 1985.

Merriam, Eve. "Apple" in *Halloween ABC*. Illus. by Lane Smith. Macmillan, 1987.

Moore, Lilian. "How the Frog Feels about It" in *Adam Mouse's Book of Poems*. Illus. by Kathleen Garry McCord. Atheneum/Macmillan, 1992.

Silverstein, Shel. "Alice" in *Where the Sidewalk Ends*. Harper, 1974.

Stilborn, Myra. "A Mosquito in the Cabin" in Booth, David. *'Til All the Stars Have Fallen*. Viking, 1990.

Watson, Clyde. *Father Fox's Pennyrhymes*. Illus. by Wendy Watson. Harper, 1971.

Wynne, Annette. "I Keep Three Wishes Ready" in Larrick, Nancy. *Piping Down the Valleys Wild*. Delacorte, 1985.

Yolen, Jane. "Caterpillar's Lullaby" in Harrison, Michael. *Splinters*. Oxford, 1988.

———. "The Used Carpet Salesman" in *Best Witches*. Illus. by Elise Primavera. Putnam, 1989.

## Retellings

Another kind of poem retells a classic story. Some of these simply tell the story in verse and are listed below followed by the word "retelling." Others rethink the classic story, given modern attitudes and opinions. Judith Viorst retells Hans Christian Andersen's tragic story, "The Little Mermaid," with the mermaid advising others not to do as she did; she might have been better off and even have won the prince if she had been true to herself. After reading and listening to some of these retellings, students may enjoy trying to write their own. Students who enjoy rap music and chants may want to try rap or chanted versions of traditional tales but with a modern twist. This version of Little Red Riding Hood was created after talking with some older children about what a "wimp" Little Red Riding Hood was. It is intended to be presented as a call-and-response story:

Here comes Little Red Riding Hood.
Isn't she good?
Isn't she good?
Walking so carefully through the wood.
Isn't she good?
Isn't she good?
In a cape with a basket over her arm.
Nice and warm.
Nice and warm.
With gifts for grandma from her mom.
Safe from harm?
Safe from harm?
Here comes Wolf who's up to no good.
Look out, "Hood"!
Look out, "Hood"!
"Going to Grandma's? Wish I could."
Look out, "Hood"!
Look out, "Hood"!
Wolf goes off and "Red" walks on.
Where's Wolf gone?
Where's Wolf gone?
She comes to Grandma's before long...
"Riding," run!
"Riding," run!
"Grandma, Grandma" (What has changed her?)
"Red," there's danger!
"Red," there's danger!
"Oh, dear Grandma, you're a stranger."
"Red," there's danger!
"Red," there's danger!
"What big teeth, big ears, big eyes!"
(Here it comes, guys)
(Here it comes, guys)
"The Better to eat you with, Wolf cries!"
(Red's demise.)
(Red's demise.)
Moral:
Little Red Riding Hood was all heart.
But not smart.
But not smart. (Chatton, 1981)

Adoff, Arnold. "Life in the Forest, or Bad News...Good News...Bad News" in *Chocolate Dreams*. Illus. by Tori MacCombie. Lothrop, 1989.

Aylesworth, Jim. *The Completed Hickory Dickory Dock*. Illus. by Eileen Christelow. Atheneum, 1990.

Bennett, Rowena. "The Gingerbread Man" in De Regniers, Beatrice Schenk. *Sing a Song of Popcorn*. Scholastic, 1988. (retelling)

Bourinot, Arthur S. "Paul Bunyan" in Booth, David. *'Til All the Stars Have Fallen*. Viking, 1990. (retelling)

Ciardi, John. "The Wise Hen" in *You Read to Me, I'll Read to You*. Illus. by Edward Gorey. Lippincott/Harper, 1961.

Dahl, Roald. *Rhyme Stew*. Illus. by Quentin Blake. Viking, 1989.

Esbensen, Barbara Juster. "Fairy Tale" and "Perseid Meteor Shower" (Perseus and Medusa) in *Cold Stars and Fireflies*. Illus. by Susan Bonners. Harper, 1991.

Fleischman, Paul. "The Phoenix" in *I Am Phoenix*. Illus. by Ken Nutt. Harper, 1985.

"The Hairy Toe" and "Life Story" in Harrison, Michael. *The Oxford Book of Story Poems*. Oxford, 1990.

Hay, Sara Henderson. "Interview" in Hall, Donald. *Oxford Book of Children's Verse in America*. Oxford, 1985.

Kennedy, X.J. "Mingled Yarns" in Hall, Donald. *Oxford Book of Children's Verse in America*. Oxford, 1985.

McCord, David. "Jack, Jill, Sprats, and Horner" in *One at a Time*. Little, 1986.

Marsh, James. "Frog Prince" in *Bizarre Birds and Beasts*. Dial, 1991.

Milne, A. A. "Little Bo-Peep and Little Boy Blue" in *When We Were Very Young*. Illus. by Ernest H. Shepard. Dutton, 1988.

Moore, Lilian. "The Troll Bridge" in *Something New Begins*. Illus. by Mary Jane Dunton. Atheneum/Macmillan, 1982.

"The Mouse, the Frog, and the Little Red Hen" in Hopkins, Lee Bennett. *Side by Side: Poems to Read Together*. Simon, 1988. (retelling)

Norris, Leslie. "Merlin and the Snake's Egg" in Harrison, Michael. *Oxford Book of Story Poems*. Oxford, 1990.

"The Old Man Who Lived in the Woods" in Corrin, Sara. *Once Upon a Rhyme*. Faber, 1982. (retelling)

Patten, Brian. "The Complacent Tortoise" in Harrison, Michael. *The Oxford Book of Story Poems*. Oxford, 1990.

Paxton, Tom. *Aesop's Fables*. Illus. by Robert Rayevsky. Morrow, 1988.

———. *Androcles and the Lion*. Illus. by Robert Rayevsky. Morrow, 1991.

———. *Belling the Cat*. Illus. by Robert Rayevsky. Morrow, 1990.

Potter, Beatrix. "The Old Woman" in Prelutsky, Jack. *Read Aloud Rhymes for the Very Young*. Knopf, 1986.

Rice, James. *Cajun Night before Christmas*. Pelican, 1976.

———. *Prairie Night before Christmas*. Pelican, 1986.

———. *Texas Night before Christmas*. Pelican, 1986.

Saxe, John Godfrey. "The Blind Men and the Elephant" in Corrin, Sara. *Once Upon a Rhyme*. Faber, 1982. (retelling)

Serraillier, Ian. "After Ever Happily" in Harrison, Michael. *The Oxford Book of Story Poems*. Oxford, 1990.

Sharp, Richard Scrafton. "The Country Mouse and the City Mouse" in Elledge, Scott. *Wider Than the Sky*. Harper, 1990. (retelling)

Silverstein, Shel. "In Search of Cinderella" in *The Light in the Attic*. Harper, 1981.

————. "Paul Bunyan" and "The Silver Fish" in *Where the Sidewalk Ends*. Harper, 1974.

Stafford, William. "A Story That Could Be True" in Kennedy, X.J. *Knock at a Star*. Little, 1985.

Steig, Jeanne. "Fish" in *Consider the Lemming*. Illus. by William Steig. Farrar, 1988.

Strauss, Gwen. *Trail of Stones*. Illus. by Anthony Browne. Knopf, 1990.

Viorst, Judith. "Fairy Tales" section in *If I Were in Charge of the World and Other Worries*. Illus. by Lynn Cherry. Atheneum/Macmillan, 1984.

Yolen, Jane. "The Magic House" in *Best Witches*. Illus. by Elise Primavera. Putnam, 1989.

# Parodies

Parodies are retellings in which the rhyme scheme, rhythms, and often the first line of a classic piece are "borrowed" by the poet and rewritten to tell a very different tale. Lewis Carroll's classic "Twinkle Twinkle, Little Bat" is a parody that most children can easily recognize. Several writers have parodied Joyce Kilmer's classic poem "Trees," including Ogden Nash, who uses the form to talk about billboards, and Conrad Diekmann, who uses it to talk about skiing.

Arnold Lobel and Clyde Watson have used the rhythms and sometimes the first lines of nursery rhymes to create their own verse, a form of simple parody younger children can enjoy. Children who know the nursery rhymes and recognize these verses may want to try writing their own revised versions.

"The Boy Stood on the Burning Deck," "Humpty Dumpty," "Mary Had a Little Lamb," and "Somebody Said It Couldn't Be Done" in Prelutsky, Jack. *For Laughing Out Loud*. Knopf, 1991.

Carroll, Lewis. "Twinkle, Twinkle, Little Bat" in Prelutsky, Jack. *Read Aloud Rhymes for the Very Young*. Knopf, 1986.

————. "You Are Old Father William" in Elledge, Scott. *Wider Than the Sky*. Harper, 1990.

Ciardi, John. "Ode" in *Mummy Took Cooking Lessons*. Illus. by Merle Nacht. Houghton, 1990.

Dehn, Paul. "Hey Diddle Diddle" and "Little Miss Muffet" in Dunning, Stephen. *Reflections on a Gift of Watermelon Pickle*. Lothrop, 1966.

Diekmann, Conrad. "Winter Trees" in Morrison, Lillian. *Sprints and Distances*. Crowell/Harper, 1990.

Fatchen, Max. "Rockabye Baby" in Foster, John. *A Third Poetry Book*. Oxford, 1987.

"Humpty Dumpty" and "Mary Had a Little Lamb" in Foster, John. *A Third Poetry Book*. Oxford, 1987.

Kennedy, X.J. "Takeoffs" section in *Knock at a Star*. Little, 1985.

Lobel, Arnold. "Orson Porson Pudding and Pie" in *Whiskers and Rhymes*. Greenwillow, 1985.

McNaughton, Colin. "Monday's Child Is Red and Spotty" in Prelutsky, Jack. *For Laughing Out Loud*. Knopf, 1991.

"Mary Had a Little Lamb" in Prelutsky, Jack. *Poems of A. Nonny Mouse*. Knopf, 1989.

Merriam, Eve. "A New Song for Old Smokey" in *A Poem for a Pickle*. Illus. by Sheila Hamanaka. Morrow, 1989.

Nash, Ogden. "Song of the Open Road" in Janeczko, Paul. *Pocket Poems*. Bradbury/ Macmillan, 1985.

O'Donnell, Elizabeth Lee. *The Twelve Days of Summer*. Illus. by Karen Lee Schmidt. Morrow, 1991.

Rosen, Michael. "Humpty Dumpty Went to the Moon" in Foster, John. *A Very First Poetry Book*. Oxford, 1980.

Silverstein, Shel. "One Two" and "Squishy Touch" in *A Light in the Attic*. Harper, 1981.

"Teasing" and other nursery rhyme parodies, in Clark, Emma C. *I Never Saw a Purple Cow*. Little, 1991.

Watson, Clyde. *Father Fox's Pennyrhymes*. Illus. by Wendy Watson. Harper, 1971.

## Plot and Poetry

Some poems use plot patterns that are also used in stories. One plot that children recognize is the cumulative story, which relates a series of similar plot events in a simple chain. Stories such as *The Little Red Hen* and *Chicken Little* use this plot form. Poems such as *I Know an Old Lady* and *This Is the House That Jack Built* use cumulative plots. Verna Aardema's *Bringing the Rain to Kapiti Plain* echoes not only the cumulative plot of *This Is the House That Jack Built* but uses the same rhythmic pattern. The cumulative plot is enjoyed by older students when it is used in ghost stories. Harve Zemach's picture book "horror" story, *The Judge*, uses the cumulative form and a new poem in picture book form, *Look Out, Look Out, It's Coming!* by Laura Geringer, tells a similar story.

Many traditional stories and fantasies have circular plots involving a journey in which the hero leaves home on a kind of quest and returns home changed from that experience. *Hansel and Gretel* and *Jack and the Beanstalk* are examples of circular stories. *Valentine and Orson*, Nancy Ekholm Burkert's extended retelling of a medieval legend uses this circular plot pattern as do many of the story poems in *The Oxford Book of Story Poems* and *Sing a Song of Popcorn*.

After sharing a number of these types of plots with her first graders and helping them to see the patterns in these plots, one teacher then shared Dr. Seuss's "Too Many Daves" and asked them about that plot pattern. The children were shocked to notice that this plot stops in the middle.

Aardema, Verna. *Bringing the Rain to Kapiti Plain*. Illus. by Beatriz Vidal. Dial, 1981.
Burkert, Nancy Ekholm. *Valentine and Orson*. Farrar, 1989.

De Regniers, Beatrice Schenk, et al., sels. "Story Poems" in *Sing a Song of Popcorn.* Illus. by nine Caldecott artists. Scholastic, 1988.

Dr. Seuss. "Too Many Daves" in *The Sneetches*. Random, 1961. (fiction)

Geringer, Laura. *Look Out, Look Out, It's Coming!* Illus. by Sue Truesdell. Harper, 1992.

Harrison, Michael, and Christopher Stuart-Clark. *The Oxford Book of Story Poems.* Oxford, 1990.

Zemach, Harve. *The Judge: An Untrue Tale*. Illus. by Margot Zemach. Farrar, 1988. (fiction)

# REFERENCES

Chatton, B. (1981). Poem written for a class at Ohio State University.

Kennedy, X.J. and D. Kennedy. (1982). "Takeoffs" *Knock at a Star: A Child's Introduction to Poetry*. Boston: Little.

Robertson, B. (1992). Journal Entry.

Yolen, J. (1981). *Touch Magic*. New York: Philomel/Putnam, p. 15.

used in conjunction with music and providing sound and visual imagery, poems sometimes describe the act of playing an instrument or singing. Sometimes they describe the act of listening to music. One poem in book format, Richard Lewis' *All of You Was Singing*, is a retelling of the Aztec myth of how music came to the earth.

Doyle, Marion Stauffer. "The Wind" in Bober, Natalie S. *Let's Pretend*. Viking, 1986.

Johnston, Tony. "Aerial Sheet Music" in *I'm Gonna Tell Mama I Want an Iguana*. Illus. by Lillian Hoban. Putnam, 1990.

Lewis, Richard. *All of You Was Singing*. Illus. by Ed Young. Atheneum/Macmillan, 1991.

Merriam, Eve. "Quaking Aspen" in *Fresh Paint*. Illus. by David Frampton. Macmillan, 1986.

———. "Rainbow Writing" and "Starry Night I" in *The Singing Green*. Illus. by Kathleen Collins Howell. Morrow, 1992.

Norman, Charles. "A Parlement of Swallows" in *The Hornbeam Tree*. Illus. by Ted Rand. Holt, 1988.

Yolen, Jane. "Song/Birds" in *Bird Watch*. Illus. by Ted Lewin. Philomel/Putnam, 1990.

## Song Picture Books

The song picture book is a popular form of poetry for children. In these books the lyrics for a song are used as the poetic text for a picture book and the music is included in the back. Song picture books include patriotic songs such as *The Star Spangled Banner* and *Yankee Doodle*, contemporary songs, songs from musical comedy such as *A Real Nice Clambake* or *The Happy Hippopotamus*, and traditional songs.

*The Balancing Act: A Counting Song*. Illus. by Merle Peek. Clarion/Ticknor and Fields, 1987.

Bangs, Edward. *Yankee Doodle*. Illus. by Steven Kellogg. Four Winds/Macmillan, 1984.

Brebeuf, Jean de. *The Huron Carol*. Illus. by Frances Tyrrell. Dutton, 1992.

*Casey Jones*. Illus. by Francis Balistreri. Raintree, 1987.

Child, Lydia Maria. *Over the River and Through the Wood*. Illus. by Brinton Turkle. Coward/Putnam, 1975.

———. *Over the River and through the Wood*. Illus. by Iris Van Rynback. Morrow, 1992.

Craver, Mike. *Beaver Ball at the Bug Club*. Illus. by Joan Kaghan. Farrar, 1992.

Davis, Katherine, Henry Onorati, and Harry Simeone. *The Little Drummer Boy*. Illus. by Ezra Jack Keats. Collier/Macmillan, 1968.

*The Erie Canal*. Illus. by Peter Spier. Doubleday, 1970.

*A Farmyard Song*. Illus by Christopher Manson. North-South, 1992.

Fertig, Dennis. *Take Me Out to the Ball Game*. Illus. by William McMahon. Albert Whitman, 1987.

Flanders, Michael, and Donald Swan. *The Hippopotamus Song: A Muddy Love Story*. Illus. by Nadine Bernard Westcott. Little, 1991.

*Fox Went Out on a Chilly Night: An Old Song.* Illus. by Peter Spier. Doubleday, 1961.

*The Friendly Beasts: A Traditional Christmas Carol.* Illus. by Sarah Chamberlain. Dutton, 1991.

*The Friendly Beasts.* Illus. by Tomie DePaola. Putnam, 1981.

*Frog Went A-Courting.* Retold by John Langstaff. Illus. by Feodor Rojankovsky. Harcourt, 1955.

*Frog Went A-Courtin'.* Illus by Wendy Watson. Lothrop, 1990.

Gag, Wanda. *The ABC Bunny.* Coward/Putnam, 1978.

*Go Tell Aunt Rhody.* Illus. by Aliki. Macmillan, 1986.

*Go Tell Aunt Rhody.* Illus. by Robert Quackenbush. Harper, 1973.

Hale, Sarah Josepha. *Mary Had a Little Lamb.* Illus. by Tomie De Paola. Holiday, 1984.

———. *Mary Had a Little Lamb.* Illus. by Bruce McMillan. Scholastic, 1990.

Hammerstein, Oscar and Richard Rodgers. *A Real Nice Clambake.* Illus. by Nadine Bernard Westcott. Little, 1992.

Hurd, Thatcher. *Mama Don't Allow.* Harper, 1984.

*Hush Little Baby: A Folk Lullaby.* Illus. by Aliki. Simon, 1968.

*Hush Little Baby: From a Traditional Lullaby.* Illus. by Jeanette Winter. Pantheon, 1984.

Ivemey, John W. *Three Blind Mice.* Illus. by Lorinda Bryan Cauley. Putnam, 1991.

———. *Three Blind Mice.* Illus. by Victoria Chess. Little, 1990.

———. *Three Blind Mice.* Illus. by Paul Galdone. Clarion, 1987.

Kennedy, Jimmy. *The Teddy Bears' Picnic.* Illus. by Michael Hague. Holt, 1992.

———. *The Teddy Bears' Picnic.* Illus. by Alexandra Day. Green Tiger Press, 1989.

Key, Francis Scott. *The Star Spangled Banner.* Illus. by Peter Spier. Doubleday, 1973.

Langstaff, John. *Oh, A-Hunting We Will Go.* Illus. by Nancy Winslow Parker. M.K. McElderry/Macmillan, 1983.

*London Bridge Is Falling Down.* Illus. by Peter Spier. Doubleday, 1972.

McCarthy, Bobette. *Buffalo Girls.* Crown, 1987.

McNally. Darcie. *In a Cabin in a Wood.* Illus. by Robin Michal Koontz. Cobblehill/ Dutton, 1989.

Moss, Marissa. *Knick, Knack, Paddywack.* Houghton, 1992.

*Old MacDonald Had a Farm.* Illus. by Prue Theobalds. Bedrick, 1991.

Peek, Merle. *Mary Wore Her Red Dress and Henry Wore His Green Sneakers.* Clarion/ Ticknor and Fields, 1985.

Raffi. *Baby Beluga.* Illus. by Ashley Wolff. Crown, 1990.

*Ridin' That Strawberry Roan.* Illus. by Marcia Sewell. Puffin, 1987.

*Roll Over!* Illus. by Merle Peek. Houghton, 1981.

*She'll be Comin' 'Round the Mountain.* Illus. by Robert Quackenbush. Harper, 1973.

Staines, Bill. *All God's Critters Got a Place in the Choir.* Illus. by Margot Zemach. Dutton, 1989.

Taylor, Jane. *Twinkle, Twinkle, Little Star.* Illus. by Michael Hague. Morrow, 1992.

———. *Twinkle, Twinkle, Little Star.* Illus. by Julia Noonan. Scholastic, 1992.

*Ten in a Bed.* Illus. by Mary Rees. Joy Street/Little, 1988.

*There's a Hole in the Bucket.* Illus. by Nadine Bernard Westcott. Harper, 1990.

*This Old Man.* Illus. by Carol Jones. Houghton, 1990.

*This Old Man: The Counting Song.* Illus. by Robin M. Koontz. Putnam, 1988.

Titherington, Jeanne. *Baby's Boat.* Greenwillow, 1992.

*The Twelve Days of Christmas.* Illus. by Joanna Isles. Hyperion, 1992.

Wadsworth, Olive A. *Over in the Meadow.* Illus. by Ezra Jack Keats. Scholastic, 1985.

———. *Over in the Meadow.* Illus. by Feodor Rojankovsky. Harcourt, 1957.

Watson, Clyde and Wendy. *Father Fox's Feast of Songs.* Philomel/Putnam, 1983.

Westcott, Nadine Bernard. *I Know an Old Lady Who Swallowed a Fly.* Little, 1980.

———. *Skip to My Lou.* Little, 1989.

*The Wheels on the Bus.* Illus. by Paul O. Zelinsky. Dutton, 1990.

*The Wheels on the Bus.* Illus. by Maryann Kovalskii. Joy Street/Little, 1990.

Young, Ruth. *Golden Bear.* Illus. by Rachel Isadora. Viking, 1992.

*The Zebra-Riding Cowboy: A Folk Song from the Old West.* Col. by Angela Shelf Medearis. Illus. by Maria Christina Brusca. Holt, 1992.

## Collections of Folk Rhymes Set to Music

Cole, Joanna, and Stepanie Calmenson, sels. *The Eentsy, Weentsy Spider: Finger Plays and Action Rhymes.* Morrow, 1991.

Delacre, Lulu, sel. *Arroz Con Leche: Popular Songs and Rhymes from Latin America.* Scholastic, 1989.

Glazer, Tom, sel. *Eye Winker, Tom Tinker, Chin Chopper: Fifty Musical Fingerplays.* Illus. by Ronald Himler. Doubleday, 1973.

Larrick, Nancy, sel. *Songs from Mother Goose, with the Traditional Melody for Each.* Illus. by Robin Spowart. Harper, 1989.

Schwartz, Alvin, sel. *And the Green Grass Grew All Around.* Illus. by Sue Truesdell. Harper, 1992.

Yolen, Jane, sel. *Jane Yolen's Mother Goose Songbook.* Illus. by Rosekrans Hoffman. Caroline/Boyds Mills, 1992.

## Musical Performances

Some poems are about playing a musical instrument or singing. Some poems concern the experience of "doing" music in school or taking music lessons. As with poems on creating art, these poems describe both positive and negative experiences. Jeanne Steig captures my own feelings about piano lessons when I was growing up in "A Pianist Plummets," in which a mother reminds her daughter that playing dead and falling off the piano bench only postpones her practicing of scales. Others show positive experiences with playing and listening to music, which can help us feel, or relieve our feelings.

Several children's books focus on children who make music of one kind or another, which can be linked with poetry about playing and appreciating music. Robert McCloskey's *Lentil* plays the harmonica in his small town in Ohio in this classic picture book. In a more recent free verse picture book, *The Finest Horse in Town,* based on stories told about her great aunts,

Jacqueline Briggs Martin features a horse who has been taught to dance to the music of a harmonica. In Eth Clifford's novel, *Summer of the Dancing Horse*, a beautiful palomino does the same thing.

Patricia MacLachlan's *Facts and Fictions of Minna Pratt* focuses on a young cellist who is struggling to learn her vibrato. Richard Lester's poem, "My Cello Big and Fat," is shaped like a cello and also concerns the learning of the vibrato. Rachel Isadora's *Ben's Trumpet* and Vera B. Williams' *Music, Music for Everyone* also focus on musicians. These and other novels featuring music can be read along with poetry as we listen to different styles and forms of music.

Blake, Quentin. "All Join In" in *All Join In*. Little, 1991.

Bryan, Ashley. "My Dad" in *Sing to the Sun*. Harper, 1992.

Clayton, Candyce. "Piano Lessons" in Lueders, Edward. *Zero Makes Me Hungry*. Scott, Foresman, 1976.

Clifford, Eth. *Summer of the Dancing Horse*. Illus. by Mary Beth Owens. Houghton, 1991. (fiction)

Giovanni, Nikki. "The Drum" in *Spin a Soft Black Song*. Illus. by George Martins. Hill, 1985.

Greenfield, Eloise. "Fun" in *Honey, I Love*. Illus. by Leo and Diane Dillon. Crowell/Harper, 1978.

Hillyer, Robert. "The Fireflies Wink and Glow" in Gordon, Ruth. *Time Is the Longest Distance*. Harper, 1991.

Hines, Carl Wendall, Jr. "From Two Jazz Poems" in Dunning, Stephen. *Reflections on a Gift of Watermelon Pickle*. Lothrop, 1966.

Isadora, Rachel. *Ben's Trumpet*. Greenwillow, 1979. (fiction)

Kennedy, X.J. "The Girl Who Makes the Cymbals Bang" in *The Kite That Braved Old Orchard Beach*. Illus. by Marion Young. M.K. McElderry/Macmillan, 1991.

Kuskin, Karla. "Lewis Has a Trumpet" in *Dogs and Dragons, Trees and Dreams*. Harper, 1980.

Lester, Richard. "My Cello Big and Fat" in Moss, Elaine. *From Morn to Midnight*. Illus. by Satomi Ichikawa. Crowell/Harper, 1977.

Lobel, Arnold. "Friendly Frederick Fuddlestone" in *Whiskers and Rhymes*. Greenwillow, 1985.

MacLachlan, Patricia. *The Facts and Fictions of Minna Pratt*. Harper, 1988. (fiction)

McCloskey, Robert. *Lentil*. Viking, 1940. (fiction)

McCurdy, Michael. *The Old Man and the Fiddle*. Putnam, 1992.

Martin, Jacqueline Briggs. *The Finest Horse in Town*. Illus. by Susan Gaber. Harper, 1992.

Service, Robert W. *The Shooting of Dan McGrew*. Illus. by Ted Harrison. Godine, 1988.

Steig, Jeanne. "A Pianist Plummets" in *Alpha Beta Chowder*. Illus. by William Steig. Harper, 1992.

Updike, John. "Recital" in Morrison, Lillian. *Rhythm Road*. Lothrop, 1988.

Williams, Vera B. *Music, Music for Everyone*. Greenwillow, 1984. (fiction)

Worth, Valerie. "Bell" in *All the Small Poems*. Illus. by Natalie Babbitt. Farrar, 1987.

# Poems about Singing and Song

Quentin Blake's picture book *All Join In* invites children to participate in singing and creating sound effects for their own songs. This joy in singing is also apparent in many of the poems in Ashley Bryan's *Sing to the Sun*. Sometimes the sound of the voices of a choir raised in song is enriching, as Eloise Greenfield suggests in "In the Church." Poets often write about nature singing, as Paul Fleischman does in "Cicadas," describing their "jubilant" hymn to the sun after time spent underground. Walt Whitman's poem in praise of American diversity, *I Hear America Singing,* finds music in the daily activities of Americans of his time.

Blake, Quentin. *All Join In.* Little, 1991.

Brooks, Gwendolyn. "Gertrude" in *Bronzeville Boys and Girls.* Illus. by Ronni Solbert. Harper, 1967.

Bryan, Ashley. *Sing to the Sun.* Harper, 1992.

Fleischman, Paul. "Cicadas" in *Joyful Noise.* Illus. by Eric Beddows. Harper, 1988.

Greenfield, Eloise. "In the Church" in *Night on Neighborhood Street.* Illus. by Jan Spivey Gilchrist. Dial, 1991.

―――. "Nathaniel's Rap" and "Nathaniel's Rap (Reprise)" in *Nathaniel Talking.* Illus. by Jan Spivey Gilchrist. Black Butterfly/Writers and Readers, 1988.

Lobel, Arnold. "Sing, Sing" in *Whiskers and Rhymes.* Greenwillow, 1985.

"Sing a Song of Sixpence." Many nursery rhyme collections.

Turner, Nancy Byrd. "From... A Popcorn Song" in De Regniers, *Sing a Song of Popcorn.* Scholastic, 1988.

Whitman, Walt. *I Hear America Singing.* Illus. by Robert Sabuda. Philomel/Putnam, 1991.

# Appreciating Music

Along with songs and playing music, we need to listen to many styles of music and instruments to learn to appreciate them. The following poems describe particular kinds of music or a particular musician. Because they were written in response to music, they can be shared before, after, or along with the pieces of music they describe. Some ideas for using poetry and music together are discussed in Chapter 8.

Birchman, David F. *Brother Billy Bronto's Bygone Blues Band.* Illus. by John O'Brien. Lothrop, 1992.

Cole, William. "Here Comes the Band" in De Regniers, Beatrice Schenk. *Sing a Song of Popcorn.* Scholastic, 1988.

Fleischman, Paul. *Rondo in C.* Illus. by Janet Wentworth. Harper, 1988.

Greenfield, Eloise. "Grandma's Bones," "My Daddy," and "Who the Best" in *Nathaniel Talking.* Illus. by Jan Spivey Gilchrist. Black Butterfly/Writers and Readers, 1988.

―――. "Way Down in the Music" in *Honey, I Love.* Illus. by Leo and Diane Dillon. Crowell/Harper, 1978.

Hru, Dakari Kamau. "John Coltrane Ditty" in Slier, Deborah. *Make a Joyful Sound.* Checkerboard, 1991.

Joseph, Lynn. "Steel Drum" in *Coconut Kind of Day.* Illus. by Sandra Speidel. Lothrop, 1992.

Komaiko, Leah. *I Like the Music.* Harper, 1989.

Merriam, Eve. "A Short Note" in *A Sky Full of Poems.* Illus. by Walter Gaffney-Kessell. Dell, 1986.

Raschka, Chris. *Charlie Parker Played Be Bop.* Orchard, 1992.

Shapiro, Karl. "Piano" in Morrison, Lillian. *Rhythm Road.* Lothrop, 1988.

"Ten Tom-Toms" in Morrison, Lillian. *Rhythm Road.* Lothrop, 1988.

Wayland, April Halprin. "When Mom Plays Just for Me" in Livingston, Myra Cohn. *Poems for Mothers.* Holiday, 1988.

## PHYSICAL EDUCATION

Physical education is more than recess. Children practice physical education in science, social studies, music, and art. The rhythmic qualities of poetry invite students to respond physically, making a natural link between poetry and awareness of how human bodies move and work. Children jump, clap, pose, imitate, and pantomime spontaneously as images of movement are shared in poems.

### Jump Rope Rhymes

Children use poetry regularly on the playground as they recite traditional songs and chants to accompany jump rope, hand clapping, and other games. Jump rope fans enjoy looking at collections of traditional jump rope rhymes such as *Anna Banana: 101 Jump Rope-Rhymes* and *Jump! The New Jump Rope Book.* They discover that their versions of these rhymes differ somewhat from versions collected in other places. Sometimes it is just a difference in one or two words, sometimes there are more verses, and sometimes the same rhythmic beat is used but with entirely different words. Students might collect versions of these jump rope rhymes that their parents and teachers remember to compare with their own. Poets like the rhythms of jump rope games and have created their own jump rope poems. Eve Merriam particularly enjoys the rhythms of jump rope rhymes and includes one in nearly all of her collections of poetry. Clyde Watson has written "Uptown, Downtown," a verse with the rhythms of traditional jump rope rhymes. Several jump rope rhymes have been illustrated in picture book form including *A, My Name Is Alice* and *The Lady with the Alligator Purse.* Students might want to add new verses to these rhymes or to make their own illustrated book featuring one of their own favorite rhymes.

Bayer, Jane. *A, My Name Is Alice*. Illus. by Steven Kellogg. Dial, 1984.

Cole, Joanna, sel. *Anna Banana: 101 Jump-Rope Rhymes*. Illus. by Alan Tiegreen. Morrow, 1989.

Greenaway, Kate. "Jump-Jump-Jump" in Hopkins, Lee Bennett. *Side by Side: Poems to Read Together*. Simon, 1988.

Greenfield, Eloise. "Rope Rhyme" in *Honey, I Love*. Illus. by Leo and Diane Dillon. Crowell/Harper, 1978.

"Jose Canseco (Jump Rope Rhyme)" in Morrison, Lillian. *At the Crack of the Bat*. Illus. by Steve Cieslawski. Hyperion, 1992.

Kalbfleisch, Susan. *Jump! The New Jump Rope Book*. Illus. by Laurie McGugan. Beech Tree/Morrow, 1987.

Merriam, Eve. "A Rhyme Is a Jump Rope" and "Supermarket, Supermarket (A Jump Rope Rhyme)" in *The Singing Green*. Illus. by Kathleen Collins Howell. Crowell, 1992.

———. "Skip Rope Rhyme" in *A Poem for a Pickle*. Illus. by Sheila Hamanaka. Morrow, 1989.

———. "Skip Rope Rhyme for Our Time" in *Fresh Paint*. Illus. by David Frampton. Macmillan, 1986.

Rice, John. "Skipping Rhyme" in Foster, John. *A Very First Poetry Book*. Oxford, 1980.

Turner, Ann. "Red-Dress Girl" in *Street Talk*. Houghton, 1986.

Watson, Clyde. "Uptown, Downtown" in *Father Fox's Pennyrhymes*. Illus. by Wendy Watson. Harper, 1971.

Westcott, Nadine Bernard. *The Lady with the Alligator Purse*. Joy Street/Little, 1988.

## Other Traditional Games

Sometimes the lyrics used in jump rope rhymes are also used for clapping games and for sassy chants on the playground. Other games have their own particular chants. Several of these traditional chants have been collected in Joanna Cole's *Miss Mary Mack: Children's Street Rhymes* and Jane Yolen's *Street Rhymes around the World*. Because of the popularity of rap music, many children are using its strong beat and creating their own lyrics for both informal games and more formal presentations in their classrooms.

While jump rope rhymes and street rhymes generally are passed from child to child, other traditional rhymes and chants are passed from adults to children. Mother Goose rhymes are often accompanied by rhythmic activities. Other traditional games that include rhymes and activities may be learned through camp, scouting, or other organized group activities. Michael Rosen has created a version of *We're Going on a Bear Hunt*, which comes complete with actions. Songs such as "My Hat It Has Three Corners" and "The Hokey Pokey" also include actions. The song picture book section of this chapter includes other songs that lend themselves to rhythmic movements.

Bronner, Simon J. *American Children's Folklore*. August House, 1990.

Brown, Marc. *Finger Rhymes*. Dutton, 1980.

———. *Hand Rhymes*. Dutton, 1985.

Cole, Joanna, and Stephanie Calmenson, sels. *The Eentsy, Weentsy Spider*. Illus. by Alan Tiegreen. Morrow, 1991.

———. *Miss Mary Mack and Other Children's Street Rhymes*. Illus. by Alan Tiegreen. Morrow, 1990.

———. *Pat-a-Cake and Other Play Rhymes*. Illus. by Alan Tiegreen. Morrow, 1992.

Glazer, Tom, sel. *Eye Winker, Tom Tinker, Chin Chopper: Fifty Musical Fingerplays*. Doubleday, 1973.

Hastings, Scott E., Jr. *Miss Mary Mack All Dressed in Black*. August House, 1990.

Lamont, Priscilla, sel. *Ring-a-Round-a-Rosy*. Little, 1992.

Opie, Iona, and Peter Opie, sels. *I Saw Esau: The Schoolchild's Pocket Book*. Illus. by Maurice Sendak. Candlewick, 1992.

Rosen, Michael. *We're Going on a Bear Hunt*. Illus. by Helen Oxenbury. M.K. McElderry/Macmillan, 1989.

Schwartz, Alvin, sel. "Fun and Games" section in *And the Green Grass Grew All Around*. Illus. by Sue Truesdell. Harper, 1992.

Withers, Carl, sel. *A Rocket in My Pocket*. Holt, 1988.

Wyndham, Robert, sel. *Chinese Mother Goose Rhymes*. Illus. by Ed Young. Philomel/ Putnam, 1989.

Yolen, Jane. *Street Rhymes around the World*. Illus. by Jeanette Winter and 17 international artists. Wordsong/ Boyds Mills, 1992.

## Rhythmic Play

Some poems encourage kinetic activity, inviting children through rhythm and imagery to "act out" what they hear and see. Jean Marzollo's *Pretend You're a Cat* is a rhymed picture book text that asks children to pretend they are various animals and is accompanied by Jerry Pinkney's lively paintings of actual children who "pretended" for him. Eve Merriam's "On Our Way" and "I'm a Prickly Crab" echo this picture book as they invite children to walk like the animals. Another Merriam poem that can be acted out, "Will You?" combines the animals' actions with sounds they might make. This activity might even be paired with the animal-like yoga positions suggested for children in *Be a Frog, a Bird, or a Tree*. Irene Smalls-Hector's *Jonathan and His Mommy* invites children to take a walk with this pair as they hop, jump, and dance down the streets to the rhythmic text.

Like the jump rope rhymes listed above, some poems imitate the movements of actual play and games. Harry Behn's "Follow the Leader" is a chanted poem that demands movement. Lorinda Bryan Cauley's *Clap Your Hands* is a kind of follow-the-leader game for young children as a narrator chants the various actions in the lines of the poem and children join in. Some poems describe a rhythmic movement so effectively, we are moved to imitate it. When reading *Up and Down on the Merry-Go-Round*, by Bill

Martin, Jr., and John Archambault, children can become the animals on the merry-go-round and try to move together rhythmically. Eve Merriam's "Autumn Leaves" describes the actions of both leaves and those who play in them in a poem designed for movement. Other examples of rhythmic poems that invite motion are included in Chapter 8.

Behn, Harry. "Follow the Leader" in Hopkins, Lee Bennett. *Side by Side: Poems to Read Together.* Illus. by Hilary Knight. Simon, 1988.

Carr, Rachel. *Be a Frog, a Bird, or a Tree.* Illus. by Edward Kimball, Jr., and Don Hedin. Harper, 1973. (nonfiction)

Cauley, Lorinda Bryan. *Clap Your Hands.* Putnam, 1992.

Martin, Bill, Jr., and John Archambault. *Up and Down on the Merry-Go-Round.* Illus. by Ted Rand. Holt, 1988.

Marzollo, Jean. *Pretend You're a Cat.* Illus. by Jerry Pinkney. Dial, 1990.

Merriam, Eve. "Autumn Leaves" in *Jamboree.* Illus. by Walter Gaffney-Kessell. Dell, 1984.

———. "I'm a Prickly Crab" in *Blackberry Ink.* Illus. by Hans Wilhelm. Morrow, 1985.

———. "On Our Way" in De Regniers, Beatrice Schenk. *Sing a Song of Popcorn.* Scholastic, 1988.

———. "Will You?" in Hopkins, Lee Bennett. *Side by Side: Poems to Read Together.* Illus. by Hilary Knight. Simon, 1988.

Smalls-Hector, Irene. *Jonathan and His Mommy.* Illus. by Michael Hayes. Little, 1992.

## Sports

Sports are a popular subject of poetry and collections of sports poems may interest students who might not otherwise choose to read poetry. Sharon Bell Mathis' *Red Dog, Blue Fly* features poems about playing football from the point of view of young players. Lillian Morrison's *At the Crack of the Bat* contains poems about all aspects of baseball, including biographical poems and poems about famous games and plays. Her *Sprints and Distances* and Arnold Adoff's *Sports Pages* include poems about all sports.

Students may also enjoy searching through other collections for poems about a favorite sport. A short list of poems that could get a student started are included here. (The sport is listed in parentheses if the title is not clear.) Girls' opportunities for participation in sports are the subject of several poems. A list of these is included here as well.

### *Collections of Sports Poems*

Adoff, Arnold. *Sports Pages.* Illus. by Steve Kuzma. Lippincott/Harper, 1986.

Ferris, Helen, sel. "It's Fun to Play" section in *Favorite Poems Old and New.* Doubleday, 1957.

Mathis, Sharon Bell. *Red Dog, Blue Fly: Football Poems.* Viking, 1991.

Morrison, Lillian, sel. *At the Crack of the Bat: Baseball Poems*. Illus. by Steve Cieslawski. Hyperion, 1992.

————. *The Break Dance Kids: Poems of Sport, Motion, and Locomotion*. Lothrop, 1988.

————. *Sprints and Distances: Sports in Poetry and the Poetry in Sport*. Crowell/ Harper, 1990.

Prelutsky, Jack, sel. *Random House Book of Poetry for Children*. Random, 1983. (See subject index under "Games and Sports.")

## Sports Poems

Francis, Robert. "The Base Stealer" in Dunning, Stephen. *Reflections on a Gift of Watermelon Pickle*. Lothrop, 1966.

George, Kristine O'Connell. "Skating in the Wind" in Livingston, Myra Cohn. *Poems for Brothers, Poems for Sisters*. Holiday, 1991.

Giovanni, Nikki. "Basketball" in *Spin a Soft Black Song*. Illus. by George Martins. Hill, 1985.

Hoey, Edwin A. "Foul Shot" in Dunning, Stephen. *Reflections on a Gift of Watermelon Pickle*. Lothrop. 1966. (basketball)

Johnston, Tony. "Overdog" in *I'm Gonna Tell Mama I Want an Iguana*. Illus. by Lillian Hoban. Putnam, 1990. (baseball)

Livingston, Myra Cohn. "History" in Hopkins, Lee Bennett. *Morning, Noon, and Nighttime, Too*. Harper, 1980. (baseball)

———— "Skating Song" in *A Song I Sang to You*. Harcourt, 1984. (roller skating)

Mason, Walt. "Football" in Kennedy, X.J. *Knock at a Star*. Little, 1985.

Merriam, Eve. "Associations" in *The Singing Green*. Illus. by Kathleen Collins Howell. Morrow, 1992. (baseball)

————. "Ping-Pong" in *A Sky Full of Poems*. Illus. by Walter Gaffney-Kessell. Dell, 1986.

Owen, Gareth. "The Commentator" in Foster, John. *A Third Poetry Book*. Oxford, 1987. (soccer)

Prelutsky, Jack. "Stringbean Small" in *The New Kid on the Block*. Illus. by James Stevenson. Greenwillow, 1984. (basketball)

Souster, Raymond. "The Roundhouse" in Booth, David. *'Til All the Stars Have Fallen*. Viking, 1990. (baseball)

Swenson, May. "Analysis of Baseball" in Kennedy, X.J. *Knock at a Star*. Little, 1985.

Troupe, Quincy. "A Poem for Magic" in Slier, Deborah. *Make a Joyful Sound*. Checkerboard, 1991.

Whitman, Walt. "The Runner" in Kennedy, X.J. *Knock at a Star*. Little, 1985.

## Girls' Roles in Sports

Hopkins, Lee Bennett. "Girls Can, Too!" in *Morning, Noon, and Nighttime, Too*. Harper, 1980.

Jacobs, Leland B. "Queenie" in Prelutsky, Jack. *The Random House Book of Poetry for Children*. Random, 1983.

Joseph, Lynn. "All Star Boys" in *Coconut Kind of Day*. Illus. by Sandra Speidel. Lothrop, 1990.

Mathis, Sharon Bell. "Ebonee" in *Red Dog, Blue Fly: Football Poems*. Viking, 1992.

Prelutsky, Jack. "No Girls Allowed" in *The Random House Book of Poetry for Children*. Random, 1983.

## No Good at Sports

No matter how we try, some of us are not good at athletic pursuits. Arnold Adoff's poem, "The Coach Said," about a round stomach that keeps a child off of the basketball team and Jean Little's "Cartwheel" about a child's inability to do one, will appeal to non-athletes. Even children who like sports may not particularly like physical education classes. Kalli Dakos speaks to this in "I'm Going to Die."

Adoff, Arnold. "The Coach Said" in *Eats*. Illus. by Susan Russo. Lothrop, 1979.

Armour, Richard. "Good Sportsmanship" in Kennedy, X.J. *Knock at a Star*. Little, 1985.

Dakos, Kalli. "I'm Going to Die" in *If You're Not Here, Please Raise Your Hand*. Illus. by G. Brian Karas. Four Winds/Macmillan, 1990.

Little, Jean. "Cartwheels" in *Hey World, Here I Am!* Illus. by Sue Truesdell. Harper, 1989.

## Dance

Dance is a physical activity done both formally and informally in schools. It may be used in conjunction with music studies or with physical education. Lillian Morrison has written poems about break dancing and other informal dances in *The Break Dance Kids*. Other poets have looked at more formal dancing. Bill Martin, Jr., and John Archambault have written *Barn Dance!* which is full of the rhythms and sounds of square dances. Jane Yolen has written tongue-in-cheek poems for *Dinosaur Dances* in which she describes the types of formal dances dinosaurs might do. There are poems about dance in ethnic traditions such as Angela Shelf Medearis' picture book poem, *Dancing with the Indians*, about attending a Seminole dance in Oklahoma and Leah Komaiko's *Aunt Elaine Does the Dance from Spain*.

Some poems describe the kind of wonderful free-form dancing that some of us do to express ourselves. James Skofield's *Nightdances* describes a family who loves to go out into the night to celebrate with improvisational dancing. Claudia Lewis talks about dressing up in colored strips of cheesecloth, imagining herself as various characters and dancing, in "The Best Birthday Present: From My Mother." Children might want to create their own expressive dances in response to poems and music they enjoy.

Bryan, Ashley. "Taste the Air" in *Sing to the Sun*. Harper, 1992.

Craver, Mike. *Beaver Ball at the Bug Club*. Illus. by Joan Kaghan. Farrar, 1992.

Giovanni, Nikki. "Dance Poem" in *Spin a Soft Black Song*. Illus. by George Martins. Hills, 1985.

Greenfield, Eloise. "Buddy's Dream" in *Night on Neighborhood Street*. Illus. by Jan Spivery Gilchrist. Dial, 1991.

———. "Way Down in the Music" in *Honey, I Love*. Illus. by Leo and Diane Dillon. Crowell/Harper, 1978.

Hughes, Langston. "Song for a Banjo Dance" in Sullivan, Charles. *Children of Promise*. Abrams, 1989.

Jabar, Cynthia, sel. *Shimmy Shake Earthquake*. Joy Street/Little, 1992.

Komaiko, Leah. *Aunt Elaine Does the Dance from Spain*. Illus. by Petra Mathers. Doubleday, 1992.

Lewis, Claudia. "The Best Birthday Present: From Mother" in *Up in the Mountains*. Illus. by Joel Fontaine. Harper, 1991.

Martin, Bill, Jr., and John Archambault. *Barn Dance*. Illus. by Ted Rand. Holt, 1986.

Medearis, Angela Shelf. *Dancing with the Indians*. Illus. by Samuel Byrd. Holiday, 1991.

Morrison, Lillian. "The Break Dance Kids or No More Gang Wars" in *The Break Dance Kids*. Lothrop, 1985.

———. "The Twirl and the Swirl: Poems to Dance To" in *Rhythm Road*. Lothrop, 1988.

Sandburg, Carl. "From...Lines Written for Gene Kelly to Dance To" in Hopkins, Lee Bennett. *Rainbows Are Made*. Harcourt, 1982.

Skofield, James. *Nightdances*. Illus. by Karen Gundersheimer. Harper, 1981.

Turner, Ann. "Breakin'" in *Street Talk*. Houghton, 1986.

Williams, William Carlos. "The Artist" in Lueders, Edward. *Zero Makes Me Hungry*. Scott, Foresman, 1976.

Yolen, Jane. *Dinosaur Dances*. Illus. by Bruce Degen. Putnam, 1990.

# HEALTH

The study of the human body takes place in science and health lessons throughout the elementary school years. Various poetry activities can be done in conjunction with this unit. A great number of poems describe the attributes of the human body, from simple poems for young children such as the classic "Hands, Hands, Fingers, Toes," to poems that encourage children to think about the systems of their bodies and how they work.

Many phrases in our language use parts of the body in interesting ways. A person may need, for example, "elbow room" or "breathing space." A person may act "nosy" or "footloose." A person may "lend an ear," or "lend a hand," or be unable "to stomach" something. A full-size chart of the human body used in anatomy classes or a photograph or drawing of a person blown up to poster size and laminated can be used to share group knowledge of these "body parts" of our language. As these and other idioms are brainstormed, they can be added to the "person" poster. The poster can be left up for a period of time so that children can add to it as they think of more "body language." Students can also name articles of clothing that include parts of the body in their names such as earmuffs and elbow patches. Both of these activities may lead students to do some language research on the origins of these expressions. Our language often reflects the fact that we see the world in human terms and these activities with body and clothing words help students see this connection more clearly.

Sometimes we need a little help from poetry when we study body parts. Students might ask parents, older brothers and sisters, or teachers who have taken anatomy courses to share the mnemonic devices they used to memorize the bones and muscles of the body. Many times these lists are rhythmic, rhymed, or topical so that they are easier to remember, and they constitute a kind of changing folk poetry of the classroom. Children might then want to make up their own mnemonics as they study bones and muscles.

Sometimes a particular part of the body gets enough attention that a mini-unit can be developed around it. Two stories, *Johnny Longnose* and *The Nose Tree*, feature characters whose noses grow in a manner reminiscent of Pinocchio. Ian Chrichton Smith has told another nose story in his poem "The Nose," and Jack Prelutsky has written a humorous poem, "Be Glad Your Nose Is on Your Face," as has Colin West in "Norman Norton's Nostrils." Students might compile collections of "nose facts" along with stories and poems for this unit. Poems, stories, and facts can also be easily collected on the eyes, hands, and feet. Michael Rosen's *Freckly Feet and Itchy Knees* is an extended poem on body parts. The other poems listed here are about individual body parts. When the subject of the poem is not clear, it is listed in parentheses.

Adoff, Arnold. "These Knees" in *Sports Pages*. Illus. by Steve Kuzma. Harper, 1986.

Burgess, Gelett. "On Digital Extremities" in Ferris, Helen. *Favorite Poems Old and New*. Doubleday, 1957.

Chandra, Deborah. "Skeleton" and "Tent" (skin) in *Balloons*. Illus. by Leslie Bowman. Farrar, 1990.

Ciardi, John. "Someone's Face" in Prelutsky, Jack. *Read-Aloud Rhymes for the Very Young*. Knopf, 1986.

Dacey, Phillip. "Thumb" in Kennedy, X.J. *Knock at a Star*. Little, 1985.

Dakos, Kalli. "Is Your Head on Nice and Tight?" in *If You're Not Here, Please Raise Your Hand*. Illus. by G. Brian Karas. Four Winds/Macmillan, 1990. (whole body)

Fisher, Aileen. "But Then" in *Always Wondering*. Illus. by Joan Sandin. Harper, 1991. (teeth)

"The Hairy Toe" in Harrison, Michael. *The Oxford Book of Story Poems*. Oxford, 1990.

Hutton, Warwick. *The Nose Tree*. Atheneum, 1981. (traditional)

Hymes, Lucia, and James L. Hymes. "Ears Hear" in Prelutsky, Jack. *Read Aloud Rhymes for the Very Young*. Knopf, 1986.

Kruss, James, and Naomi Lewis. *Johnny Longnose*. Illus. by Stasys Eidrigevicius. North-South, 1990.

Kuskin, Karla. "Me" in *Dogs and Dragons, Trees and Dreams*. Harper, 1980.

———. *Soap Soup and Other Verses*. Harper, 1992.

Merriam, Eve. "Thumbprint" in *A Sky Full of Poems*. Illus. by Walter Gaffney-Kessell, Dell, 1986.

———. "Xylophone" in *Halloween ABC*. Illus. by Lane Smith. Macmillan, 1987. (bones)

Moore, Lilian. "Sometimes" in Hopkins, Lee Bennett. *Morning, Noon, and Nighttime, Too*. Harper, 1980. (heart)

O'Neill, Mary. "My Fingers" in Kennedy, X.J. *Knock at a Star*. Little, 1985.

Prelutsky, Jack. "Be Glad Your Nose Is on Your Face" in *The New Kid on the Block*. Illus. by James Stevenson. Greenwillow, 1984.

———. "Dance of the Thirteen Skeletons" in *Nightmares*. Illus. by Arnold Lobel. Greenwillow, 1976.

Rosen, Michael. *Freckly Feet and Itchy Knees*. Illus. by Sami Sweeten. Doubleday, 1990.

Sandburg, Carl. "Phizzog" (face) and "Choose" (hands) in Hopkins, Lee Bennett. *Rainbows Are Made*. Harcourt, 1982.

Silverstein, Shel. "Senses" in *A Light in the Attic*. Harper, 1981.

Smith, Ian Crichton. "The Nose" in Harrison, Michael. *Oxford Book of Story Poems*. Oxford, 1990.

Ulrich, George. "Say Cheese, Please" in *The Spook Matinee*. Delacorte, 1992. (skull)

West, Colin. "Norman Norton's Nostrils" in Prelutsky, Jack. *For Laughing Out Loud*. Knopf, 1991.

## ILLNESS

Sometimes poets describe children's feelings about illness, although few have written about the lives and feelings of very sick children. Some of these children have described their own lives eloquently in two nonfiction works, Jill Krementz' *How It Feels to Fight for Your Life* and Erma Bombeck's *"I Want to Grow Hair, I Want to Grow Up, I Want to Go to Boise": Children Surviving Cancer*. Poets have described children's illnesses in a more lighthearted manner. Shel Silverstein's classic "Sick," in which the child narrator feels terrible and gives a long list of ailments and woes until discovering that it is Saturday, is typical of this type of poem. Judith Viorst's "Oh, Wow! Book" suggests that when you are sick the best thing for you is a great book. Many classic poems have been written about being ill, including Robert Louis Stevenson's "Land of Counterpane" and A.A. Milne's "Sneezles." Poems such as Silverstein's that show children feigning illness to avoid problems at school are very popular and may provide interesting fodder for discussion.

More serious poems often deal with a child's reaction to the illness of another. Myra Cohn Livingston's "Olive Street" tells of a child's memories of happier times before a father became ill and in "Aunt Ruth" she tells the story of an aunt who has been ill all of her life. Gwendolyn Brooks' Jim, in "Jim," gives up his beloved baseball to take care of his sick mother.

Bombeck, Erma. *"I Want to Grow Hair, I Want to Grow Up, I Want to Go to Boise":
Children Surviving Cancer.* Harper, 1989. (nonfiction)

Brooks, Gwendolyn. "Charles" and "Jim" in *Bronzeville Boys and Girls.* Illus. by
Ronni Solbert. Harper, 1967.

De la Mare, Walter. "Bones" in Dunning, Stephen. *Reflections on a Gift of Watermelon
Pickle.* Lothrop, 1966.

Hoban, Russell. "Sick in Winter" in *Egg Thoughts and Other Frances Songs.* Illus. by
Lillian Hoban. Harper, 1972.

Hoberman, Mary Ann. "Sick Days" in *Fathers, Mothers, Sisters, Brothers.* Illus. by
Marylin Hafner. Little, 1991.

Hughes, Shirley. "Sick" in *Out and About.* Lothrop, 1988.

Kennedy, X.J. "Sister Has a Blister" in Livingston, Myra Cohn. *Poems for Brothers,
Poems for Sisters.* Holiday, 1991.

Krementz, Jill. *How It Feels to Fight for Your Life.* Joy Street/Little, 1989. (nonfiction)

Kumin, Maxine. "Sneeze" in Prelutsky, Jack. *Read Aloud Rhymes for the Very Young.*
Knopf, 1986.

Livingston, Myra Cohn. "Aunt Ruth" in *Worlds I Know and Other Poems.* Illus. by Tim
Arnold. M.K. McElderry/Macmillan, 1985.

————. "Olive Street" in *There Was a Place and Other Poems.* M.K. McElderry/
Macmillan, 1988.

McCord, David. "The Doctor" and "Tooth Trouble" in *One at a Time.* Little, 1986.

Margolis, Richard. "Soups and Juices" in Livingston, Myra Cohn. *Poems for Brothers,
Poems for Sisters.* Holiday, 1991.

Merriam, Eve. "Bella Had a New Umbrella" in *Blackberry Ink.* Illus. by Hans
Wilhelm. Morrow, 1985.

Milne, A.A. "Sneezles" in *Now We Are Six.* Illus. by Ernest H. Shepard. Dutton, 1988.

Prelutsky, Jack. "I've Got an Incredible Headache" in *The New Kid on the Block.* Illus.
by James Stevenson. Greenwillow, 1984.

Reader, Willie. "When Paul Bunyan Was Ill" in Kennedy, X.J. *Knock at a Star.* Little,
1985.

Silverstein, Shel. "Sick" in *Where the Sidewalk Ends.* Harper, 1974.

Smaridge, Norah. "Fair Warning" in Hopkins, Lee Bennett. *The Sky Is Full of Song.*
Harper, 1983.

Starbird, Kaye. "Measles" in Prelutsky, Jack. *The Random House Book of Poetry for
Children.* Random, 1983.

Stevenson, Robert Louis. "The Land of Counterpane" in *A Child's Garden of Verses.*
Illus. by Michael Foreman. Delacorte, 1985.

Viorst, Judith. "My Oh-Wow!-Book" in *If I Were in Charge of the World and Other
Worries.* Illus. by Lynn Cherry. Atheneum/Macmillan, 1981.

West, Colin. *The King's Toothache.* Illus. by Anne Dalton. Lippincott/Harper, 1988.

Westcott, Nadine Bernard. *The Lady with the Alligator Purse.* Joy Street/Little, 1988.

Because art, music, physical education, and health encourage self-expression in various ways they have strong ties to poetry. The poet tries to express a feeling, thought, or idea using words, rhythms, sounds, and images. The dancer, artist, or athlete expresses these feelings and thoughts in different ways. When poetry, the arts, physical education, and health are linked we can highlight students' strengths and help them see the range of ways we communicate.

## REFERENCES

Elleman, B. (1992)."Colors." *Booklinks* 1 (July): 31–34.

Grossman, F. (1982). "Lists." *Getting from Here to There*. Montclair, NJ: Boynton/ Cook, 7–9.

"Music Web" *The Web* 8 (Spring 1984): 14–18.

Wiseman, C. (1992). "Singing the book." *Booklinks* 1 (March): 56–59.

# Chapter 8:
# Sharing Poetry

Sharing a poem is powerful. When we read a poem that moves us or makes us laugh it is natural to want to share that experience with others. You may know children who have fallen in love with a poem and read or recited it to anyone who would listen. You may know a teacher or librarian who can provide a line of poetry or a line from a song that fits the mood on any given occasion. We need to create an environment in schools that encourages children to share poetry. We can begin by sharing poetry frequently ourselves and by encouraging others to share poems they like. We might invite parents, community leaders, and poetry lovers into our classrooms and libraries to share poems with us.

We might listen to poets read their own poems aloud. Some poets talk about their poems, how they write them, and then read their poetry in a matter-of-fact way that allows us to know their poems, as Karla Kuskin does in *Poetry Explained*. Some poets share their reverence for their subject as they read, as Byrd Baylor does in readings from her works. Some poets take on the voice of a child and present their poems dramatically as Jack Prelutsky does when he reads from *The New Kid on the Block*. These poets help us see that there is no one right way to read or present a poem. Audiovisual materials that feature poets reading from their own works are included in the list of biographical materials at the end of this chapter.

How do you prepare to share a poem? First, choose a poem that has affected you in some way. You want to convey that experience of the poem to your listeners. Read the poem over several times. As you read, think about what the poet is trying to say. What words help convey that meaning? Are there sounds that help you hear the images of the poem? Does the rhythm of the poem convey its meaning? How could you use pauses and accent various words or syllables to convey that meaning?

A common error students make in reading poetry aloud is to fall into a kind of sing-song rhythm with alternating beats accented and a hard stop at the end of each line so that every poem sounds the same. The presenter's job is to help convey the poet's meaning. It is probably better to err on the side of not breaking lines when a full thought takes several lines if the meaning is clearer in this way. But take time to think about those breaks. Why did the poet break the line in a certain place? Should there be a brief pause or none at all? Dramatic presentations reveal the richness of poems by highlighting the sounds, rhythms, and images used by the poet. We need time to read and reflect on poems in order to plan the most effective way of presenting them to others.

In any kind of dramatic presentation you rely on vocal qualities and sometimes even physical gestures to help convey meaning. Perhaps a poem requires a quiet voice. Charlotte Pomerantz has written a lullaby poem that suggests a quiet presentation, titled "A Little Lullaby to Be Read a Little Bit Out Loud." Sometimes they call for voices to be louder and then softer in response to the emotion of the poem, such as A.A. Milne's "Disobedience," which instructs the reader in parentheses: "(Now then, very softly)." Other poems, often those that express anger or frustration, require a loud voice. Perhaps the poem requires hurried speech. One of my favorite poems to share by speaking quickly is Judith Viorst's "Talking," in which the narrator shows through a long list of strange items how easy it is to talk too much. A poem such as Carmen Bernos de Gasztold's "Prayer of the Tortoise" can be read slowly. Sometimes we change the pace of the poem to reflect changing action or emotion. The "References" section at the end of this chapter lists additional materials for helping us to share poetry.

## PANTOMIME

Pantomime is one way to dramatically present a poem using body language. A narrator reads the poem as one, several, or a whole class of children silently act out the motions and emotions. Children respond easily with gestures when the narration of a poem calls for them, acting out movements and rhythms for action-oriented nursery rhymes such as "The Grand Old Duke of York," "Pat-a-cake, Pat-a-cake," or clapping games. Pantomime is effective with poems that show action and movement. Poems about sports, walking, running, the movements of animals, parades, and marching all lend themselves to pantomime. Sharon Bell Mathis' "Touchdown," which describes a series of motions involved in making a winning football play, for example, could be pantomimed effectively. The words and rhythms of the picture book *Thump, Thump, Rat-A-Tat-Tat* so clearly evoke a marching band as it approaches and then moves away from parade watchers that children might want to try to pantomime these movements. Other actions such as rolling and tumbling, somersaults, swinging, searching for something, or hiding from something can be pantomimed success-fully. Younger children delight in actually acting out the movements of the classic song-rhyme *Roll Over.*

Some poems pantomime a small movement or gesture and are fun to do as a kind of interlude in class activities or between poems. John Ciardi's "Read This with Gestures" describes so perfectly the infectious movement of reaching for a handful of snow, creating a snowball, and throwing it that the pantomime comes almost automatically. Eve Merriam's "Uncle Dick," a brief poem in which Uncle Dick leaps up and clicks his heels, is another mini-pantomime. William Cole's brief "It's Such a Shock I Almost Screech" about finding a worm in his peach also would make a brief pantomime can also be performed this way.

Other poems require more complex pantomime movements. John Ciardi's "How I Helped the Traveler" is a poem about giving directions that turn out to be unclear. Students might enjoy trying to create pointing motions that add to the confusion in this poem. Constance Levy's "Out" is filled with the motions of going in and out, which are popular in jump rope rhymes and would involve creative jumping movements. In "All the Colors of the Race," Arnold Adoff uses lines and circles along with several other motions to represent togetherness with each other and our past. These could be pantomimed to convey his quiet message. His "I Know the Rules" includes references to faces and hands that seem designed for simple pantomime. Other poems describing body movements and activities in sports are included in Chapter 7.

Creating pantomimes to show emotions requires more practice than do those that show physical movements. It is easy to fall into the trap of using one sad or glad expression for an entire poem. The best emotional poems to use with pantomime are those showing increasing emotion as the poem goes on or showing changes in feelings, because these can be conveyed with body movement changes instead of relying on facial expression. Karla Kuskin's "I Woke Up This Morning" shows this development of emotion effectively. Children can use increasingly large physical gestures to show the growing anger of the child narrator.

Adoff, Arnold. "All the Colors of the Race" and "I Know the Rules" in *All the Colors of the Race*. Illus. by John Steptoe. Lothrop, 1982.

Baer, Gene. *Thump, Thump, Rat-A-Tat-Tat.* Harper, 1989.

Ciardi, John. "How I Helped the Traveler" in *Doodle Soup*. Illus. by Marle Nacht. Houghton, 1985.

———. "Read This with Gestures" in *Fast and Slow*. Houghton, 1978.

Cole, William. "It's Such a Shock I Almost Screech" in *Poem Stew*. Lippincott, 1981.

De Gasztold, Carmen Bernos. "Prayer of the Tortoise" in *Prayers from the Ark*. French and European, n.d.

Kuskin, Karla. "I Woke Up This Morning" in *Dogs and Dragons, Trees and Dreams*. Harper, 1980.

Levy, Constance. "Out" in *I'm Going to Pet a Worm Today*. Illus. by Ronald Himler. M.K. McElderry/Macmillan, 1991.

Mathis, Sharon Bell. "Touchdown" in *Red Dog, Blue Fly: Football Poems*. Viking, 1991.

Merriam, Eve. "Uncle Dick" in *A Poem for a Pickle*. Illus. by Sheila Hamanaka. Morrow, 1989.

Milne, A.A. "Disobedience" in *When We Were Very Young*. Illus. by Ernest H. Shepard. Dutton, 1988.

Pomerantz, Charlotte. "A Little Lullaby to Be Read a Little Bit Out Loud" in *The Tamarindo Puppy*. Illus. by Brian Barton. Greenwillow, 1980.

*Roll Over! A Counting Song*. Illus. by Merle Peek. Crown, 1988.

*Ten in a Bed*. Illus. by Mary Rees. Joy Street/Little, 1988.

Viorst, Judith. "Talking," in *If I Were in Charge of the World and Other Worries*. Illus. by Lynn Cherry. Atheneum/Macmillan, 1984.

# CHORAL READING AND SPEAKING

Shared choral reading and speaking are effective ways to bring creative dramatics into the classroom. In choral reading, a reading "choir" performs a poem. Choral reading requires enough practice so that students can share a poem in unison and pay attention to sound and rhythm. Choral speaking is a memorized presentation of a poem. The transition from choral reading to choral speaking often happens naturally and inevitably in the process of working on a poem for presentation. Young children will pick up verses and refrains quickly and begin to recite action songs and rhymes after only one or two readings. In the course of practicing for presentation, older children frequently commit poems to memory as well. Generally, those of us who do not care to memorize poems were forced to present poems of someone else's choosing. When students are allowed to select the poem they present to others, they are more likely to want to commit the poem to memory, and their presentation is likely to be of better quality.

Choral reading or speaking can take many forms. One person may read a poem or a group may read a poem in unison. Sometimes choral reading is antiphonal, using two voices or two groups who read various parts of the poem as a conversation. Some poems lend themselves to a cumulative presentation in which more and more voices are added until there is a dramatically loud climax. Within the choral presentation, certain parts may be picked out for a solo or small group reading. Some groups like to try to "read-around," where each child reads one line of a poem.

## Monologues and Dialogues

Poems written in the first person seem designed to be monologues, presented by a single powerful voice. Sometimes the poem is a demanding question, such as "Who shrank my grandmother's house?" in "The Visit" by Barbara Juster Esbensen. Sometimes the poem is a sad moment, such as Myra Cohn Livingston's "Grandfather I Never Knew." These first person poems can be effectively presented as a monologue. Many times the emotions of the speaker in the poem are so genuinely felt by a group of children that they can perform these first person monologues as a team. Beatrice Schenk de Regniers" "Mean Song," in which the single narrator uses many mean words and sound effects can be dramatically presented as a monologue or using several voices.

Dialogues are also an effective way to dramatically present poetry. Dialogues can consist of two voices or two sets of voices. Paul Fleischman's two books of poetry, *I Am Phoenix: Poems for Two Voices* and *Joyful Noise: Poems for Two Voices* were created for dialogue presentations. In some of these poems the two voices give different points of view. Many poems are written as a dialogue between two people or a person and a thing. Some poems are written as questions and answers, some are conversations, and some provide echoes. In some of the poems in Paul Fleischman's collections the two voices create a rhythm or call-and-response. Poems in which part of the poem appears in italics seem designed for this kind of presentation. In David McCord's simple poem "Jamboree," one voice asks question's such as "A rhyme for ham?" and the other gives brief answers such as "Jam." Eve Merriam's "Hurry" uses a voice like a conscience speaking in the background. Ashley Bryan, who has encouraged so many students and teachers to try poetry through his use of call-and-response, includes "Granny" in his own collection of poems, a poem that particularly invites this type of shared reading.

Sometimes poems lend themselves to two voices because of their structure. Charlotte Zolotow's rhymed picture book, *Some Things Go Together*, describes pairs of things that naturally go together and seems designed to be presented by two voices. In Arnold Adoff's "A Song," two sisters talk about their sisterhood. In this poem for two voices, the voices are not antiphonal but in harmony with one another. Poems for dialogue presentations are discussed more fully in "Conversations" in Chapter 1.

Adoff, Arnold. "A Song" in *All the Colors of the Race.* Illus. by John Steptoe. Lothrop, 1982.

Bryan, Ashley. "Granny" in *Sing to the Sun.* Harper, 1992.

De Regniers, Beatrice Schenk. "Mean Song" in *The Way I Feel...Sometimes.* Illus. by Susan Meddaugh. Clarion/Ticknor and Fields, 1980.

Esbensen, Barbara Juster. "The Visit" in *Who Shrank My Grandmother's House?* Illus. by Eric Beddows. Harper, 1992.

Fleischman, Paul. *I Am Phoenix.* Illus. by Ken Nutt. Harper, 1985.

———. *Joyful Noise: Poems for Two Voices.* Illus. by Eric Beddows. Harper, 1988.

Livingston, Myra Cohn. "The Grandfather I Never Knew" in *Worlds I Know and Other Poems*. Illus. by Tim Arnold. M.K. McElderry/Macmillan, 1985.

McCord, David. "Glowworm" in *All Small*. Illus. by Madelaine Gill Linden. Little, 1986.

———. "Jamboree" in *One at a Time*. Little, 1986.

Merriam, Eve. "Hurry" in *The Singing Green*. Illus. by Kathleen Collins Howell. Morrow, 1992.

———. "Notice to Myself" in *Fresh Paint*. Illus. by David Frampton. Macmillan, 1986.

Zolotow, Charlotte. *Some Things Go Together*. Illus. by Karen Gundersheimer. Crowell/Harper, 1983.

## Other Styles of Presentation

Other poems lend themselves to other dramatic styles. Sometimes three voices seem appropriate. In Eve Merriam's "1,2,3," she uses three repetitions of the last word of each line, each of which could be repeated by a separate voice. Other poems may use three verses or three points of view, each of which can be presented by a different speaker. Several poems have four characters and might be presented by four voices. A.A. Milne's "The Four Friends" about four animals of various sizes might be presented by four people, each of whom can use a voice appropriate to the size of their animal. Jack Prelutsky's "Four Vain and Ancient Tortoises" uses dialogue and could be performed in a similar way.

Sometimes poems are intended to be presented by a mixture of solo and choral voices. James Reeves' "Ceremonial Band" includes a note at the top: "To be said out loud by a chorus and solo voices." Sometimes many voices are used but occasionally there is a single clear voice to add power to the words. In Eve Merriam's "Cheers" a first person narrator sets the scene for the football cheers that follow with two lines of explanation. A single voice could read these lines then a group of voices could join in her nonsense cheers. David McCord includes another cheerleader's yell, "Bananas and Cream," which could be presented with a variety of single and group voices sharing the lines. Mary Ann Hoberman's "Splendid Lion" includes one word in each stanza printed in all capital letters, which can be shouted by lots of children while only one or a few voices read the rest of the lines. Sometimes various voices read parts of the poem but all chime in on a chorus or a final line for emphasis. Mary Ann Hoberman's "What Is a Family?" includes a chorus that could be for many voices and her "Fine Fat Pig" has a chorus that younger children would enjoy. Jack Prelutsky's "Dance of the Thirteen Skeletons" has a lengthy chorus that would appeal to older students who want to try a variety of voices in their reading.

Some poems seem to be most effectively presented cumulatively, that is, with an increasing number of voices or a decreasing number of voices as the poem progresses. Counting out rhymes can be presented cumulatively with more voices chiming in as the numbers get larger. Children might also try presenting Molly Bang's *Ten, Nine, Eight* with the number of voices decreasing and becoming softer as the numbers descend to the final "one." Another "bedtime story" poem, Deborah Chandra's "Snowfall," also moves toward this quiet closing. Some poems such as Betsy Lewin's picture book with rhymed text, *Cat Count*, involve not just counting but addition. More voices and louder voices could reinforce the addition of cats in this rhyme. Cumulative stories in verse also work well with this kind of presentation.

Cumulative stories make effective read-around presentations, with each student taking a line. Popular cumulative rhymes such as *I Know an Old Lady Who Swallowed a Fly* can be presented as read-arounds in which each student speaks one part and the climax is shared by all voices. Alphabet books and poems can also be presented effectively in this manner. Jim Aylesworth's *Old Black Fly*, an alphabet book with a chorus, encourages single parts in read-around with a chorus of voices on "Shoo Fly! Shoo Fly! Shooo." Nancy Van Laan's rhythmic picture book rhyme, *Possum Come a Knockin'*, has many small spoken parts that could be performed by various characters. Litany or list poems also work well for read-around presentations. Karla Kuskin's "Spring," for example, is filled with the joyous movements and activities to welcome spring. Each of these lines can be read by a different voice with all chiming in on the final "And welcoming spring!" Litany and list poems are included in Chapter 5.

Aylesworth, Jim. *One Black Fly*. Illus. by Stephen Gammell. Holt, 1992.

Bang, Molly. *Ten, Nine, Eight*. Greenwillow, 1983.

Chandra, Deborah. "Snowfall" in *Balloons*. Illus. by Leslie Bowman. Farrar, 1990.

Hoberman, Mary Ann. "A Fine Fat Pig" and "The Splendid Lion" in *A Fine Fat Pig*. Illus. by Malcah Zeldis. Harper, 1991.

———. "What Is a Family?" in *Fathers, Mothers, Sisters, Brothers*. Illus. by Marylin Hafner. Little, 1991.

*I Know an Old Lady Who Swallowed a Fly*. Illus. by Glen Rounds. Holiday, 1991.

Kuskin, Karla. "Spring!" in *Dogs and Dragons, Trees and Dreams*. Harper, 1980.

Lewin, Betsy. *Cat Count*. Putnam, 1981.

McCord, David. "Bananas and Cream" in *One at a Time*. Little, 1986.

Merriam, Eve. "Cheers" in *The Singing Green*. Illus. by Kathleen Collins Howell. Morrow, 1992.

———. "1,2,3" in *A Poem for a Pickle*. Illus. by Sheila Hamanaka. Morrow, 1989.

Milne, A.A. "The Four Friends" in *When We Were Very Young*. Illus. by Ernest H. Shepard. Dutton, 1988.

Prelutsky, Jack. "Dance of the Thirteen Skeletons" in *Nightmares*. Illus. by Arnold Lobel, Greenwillow, 1976.

————. "Four Vain and Ancient Tortoises" in *Something Big Has Been Here*. Illus. by James Stevenson. Greenwillow, 1990.

Reeves, James. "The Ceremonial Band" in Corrin, Sara. *Once Upon a Rhyme*. Faber, 1982.

Van Laan, Nancy. *Possum Come a Knockin'*. Illus. by George Booth. Knopf, 1990.

## Rhythm and Sound

Rhythm and sound are two elements of poetry that can be highlighted in dramatic presentations of poems. Rhythmic poems can be presented with dramatic gestures and backed by rhythm instruments. Examples of poems that can be used for rhythmic presentations are included in the section on pantomime in this chapter and in Chapter 7.

One way to highlight the rhythms and sounds of poetry is to use musical sound effects in poetry presentations. Background music, bells, drums, vocal sound effects, clapping, and rhythm instruments such as triangles, rattles, and sandpaper sticks can be used to accentuate the beat in a rhythmic poem. Students might want to try using spoons to capture the clicking sounds of skeleton bones in Jack Prelutsky's "Dance of the Thirteen Skeletons" or the "bones" that Nathaniel's grandmother plays in "Grandma's Bones." Sound effects can be combined with pantomime, dialogue, and choral reading of poems.

Music enhances not only the rhythmic qualities of poems, but also the sounds they use and the images they present. Children might want to listen for the perfect piece of music to play while a poem is being presented dramatically. Some poets actually describe or refer to a type of music, as Eloise Greenfield does in "My Daddy" and Geoffrey Summerfield does in "Tap-Dancing." Some poets write about a musician, as Chris Raschka does in *Charlie Parker Played Be Bop,* and students might listen to Charlie Parker's recordings for a piece of music that they feel enhances this poem picture book. Other poems may be about a certain place and music from that place can be played as the poem is shared. A reading of Leah Komaiko's *Aunt Elaine Does The Dance from Spain* can be accompanied by castanets and Spanish guitar music. Some may be accompanied by music composed on the same subject. Parts of Vivaldi's *Four Seasons* might be used with the season poems in Jane Yolen's *Ring of Earth* or other poems about the seasons. Music teachers might help students find the perfect piece of music even for some difficult poems. For example, what music might capture the mood of "Dance of the Mushrooms" by J. Patrick Lewis?

Sound effects can be highlighted by music and musical instruments and also by the voice. Some poets combine rhythmic and sound effects, as David

McCord does in his classics "The Pickety Fence" and "Song of the Train," both of which use repetition of sounds. Some poems use particular sound qualities that children can feature in dramatic presentation. Everyone loves to try tongue twisters. Alliterative poems, like tongue twisters, must be well practiced to be shared effectively. Karla Kuskin's "Thistles," for example, contains wonderful descriptions, but "thirty thirsty thistles" takes practice to present without mistakes. A list of alliterative or tongue-twisting poems is included in Chapter 5.

Children will also enjoy presenting poems that use onomatopoeia. Deborah Chandra's "Fireworks" and Zaro Weil's "Mud" are examples of poems filled with great, impressive words to pronounce and share. Jack Prelutsky's "Bullfrogs," which contains words that sound as if a bullfrog would say them, can be presented dramatically. Jeanne Steig's collection of poems, *Alpha Beta Chowder*, is full of poems about particular people. The onomatopoetic words used in each poem help the listener to imagine what the person is like and a dramatic presentation would highlight these words.

Chants can highlight the repetitive sound qualities of many poems. Eve Merriam's "Grump," a poem filled with "grumps," is a fine one for group chanting. Other poems, such as David McCord's "Bananas and Cream" and Eve Merriam's "Cheers," are designed to sound like football yells and can be presented as chants. Sometimes a poem might benefit from actual sound effects, such as animal sounds or the sound of an automobile horn in Eve Merriam's "The Stuck Horn."

Choral reading or speaking, when done effectively, highlights the beauty of language. Presentations of poems in the languages spoken by children in the classroom can help all students to recognize the beauty of language and to honor the traditions of all students. Some books and spoken-language recordings provide poems in other languages. *Where I Come From! Songs and Poems from Many Cultures* is a collection on cassette tape of songs and poems presented in thirteen different languages. Some provide bilingual presentations of materials ready for presentation. Students can also share poems from their own backgrounds, perhaps providing their own poetic translations of them. Students might translate a favorite English-language poem into another language to share. When these poems are presented chorally by small groups or whole classes, children get the chance to experience speaking the sounds and rhythms of several languages.

Eve Merriam's "Conversation" includes four participants speaking Spanish, French, Italian, and English. Students could add more lines to the poem by including the simple phrases for "Good morning," "Good night," and "See you later" in other languages they know, or they could add verses to the poem by including more phrases from each of these and other languages. Students might want to create a circle of languages in classrooms with children from many language backgrounds. Names of animals, objects, verbs, simple phrases, and even the sounds animals make in different languages can be shared around the circle. Some poems in other languages or with words in other languages are listed in Chapter 5.

Chandra, Deborah. "Fireworks" in *Balloons*. Illus. by Leslie Bowman. Farrar, 1990.
Greenfield, Eloise. "Grandma's Bones" and "My Daddy" in *Nathaniel Talking*. Illus. by Jan Spivey Gilchrist. Black Butterfly/Writers and Readers, 1988.
Komaiko, Leah. *Aunt Elaine Does the Dance from Spain*. Illus. by Petra Mathers. Doubleday/Delacorte, 1992.
Kuskin, Karla. "Thistles" in *Dogs and Dragons, Trees and Dreams*. Harper, 1980.
Lewis, J. Patrick. "Dance of the Mushrooms" in *Earth Verses and Water Rhymes*. Illus. by Robert Sabuda. Atheneum/Macmillan, 1991.
McCord, David. "Bananas and Cream," "Pickety Fence," and "Song of the Train" in *One at a Time*. Little, 1986.
Merriam, Eve. "Cheers," "Grump," and "The Stuck Horn" in *The Singing Green*. Illus. by Kathleen Collins Howell. Morrow, 1992.
———. "Conversation" in *Jamboree*. Illus. by Walter Gaffney-Kessell. Dell, 1984.
Prelutsky, Jack. "Bullfrogs" in *Ride a Purple Pelican*. Illus. by Garth Williams. Greenwillow, 1986.
———. "Dance of the Thirteen Skeletons" in *Nightmares*. Illus. by Arnold Lobel. Greenwillow, 1976.
Raschka, Chris. *Charlie Parker Played Be Bop*. Orchard, 1992.
Steig, Jeanne. *Alpha, Beta, Chowder*. Illus. by William Steig. Harper, 1992.
Summerfield, Geoffrey. "Tap-Dancing" in Jabar, Cynthia. *Shimmy Shake Earthquake*. Joy Street/Little, 1992.
Weil, Zaro. "Mud" in *Mud, Moon, and Me*. Illus. by Jo Burroughs. Houghton, 1992.
Yolen, Jane. *Ring of Earth: A Child's Book of Seasons*. Illus. by John Wallner. Harcourt, 1986.

## GETTING TO KNOW THE POETS

Many poets have written about or been interviewed about their poetry. Some poets have written short autobiographical pieces to accompany their poems and show where they get ideas, how they write, and why they write poetry.

Some of these writings appear in the poets' own works. Karla Kuskin, for example, has included comments on why she has written her poetry along with each poem in *Near the Window Tree* and *Dogs and Dragons, Trees and Dreams*. Gary Soto includes comments on his writings in *A Fire in My Hands*. Paul Janeczko interviewed a number of contemporary poets and included these interviews with a selection of each poet's work in *The Place My Words Are Looking For*. Eve Merriam includes an essay, "Writing a

Poem," on her writing and revision process for the poem "Landscape" in *A Sky Full of Poems*.

Some poets have been interviewed about why they write poetry and what they write about. Some of these interviews appear in professional journals such as *Language Arts*. Others of these interviews have appeared on audio or videotapes for children. Some poets have been taped or filmed performing their own works so that students can hear them reading.

Barbara Kiefer has edited a collection of profiles of children's authors that has appeared in *Language Arts*. This collection, titled *Getting to Know You*, includes biographies of Lillian Moore, Alvin Schwartz, Arnold Lobel, and Byrd Baylor. Some better-known poets are the subject of full-length or picture book biographies for children.

Barth, Edna. *I'm Nobody! Who Are You? The Story of Emily Dickinson*. Illus. by Richard Cuffari. Seabury Press, 1971.

Baylor, Byrd. *I'm in Charge of Celebrations*. Cheshire Book Companions, n.d. (video cassette)

Bedard, Michael. *Emily*. Illus. by Barbara Cooney. Doubleday, 1992.

Bober, Natalie S. *A Restless Spirit: The Story of Robert Frost*. Rev. and expanded version. Holt, 1991.

*Charlotte Zolotow: The Grower*. American School Publishers/Macmillan/McGraw Hill, n.d. (sound filmstrip)

Ciardi, John. *You Read to Me, I'll Read to You*. Spoken Arts, n.d. (sound cassette)

"A Conversation with Mary Ann Hoberman." *The Web* 4 (Fall, 1979): 26–28.

Giovanni, Nikki. *The Reason I Like Chocolate and Other Children's Poems*. Smithsonian/ Folkways, n.d. (sound cassette)

*Good Conversation! A Talk with Karla Kuskin*. Podell, 1991 (video cassette)

*Good Conversation! A Talk with Lee Bennett Hopkins*. Podell, 1991. (video cassette)

*Good Conversation! A Talk with Nancy Willard*. Podell, 1991. (video cassette)

Hughes, Langston. *Dream Keeper and Other Poems of Langston Hughes*. Smithsonian/ Folkways, n.d. (sound cassette)

Janeczko, Paul, sel. *The Place My Words Are Looking For*. Bradbury/Macmillan, 1990.

———. *Poetspeak: In Their Work, about Their Work*. Collier/Macmillan, 1983.

Jarrell, Randall. *The Bat Poet*. Caedmon, n.d. (audio cassette)

Kamen, Gloria. *Edward Lear, King of Nonsense*. Illus. by Edward Lear and Gloria Kamen. Atheneum, 1990.

Kiefer, Barbara, sel. *Getting to Know You: Profiles of Children's Authors Featured in Language Arts, 1985–1990*. National Council of Teachers of English, 1991.

Kuskin, Karla. *Dogs and Dragons, Trees and Dreams*. Harper, 1980.

———. *Near the Window Tree: Poems and Notes*. Harper, 1976.

———. *Poetry Explained*. Weston, CT: Weston Woods, n.d (sound filmstrip)

Livingston, Myra Cohn. "Poets of the Child's World" in *Climb into the Bell Tower: Essays on Poetry*. Harper, 1990.

*Meet Jack Prelutsky*. American School Publishers/Macmillan/McGraw Hill, n.d. (video cassette)

*Meet the Newbery Author: Arnold Lobel.* American School Publishers/Macmillan/ McGraw Hill, n.d. (video cassette, sound filmstrip)

*Meet the Newbery Author: Cynthia Rylant.* American School Publishers/Macmillan/ McGraw Hill, n.d. (video cassette, sound filmstrip)

*Meet the Newbery Author: Nancy Willard.* American School Publishers/Macmillan/ McGraw Hill, n.d. (sound filmstrip)

*Meet the Picture Book Author: Cynthia Rylant.* American School Publishers/Macmillan/ McGraw Hill, n.d. (video cassette)

Meltzer, Milton. *Langston Hughes: A Biography.* Harper, 1968.

Merriam, Eve. "Writing a Poem" in *A Sky Full of Poems.* Dell, 1986.

Mitchell, Barbara. *Good Morning, Mr. President: A Story About Carl Sandburg.* Illus. by Dane Collins. Carolrhoda, 1988.

Prelutsky, Jack. *It's Thanksgiving.* Listening Library, n.d. (audio cassette)

———. *The New Kid on the Block.* Listening Library, n.d (audio cassette)

———. *Ride a Purple Pelican.* Listening Library, n.d. (audio cassette)

*Profiles in Literature: John Ciardi, Richard Lewis, Arnold Lobel, and Eve Merriam.* Profiles in Literature, n.d. (video cassettes)

Sloan, Glenna Davis. "Profile: Eve Merriam" in *Language Arts* (1981): 957–58.

Soto, Gary. *A Fire in My Hands.* Illus. by James M. Cardillo. Scholastic, 1990.

Vardell, Sylvia. "An Interview with Jack Prelutsky." *The New Advocate* 4 (Spring, 1991): 101–111.

Walker, Alice. *Langston Hughes, American Poet.* Illus. by Don Miller. Crowell, 1974.

*Who's Dr. Seuss: Meet Ted Geisel.* American School Publishers/Macmillan/McGraw Hill, n.d. (video cassette, sound filmstrip)

Yolen, Jane. *Owl Moon.* Weston, CT: Weston Woods, n.d. (16 mm, video cassette)

## POETS IN LITERATURE FOR CHILDREN

A number of novels and picture books feature poets. These books can also introduce students to the work and life of the poet. Possibly the most famous creator of verse in literature for children is Winnie the Pooh who creates "hums" to pass the time and in honor of particular occasions. Winnie uses onomatopoeia and nonsense together to create such words as "tiddley-pom." Another small versifier is Frances, the badger heroine of Russell Hoban's books, who composes poems to herself about her everyday activities and thoughts. Her "Sunny Side Up," which concisely expresses her feelings about eggs, is included in *Egg Thoughts and Other Frances Songs*, a collection of Frances' rhymes published separately.

Several mice have been poets. Frederick, the small mouse poet of Leo Lionni's *Frederick*, stores up memories of the warmth and colors of summertime to share with the other mice when winter closes in. Miss Bianca, the pampered white mouse heroine of Margery Sharp's *The Rescuers*, is also a poet. Adam Mouse, who exchanges visits with his city mice friends in several books by poet Lilian Moore, has his own book of poetry, *Adam Mouse's Book of Poems*.

One of the most eloquent animal poets in children's literature is the bat poet in Randall Jarrell's book of the same title. This poet struggles with who his audience is, what his subjects should be, and whether he is meant to write poetry in the course of this short novel. The poems the bat poet produces, all contained in the novel, are also included in many collections.

There are even a few human poets in literature for children. Anastasia Krupnik in Lois Lowry's *Anastasia Krupnik* series keeps a notebook of poetry ideas, works hard on her drafts and revisions, and turns out some good and some not-so-good poems. She also has a father who writes and teaches poetry. Robert Burch, Betsy Byars, and Elizabeth Levy all include child poets in novels. Students may want to develop a library of books featuring poets and writers. They may also want to talk about which of these poets they think write well and which might do with some help in revision.

Sometimes a poet writes a poem about poets. These may be autobiographical or they may reflect images that we tend to have of poets. Countee Cullen's "For a Poet" is an elegy for a poet. Carl Sandburg's "From...Sketch of a Poet" is a more humorous look at how a poet spends his days. Poems about poetry in Chapter 5 may contain other poetic images of poets.

Burch, Robert. *King Kong and Other Poets*. Viking, 1986.

Byars, Betsy. *Beans on the Roof*. Illus. by Melodye Rosales. Delacorte, 1988.

Cullen, Countee. "For a Poet" in Larrick, Nancy. *Bring Me All of Your Dreams*. Evans, 1980.

Hoban, Russell. *A Baby Sister for Frances*. Illus. by Lillian Hoban. Harper, 1964.

————. *A Bargain for Frances*. Illus. by Lillian Hoban. Harper, 1970.

————. *Bedtime for Frances*. Illus. by Garth Williams. Harper, 1960.

————. *Best Friends for Frances*. Illus. by Lillian Hoban. Harper, 1969.

————. *A Birthday for Frances*. Illus. by Lillian Hoban. Harper, 1968.

————. *Bread and Jam for Frances*. Illus. by Lillian Hoban. Harper, 1965.

————. *Egg Thoughts and Other Frances Songs*. Illus. by Lillian Hoban. Harper, 1972.

Jarrell, Randall. *The Bat Poet*. Illus. by Maurice Sendak. Macmillan, 1964.

Levy, Elizabeth. *Keep Ms. Sugarman in the Fourth Grade*. Harper, 1992.

Lionni, Leo. *Frederick*. Knopf, 1967.

Lowry, Lois. *Anastasia Krupnik*. Houghton, 1979.

————. *Attaboy, Sam!* Houghton, 1992.

Milne, A.A. *Winnie the Pooh*. Illus. by Ernest H. Shepard. Dutton, 1988.

Moore, Lilian. *Adam Mouse's Book of Poems*. Illus. by Kathleen Garry McCord. Atheneum/Macmillan, 1992.

————. *Don't Be Afraid, Amanda*. Illus. by Kathleen Gary McCord. Atheneum/Macmillan, 1992.

————. *I'll Meet You at the Cucumbers*. Illus. by Sharon Wooding. Atheneum/Macmillan, 1988.

Sandburg, Carl. "From...Sketch of a Poet" in Hopkins, Lee Bennett. *Rainbows Are Made*. Harcourt, 1982.

Sharp, Margery. *The Rescuers*. Little, 1959.

## POEMS ABOUT BOOKS AND READING

Another way to make a link between poetry and other areas of the curriculum is to take advantage of the number of poems about books and reading.

Classic poems for young children such as Robert Louis Stevenson's "Land of Storybooks" describe the magic inside the covers of books, just as Myra Cohn Livingston's modern poem, "Worlds I Know," does. Others, such as Arnold Lobel's "Books to the Ceiling," portray the continuing challenge we face in trying to read everything we want to read. Still others suggest that the good long read is worth it, no matter how much time it takes, as Jean Little does in "Condensed Version." Lee Bennett Hopkins has collected his favorite poems on books and reading in *Good Books, Good Times.*

Librarians and other library lovers may also want to collect poems on libraries. Some of these reflect the stereotypes about libraries, including Shel Silverstein's poem about "Overdues." Others invite readers to consider the library as a wonderful and mystery-filled place, as Barbara Juster Esbensen does in "Bat" and "Giraffe" in *Words with Wrinkled Knees.* Any of these poems can be posted in libraries and classrooms, near reading areas for children to consider as they select books to read.

Dasgupta, Manjush. "Companion" in Nye, Naomi Shihab. *This Same Sky: A Collection of Poems From Around the World.* Four Winds/Macmillan, 1992.

Dickinson, Emily. "There is No Frigate Like a Book" in Elledge, Scott. *Wider Than the Sky.* Harper, 1990.

Esbensen, Barbara Juster. "Bat" and "Giraffe" in *Words with Wrinkled Knees.* Illus. by John Stadler. Crowell/Harper, 1987.

Fisher, Aileen. "After the End" in *Always Wondering.* Illus. by Joan Sandin. Harper, 1991.

Giovanni, Nikki. "Ten Years Old" in *Spin a Soft Black Song.* Illus. by George Martins. Hill, 1985.

Hopkins, Lee Bennett. *Good Books, Good Times!* Illus. by Harvey Stevenson. Harper, 1990.

Kennedy, X.J. "My Fishbowl Head" in *The Forgetful Wishing Well.* Illus. by Monica Incisa. M.K. McElderry/Macmillan, 1985.

———. "Summer Cooler" in *The Kite That Braved Old Orchard Beach.* M.K. McElderry/Macmillan, 1991.

Little, Jean. "Condensed Version" in *Hey World, Here I Am!* Illus. by Sue Truesdell. Harper, 1989.

Livingston, Myra Cohn. "Give Me Books, Give Me Wings" and "This Book is Mine" in *I Never Told.* M.K. McElderry/Macmillan, 1990.

———. "Picture People" in Hopkins, Lee Bennett. *More Surprises.* Harper, 1987.

——— "Reading: Fall," "Reading: Spring," "Reading: Summer," and "Reading: Winter" in *Remembering and Other Poems.* Macmillan, 1989.

———. "Worlds I Know" in *Worlds I Know.* Illus. by Tim Arnold. M.K. McElderry/Macmillan, 1985.

Lobel, Arnold. "Books to the Ceiling" in *Whiskers and Rhymes*. Greenwillow, 1985.

Merriam, Eve. "A New Song for Old Smokey" in *A Poem for a Pickle*. Illus. by Sheila Hamanaka. Morrow, 1989.

Miller, Jim Wayne. "A House of Readers" in Janeczko, Paul. *Pocket Poems*. Bradbury/Macmillan, 1985.

Moore, Lilian. "In the Library" in *Adam Mouse's Book of Poems*. Illus. by Kathleen Garry McCord. Atheneum/Macmillan, 1992.

Morrison, Lillian. "Sport" and "When I Read" in *Break Dance Kids*. Lothrop, 1985.

Silverstein, Shel. "Overdues" in *A Light in the Attic*. Harper, 1981.

Stevenson, Robert Louis. "The Land of Storybooks" and "Picture Books in Winter" in *A Child's Garden of Verses*. Illus. by Michael Foreman. Delacorte, 1985.

Worth, Valerie. "Library" in *All the Small Poems*. Illus. by Natalie Babbitt. Farrar, 1987.

## A PERSONAL POETRY COLLECTION

Most teachers and librarians have a small library of poetry books used regularly, either for their own personal use or for children. Because of my interest in American history, for example, I heavily use my copy of Sara and John Brewton's *America Forever New*. We may have collections by favorite poets. I like to pull poems from Eve Merriam's *Fresh Paint* and Barbara Juster Esbensen's *Who Shrank My Grandmother's House?* to use when I give booktalks.

In addition to favorite books of poems, many teachers and librarians have personal poetry collections. The arrangement of each collection depends entirely on the person who creates it. Some people simply add poems to their journals and writing notebooks as they find them; others collect methodically. A flexible format is important, as the poems we find are often useful in a variety of ways. One teacher collects any poem she can find on bats, a creature that fascinates her. She sometimes uses these in conjunction with Randall Jarrell's *Bat Poet*. She once used "The Bat" by Theodore Roethke during a Halloween celebration when her class talked about what a monster might be. She sometimes uses these poems during science units when she wants her students to see connections among the features of mammals.

Some people choose to write their poems on cards and keep them in boxes or in file drawers with other materials for units. Others prefer a loose-leaf binder with tabs for subjects and themes. Some librarians and teachers have made their poetry collections a shared project. They meet periodically to read through collections and share poems they like. Each member of the poetry group watches out for poems that may be of interest to other members. In a group in which I participated others knew that I was looking for poems about moose and that I loved poems about reading so they watched out for these poems for me.

The first poems that you look for as you begin your poetry collection are simply poems you like. It is all too easy to think of poems and books as "tools" to teach other subjects rather than as works that are beautiful and instructive on their own terms. You might collect poems on a favorite topic, as the teacher who likes bats does. She also encourages her students to look for poems on their favorite subjects. These might be poems about an animal, a hobby, or a favorite food.

You may look for poems you enjoyed in childhood and had perhaps forgotten until you see them again. It is a pleasant surprise to pick up collections by Robert Louis Stevenson, A. A. Milne, or Dorothy Aldis and rediscover an old friend. When you find these poems, try to remember what pleased you about them. Was it the rhythm, rhyme, or the subject matter? Sometimes these poems were so connected to our own experiences at the time we liked them that we cannot imagine sharing them. Other times we recognize that the sound and rhythmic qualities or the topic of the poems would be enjoyed by our own students as well.

Beautiful collections and single editions of nursery rhymes are being published now. Some of these are fairly comprehensive and contain many unfamiliar rhymes. Several collections contain international rhymes; some include songs and activities. Others are selective collections or single rhyme picture books done by favorite authors or illustrators. Nursery rhymes are traditionally used with young children but many of the rhymes in these collections will appeal to older students as well. You may want to spend a workshop session with other teachers and librarians renewing your acquaintance with Mother Goose and nursery rhymes.

You may want to look at other "classic" poetry for inclusion in your personal poetry collection. Typically, classic poems are of two types. There are well-known poems, actually written for adult audiences, which we expect children to recognize, such as poems by Robert Frost or Emily Dickinson. There are also poems written for children in the past that have survived several generations, such as those of Christina Rossetti and Robert Louis Stevenson. A number of collections of classic poems and selected works by classic poets are available and are listed at the end of this chapter. As you read classic poems be aware that some of these may seem out of date, old-fashioned, or reflect the values of earlier times. Sometimes a poem is a classic because of the poet's influence in a given time, not because it is still relevant or meaningful for today's children. As you select classic poems for your notebook, keep in mind that these poems should not be isolated and taught as a "classics" unit, but integrated when appropriate and when children choose them. Children enjoy classic poems when these poems make connections to their own lives and experiences. As one child told a librarian,

Carl Sandburg was an interesting and enjoyable poet "even though he was dead!"

When you first look at children's poetry you may be attracted to poems that make you laugh. Much of the light verse written for children contains humorous observations about the foibles of being a child and being human. Nothing is so satisfying as a good hearty laugh at the misunderstandings and misfortunes of our younger selves. Poems that capture the feelings of childhood are not always humorous. Modern poets write serious poems that can help us empathize with someone who is different from us, or share sadness at the plight of a person, animal, or condition of the world.

One of the hardest lessons to learn about poetry is that engagement, the struggle to make sense of a poem because it in some way moves you, even if you don't fully understand it, is greatly satisfying. The arrangement of words, the sound of language, and the sheer beauty of a turn of phrase can send shivers down your spine. That is the power of good poetry. Sadly, many of us have learned not to pay attention to language, or worse, to see engagement with meanings of language as frivolous and just too much trouble. We might look for poems for our personal poetry collection that move us even if we can't explain exactly why. These are the poems to place in our notebooks to savor again and again. As a child, I may have been one of the lucky few to enjoy Robert Frost's "Stopping by Woods on a Snowy Evening' without having it as homework. As a result, to this day, the repetition of the simple line "and miles to go before I sleep" gives me a frisson of recognition, of duty and beauty inextricably linked. The rich sadness of "The Song of Wandering Aengus" by William Butler Yeats grips me with each re-reading since I discovered it in high school. I have enjoyed sharing this poem about something forever lost and haunting with children when I tell stories of the mystical hold that the Irish fairies have over the people they kidnap.

After spending time reading poems we like and sharing them with others, the form of the poetry collection will emerge. It might have a section of classic poems and a section of childhood favorites to share with students. It may contain a section of poems kept for rereading and rethinking. There might be sections for curriculum areas. This book is organized along these curriculum lines and you will find examples of poems for use in subject areas in each chapter. Some people keep a section of poems to be used with particular school events such as holidays, field trips, science camps, an annual play, sports events, and so on. Others keep poems that reflect problems and issues that often come up in their classrooms, such as not getting along, fighting, equipment breakdowns, or thunderstorms and other natural events. These can be pulled out and shared at appropriate moments.

Many teachers keep a selection of poems to share at odd moments: waiting for the bus to start up for the field trip, leaving for lunch, or taking a poetry break from a difficult lesson on grammar or fractions. Poems in Kalli Dakos' *If You're Not Here Please Raise Your Hand*, which talk humorously about how difficult school can be, provide light breaks that can also foster discussions about why we study the subjects we study. Sometimes these poetry breaks have nothing to do with the subject at hand but provide a laugh or a thought to change our mood.

Another section of the notebook may contain poems about feelings, which can be used when children react to events inside or outside of school. These might include poems about friendship, feelings of boredom or happiness, or reactions to changing seasons. Karla Kuskin's "Spring" echoes the feelings of Wyoming school children when they finally see signs of the season long after most of the world has seen them. Her list of leapings and racings reflects their exuberance exactly. On the other hand, a short poem such as Kuskin's "It Is Grey Out" can help us sympathize when someone we know is having a sad, grey day.

Many poems address grief, despair, and pain; poets use the poem as a way to express their own strong feelings. Teachers should use these poems with care. A poem about a dog's death can be helpful to a child who remembers last year's death but may prove to be painful and embarrassing to a child who is still grieving. A poem may make a sensitive situation more difficult if listeners see it as an accusation or a simplistic solution to a problem. All too frequently poetry and stories are used as band-aids to cover the real pain children feel. "Just read this and you'll feel better" suggests that we can guarantee a child's response to such a work will be spontaneous, positive, and healing. In truth, some of this sharing, done with the best of intentions, can have the opposite effect. Poems kept in a special section of the notebook might better be shared privately with a child when we think that child might appreciate the poet's feelings.

Poems that deal with difficult topics such as grief, unfairness, anger, and despair may play a more positive role in the classroom when they are shared during literature study. Children who are moved by Mildred Taylor's *Roll of Thunder, Hear My Cry* may find that "The Lynching" by Claude McKay helps them to understand the anger and fear felt by Cassie and her family. When Leslie dies in *Bridge to Terabithia*, Langston Hughes' simple "Poem," about his love for a friend who has gone away, helps to understand Jess's feelings. Chapter 6 on poetry and literature discusses the difficulties of looking for these types of poems and gives some examples of successful connections between poems and stories.

No matter what other sections you may have in your poetry collection, it is nice to keep a section for yourself. In this section are poems to comfort us on a hard day, inspire us to be better teachers, make our spine tingle each time we read them, or help us remember a person who is important to us. One teacher shared with me that sometimes she puts a poem in her collection without knowing exactly why. Later, she'll open her poetry notebook and discover the poem perfectly captures how she is feeling.

Poetry collections are not just for teaching. They contain all manner of poems for all kinds of occasions and some poems that we just love. They are useful for teachers and librarians, but also invaluable for students who are reading poems and discovering themselves in them. The personal poetry collection allows us to make poetry our own.

## Books and Poems Mentioned

Brewton, Sara and John E. *America Forever New*. Crowell, Harper, 1989.
Dakos, Kalli. *If You're Not Here, Please Raise Your Hand*. Illus. by Brian G. Karas. Four Winds/Macmillan, 1990.
Esbensen, Barbara Juster. *Who Shrank My Grandmother's House?* Illus. by Eric Beddows. Harper, 1992.
Frost, Robert. "Stopping by Woods on a Snowy Evening" in Prelutsky, Jack. *Random House Book of Poetry for Children*. Random, 1983.
Hughes, Langston. "Poem" in Slier, Deborah. *Make a Joyful Sound*. Checkerboard, 1991.
Jarrell, Randall. *The Bat Poet*. Illus. by Maurice Sendak. M.K. McElderry/Macmillan, 1967. (fiction)
Kuskin, Karla. "It Is Grey Out" and "Spring" in *Dogs and Dragons, Trees and Dreams*. Harper, 1980.
McKay, Claude. "The Lynching" in Adoff, Arnold. *I Am the Darker Brother*. Collier/ Macmillan, 1970.
Merriam, Eve. *Fresh Paint*. Illus. by David Frampton. Macmillan, 1986.
Paterson, Katherine. *The Bridge to Terabithia*. Illus. by Donna Diamond. Crowell/ Harper, 1977. (fiction)
Roethke, Theodore. "The Bat" in Prelutsky, Jack. *The Random House Book of Poetry for Children*. Random, 1983.
Taylor, Mildred. *Roll of Thunder, Hear My Cry*. Dial, 1976. (fiction)
Yeats, William Butler. "The Song of Wandering Aengus" in Elledge, Scott. *Wider Than the Sky*. Harper, 1990.

## Collections of Classic Poems

Blishen, Edward. *Oxford Book of Poetry for Children*. Illus. by Brian Wildsmith. Oxford, 1987.
Elledge, Scott, sel. *Wider Than the Sky: Poems to Grow Up With*. Harper, 1990.
Hall, Donald, sel. *The Oxford Book of Children's Verse in America*. Oxford, 1985.

Harrison, Michael and Christopher Stuart Clark, sel. *The Oxford Book of Story Poems.* Oxford, 1990.

Koch, Kenneth and Kate Farrell, sel. *Talking to the Sun.* Holt/Metropolitan Museum of Art, 1985.

Moss, Elaine. *From Morn to Midnight.* Illus. by Satomi Ichikawa. Crowell, 1977.

*Who Has Seen the Wind?* Rizzoli/Museum of Art, Boston, 1992.

*The World's Best Poetry for Children.* Roth/Poetry Anthology Press, 1986.

## Collections of Classic Poems by Individual Poets

Cummings, E. E. *Hist Whist and Other Poems for Children.* Illus. by David Calsada. Liveright, 1983.

Dickinson, Emily. *A Brighter Garden.* Illus. by Tasha Tudor. Philomel/Putnam, 1990.

———. *I'm Nobody, Who Are You? Poems of Emily Dickinson for Children.* Illus. by Rex Schneider. Stemmer House, 1978.

———. *Poems for Youth.* Illus. by George and Doris Hauman. Little, 1934.

Frost, Robert. *A Swinger of Birches: Poems of Robert Frost for Young People.* Illus. by Peter Koeppen. Stemmer House, 1982.

———. *You Come Too: Favorite Poems for Young Readers.* Illus. by Thomas W. Nason. Holt, 1959.

Hopkins, Lee Bennett, sel. *Rainbows Are Made: Poems by Carl Sandburg.* Illus. by Fritz Eichenberg. Harcourt, 1982.

———. *Voyages: Poems by Walt Whitman.* Illus. by Charles Mikolaycak. Harcourt, 1988.

Hughes, Langston. *Dream Keeper.* Illus. by Helen Sewell. Knopf, 1962.

Lawrence, D. H. *Birds, Beasts, and the Third Thing.* Illus. by Alice and Martin Provensen. Viking, 1982.

Lear, Edward. *How Pleasant to Know Mr. Lear!* Holiday, 1982.

———. *The Nonsense Poems of Edward Lear.* Illus. by Leslie Brook. Clarion, 1991.

———. *Of Pelicans and Pussycats: Poems and Limericks.* Illus. by Jill Newton. Dial, 1990.

Millay, Edna St. Vincent. *Collected Poems.* Harper, 1981.

———. *Edna St. Vincent Millay's Poems Selected for Young People.* Illus. by Ronald Keller. Harper, 1979.

Milne, A. A. *Now We Are Six.* Illus. by Ernest H. Shepard. Dutton, 1988.

———. *When We Were Very Young.* Illus. by Ernest H. Shepard. Dutton, 1988.

Riley, James Whitcomb. *Joyful Poems for Children.* Macmillan, 1960.

Sandburg, Carl. *Sandburg Treasury: Prose and Poetry for Young People.* Illus. by Paul Bacon. Harcourt, 1970.

Stevenson, Robert Louis. *A Child's Garden of Verses.* Illus. by Jannet Messenger. Dutton, 1992.

———. *A Child's Garden of Verses.* Illus. by Michael Foreman. Delacorte, 1985.

## REFERENCES

Atwell, N. (1991). "Finding Poetry Everywhere." *Side by Side: Essays on Teaching to Learn.* Portsmouth, NH: Heinemann.

Bauer, C. F. (1992). "Promoting Poetry." *Read for the Fun of It: Active Programming with Books for Children*. Bronx, NY: H.W. Wilson.

Clark, A. "Books in the Classroom: Poetry." *Horn Book* 68 (September/October, 1992): 624–27.

Cottrell, J. (1987). *Creative Drama in the Classroom: Grades 1–3*. Lincolnwood, IL: National Textbook Company.

Cowen, J. E. (1983). *Teaching Reading through the Arts*. Newark, DE: International Reading Association.

Denman, G. A. (1988). "The Elements of Poetry... Words in Performance." *When You've Made It Your Own: Teaching Poetry to Young People*. Portsmouth, NH: Heinemann.

Gough, J. "Poems in Context: Breaking the Anthology Trap." *Children's Literature in Education* 15 (monthly, 1984): 204–10.

Hall, D. "Bring Back the Out-Loud Culture." *Newsweek* 105 (April 15, 1985):12.

Heinig, R. B. (1988). *Creative Drama for the Classroom Teacher*. 3d ed. Englewood Cliffs, NJ: Prentice-Hall.

Hopkins, L. B. (1987). *Pass the Poetry, Please!: Using Poetry in Pre-kindergarten-six Classrooms*. 2d ed. New York: Harper Collins.

Larrick, N. (1991). *Let's Do a Poem! Introducing Poetry to Children*. New York: Delacorte.

McCaslin, N. (1974). *Creative Dramatics in the Classroom*. 2d ed. New York: David McKay.

Parsons, L. (1992). *Poetry Themes and Activities: Exploring the Fun and Fantasy of Language*. Portsmouth, NH: Heinemann.

Robb, L. "More Poetry, Please!" *The New Advocate* 3 (Summer, 1990): 197–203.

Stewig, J. (1988). "Sharing Poetry with Children." *Children and Literature*. Boston: Houghton.

Winkel, Johann, R. "How Can I Help Children to Enjoy Poetry?" *Language Arts* 58 (March, 1981): 353–55.

# Appendix:
# Directory of Publisher Addresses

**Abrams**
(Harry Abrams, Inc.)
100 Fifth Avenue
New York, NY 10011

**American School Publishers**
155 N. Wacker Drive, Box 4520
Chicago, IL 60680-4520

**Atheneum**
(See Macmillan)

**Arte Publico**
Div. of University of Houston
4800 Calhoun
Houston, TX 77204

**Bantam**
(Bantam, Doubleday, Dell)
666 Fifth Ave.
New York, NY 10103

**Bedrick**
(Peter Bedrick Books)
2112 Broadway, Rm. 318
New York, NY 10023

**Beech Tree**
(See Morrow)

**Beginner**
(See Random House)

**Black Butterfly**
(See Writers and Readers)

**Boyds Mills**
(Boyds Mills Press)
910 Church Street
Honesdale, PA 18431

**Boynton Cook**
(See Heinemann)

**Bradbury**
(See Macmillan)

**Caedmon**
1995 Broadway
New York, NY 10023

**Candlewick**
(See Walker)

**Caroline**
(see Boyds Mills)

**Carolrhoda**
241 First Ave., N.
Minneapolis, MN 55401

**Checkerboard**
30 Vesey Street
New York, NY 10007

**Cheshire Book Companions**
Dept. C
PO Box 61109
Denver, CO 80206

**Children's Book Press**
1461 Ninth Ave.
San Francisco, CA 94122

**Child's Play**
137 E. 25th./9th. floor
New York, NY 10010

**Christopher-Gordon Publishers**
480 Washington Street
Norwood, MA 02062

**Chronicle Books**
275 Fifth Street
San Francisco, CA 94103

**Clarion**
(See Houghton)

**Cobblehill**
(See Viking Penguin)

**Coward**
(See Putnam)

**Crowell**
(See Harper)

**Crown**
(See Random House)

**Delacorte**
666 Fifth Ave.
New York, NY 10103

**Dial**
(See Viking Penguin)

**Disney Press**
(See Walt Disney)

**Doubleday**
(See Bantam)

**Dover**
180 Varick Street
New York, NY 10014

**Dutton**
(See Viking Penguin)

**Faber**
(Faber and Faber)
50 Cross Street
Winchester, MA 01890

**Farrar**
(Farrar, Straus & Giroux)
19 Union Square
New York, NY 10003

**Foundation Books**
PO Box 29229
Lincoln, NE 68529

**Four Winds**
(See Macmillan)

**French and European**
115 Fifth Ave.
New York, NY 10003

**Gareth Stevens**
River Center Bldg.
1555 N. River Center Dr.
Suite 201
Milwaukee, WI 53212

**Godine**
(David R. Godine)
300 Massachusetts Av.
Horticultural Hall
Boston, MA 02115

**Green Tiger Press**
200 Old Tappan Road
Old Tappan, NJ 07675-7005

**Greenwillow**
(See Morrow)

**Grosset**
(See Putnam)

**Harcourt**
(Harcourt Brace Jovanovich)
1250 Sixth Ave.
San Diego, CA 92101

**Harper**
(Harper Collins)
10 E. 53rd. St.
New York, NY 10022

**Heinemann Educational Books**
361 Hanover Street
Portsmouth, NH 03801-3959

**Hill**
(Lawrence Hill Books)
230 Park Place
Suite 6A
Brooklyn, NY 11238

**Hill and Wang**
(See Farrar)

**Houghton**
(Houghton Mifflin)
1 Beacon Street
Boston, MA 02108

**Hyperion**
(See Walt Disney)

**International Reading Association**
800 Barksdale Road
PO Box 8139
Newark, DE 19714-8139

**Joy Street**
(See Little)

**Kane-Miller**
PO Box 529
Brooklyn, NY 11231

**Knopf**
(See Random House)

**Lippincott**
(See Harper)

**Listening Library**
One Park Avenue
Old Greenwich, CT 06870-1727

**Little**
(Little, Brown)
34 Beacon St.
Boston, MA 02108

**Liveright Publishing Corporation**
500 Fifth Avenue
New York, NY 10111

**Longman**
(Div. of Addison-Wesley)
The Longman Building
10 Bank Street
White Plains, NY 10606-1951

**Lothrop**
(See Morrow)

**M. Evans**
216 E. 49th. St.
New York, NY 10017

**M.K. McElderry**
(See Macmillan)

**McKay**
(David McKay)
201 E. 50th. St.
New York, NY 10022

**Macmillan**
866 Third Ave.
New York, NY 10022

**Morrow**
(William Morrow)
1350 Avenue of the Americas
New York, NY 10019

**National Council of Teachers of English**
1111 Kenyon Road
Urbana, IL 61801

**New Rivers Press**
420 N. Fifth, Suite 910
Minneapolis, MN 55401

**North-South Books**
1133 Broadway
Suite 1016
New York, NY 10010

**Orchard Books**
387 Park Ave. S.
New York, NY 10016

**Oxford University Press**
200 Madison Avenue
New York, NY 10016

**Pantheon**
(See Random House)

**Pelican Publishing Co.**
1101 Monroe
Gretna, LA 70053

**Penguin**
(See Viking Penguin)

**Philomel**
(See Putnam)

**Podell**
(Tim Podell Productions)
Box 244
Scarborough, NY 10510

**Prentice-Hall**
(Division of Simon and Schuster)
15 Columbus Circle
New York, NY 10029

**Profiles in Literature**
Dr. Jacqueline Weiss
3023 De Kalb Blvd.
Norristown, PA 19401

**Puffin**
(See Viking Penguin)

**Putnam Publishing Group**
200 Madison Ave.
New York, NY 10016

**Random House**
201 E. 50th. St.
31st. Floor
New York, NY 10022

**Routledge**
29 W. 35th. St.
New York, NY 10001-2291

**Scott, Foresman**
(See Harper)

**Simon**
(Simon and Schuster)
1230 Avenue of the Americas
New York, NY 10020

**Smithsonian/Folkways Recordings**
416 Hungerford Drive
Suite 320
Rockville, MD 20850

**Southern Illinois University**
PO Box 3697
Carbondale, IL 62902-3697

**Spoken Arts**
10100 SBF Drive
Pinellas Park, FL 34666

**Stemmer House**
2627 Caves Rd.
Owings Mills, MD 21117

**Tamborine**
(See Morrow)

**Teachers and Writers**
5 Union Sq. W.
New York, NY 10003-3306

**Ticknor and Fields**
215 Park Ave. S.
New York, NY 10003

**Troll Associates**
100 Corporate Drive
Mahwah, NJ 07430

**Viking Penguin**
375 Hudson St.
New York, NY 10014-3657

**Walker**
720 Fifth Ave.
New York, NY 10019

**Walt Disney**
114 Fifth Ave.
New York, NY 10011

**Weston Woods**
Weston, CT 06883

**Whitman**
(Albert Whitman)

**Winston Press**
6135 Braesheather
Houston, TX 77096

**Wordsong**
(See Boyds Mills)

**Writers and Readers**
625 Broadway
Suite 903
New York, NY 10012

# Index